A Discourse on Domination in Mandate Palestine

Imperialism, Property and Insurgency

Zeina B. Ghandour

Routledge
Taylor & Francis Group

LONDON AND NEW YORK

First published 2010
by Routledge
2 Park Square, Milton Park, Abingdon, Oxon, OX14 4RN

Simultaneously published in the USA and Canada
by Routledge
711 Third Avenue, New York, NY 10017

A *GlassHouse* book
Routledge is an imprint of the Taylor & Francis Group, an informa business

First issued in paperback 2011

© 2010 Zeina B. Ghandour

Typeset in Sabon by Taylor & Francis Books

British Library Cataloguing in Publication Data
A catalogue record for this book is available from the British Library

Library of Congress Cataloguing in Publication Data
Ghandour, Zeina B., 1966-
A discourse on domination in mandate Palestine : imperialism, property and insurgency / Zeina B. Ghandour.
   p. cm.
Includes bibliographical references and index.
1. Palestine–History–1917-1948. 2. Mandates–Palestine. 3. Colonial administrators–Great Britain–Attitudes–History. 4. British–Palestine–Attitudes. 5. Palestine–Foreign public opinion, British. 6. Public opinion–Great Britain. 7. Imperialism–Government policy–Great Britain–History–20th century. I. Title.
   DS126.G47 2009
   956.94'04–dc22
                              2009012897

ISBN10: 0-415-48993-8 (hbk)
ISBN10: 0-415-68530-3 (pbk)
ISBN10: 0-203-88084-6 (ebk)

ISBN13: 978-0-415-48993-5 (hbk)
ISBN13: 978-0-415-68530-6 (pbk)
ISBN13: 978-0-203-88084-5 (ebk)

Dedicated, with sincere humility, to my elders ...

Contents

Foreword

John Comaroff

This is an unconventional book, unconventional in both its form and its content. As such, it may offend those with conventional expectations. However, it is a strikingly impressive achievement. It sets out to do two things: the first is to 'unwrite' received histories of Mandate Palestine, thus to transform radically our understanding of those histories, from a pointedly Palestinian perspective. The second is to argue, more generally, that the 'situation of the colonizer' – a 'usurper who disturbs the local order' – is illegitimate, resting, as it does on an 'urge for profit, privilege and appropriation'. Both objectives are comprehensively realized: this study yields a counter-hegemonic, convincingly alternative account of the life and times of Palestine under British domination.

The narrative logic of *A Discourse on Domination in Mandate Palestine* owes something to postmodern discursive strategies. In offering its critique of conventional histories of Mandate Palestine – indeed, a very compelling critique – it attacks those histories not merely for the story they tell but for the manner of its telling, in which inheres a large measure of its authority. The stuff of the story itself is familiar enough. It concerns the exploits of British men of civilization, peace, and reason (many of them knighted) bringing, well, civilization, peace, and reason to the benighted peoples of other worlds; in this case, to what is (mis)portrayed as the unruly Islamic world of the Middle East. All of which, argues Ghandour is a lie, an elaborate exercise in myth-making. The power of that lie, its truth-value, derives from its representation as a value-free, 'objective', logocentric, historical master-narrative, retold repeatedly and seamlessly by professional historians in the taken-for-granted, heroic mode of political history. I shall say more in a moment of the substance of its 'unwriting' by Ghandour, which is inspired by the counter-historiography of the Subaltern Studies school in South Asia and by the theory-work of such anti-colonial intellectuals as Fanon and Césaire. But the *form* of that unwriting is what gives the text a good deal of its unconventionality: eschewing a chronologically ordered account, or the pursuit of historical cause-and-effect, it weaves together an insurgent reading of the archive with sometimes lengthy (and quite extraordinary) oral testimonies – without interpretive exegesis or analytic interpellation – from colonized peoples, thereby allowing previously silenced human subjects to speak for and of themselves; testimonies of, among other things, the civil unrest in Palestine during the late 1930s and its brute suppression; the conflicts among Palestinians brought before so-called rebel courts; and the deportation of H.F. Khalidi (H.F.K.), legendary mayor of Jerusalem, to the Seychelles. Indeed, this last text, drawn from the unpublished diary of H.F.K., closes the study with a symbolic punch that bespeaks the sensibility of a fine novelist or poet: the narrative ends *not* with a scholarly conclusion, the conventional mode of closure in this genre, but with an auto-biography of the expatriation of one of Palestine's most famed personages, a polite, poignant, disempowering removal that paralleled the polite, poignant, disempowering removal of Palestine from Palestinians. Could there be a more appropriate conclusion to the story? In sum, this is an account whose aesthetic and rhetorical construction does a great deal of critical-analytic work. As a result, this is a book that demands to be widely read in cultural studies, anthropology, and literary criticism. It will also find deep resonances at the more imaginative edges of legal history, historical sociology and Middle Eastern studies. From the more conservative edges of all these disciplines it will draw the usual criticisms, and evoke the usual consternation, in much the same way as did, say, Nadia Abu El-Haj's prize-winning, extraordinary, much vilified *Facts on the Ground* (2001).

Much more is to be said about the positive accomplishments of *A Discourse on Domination in Mandate Palestine*.

Some have already been anticipated. The first, and most general, is that it *does* succeed in offering an alternative portrait of Mandate Palestine and the famous events associated with its unpleasant history; this primarily by dislodging a number of long accepted truths about that history and the manner of its inscription. No longer will we be able to read of the epic exploits of the higher officers of the British administration without taking into account their brutal violence and the often cynical interests they served; no longer can we accept the standard view that Palestinians were wracked by internal divisions, not to mention an irreconcilable fissure between Husseinis and Nashashibis, without understanding that these had more to do with colonial provocation and power-management strategies than with an 'endemic' Arab tendency toward factionalism and infighting; indeed, no longer will we be able to read the history of Palestine innocent of the knowledge of quite how complex and subtle were political relations among the various sectors of its indigenous population. This extends, with equal profundity, to the question of religion; in particular, to the reduction by the British administration of 'Arab' to 'Muslim' – thence to irrational, primitive, 'tribal,' violent native – a misconstrual that made a mockery of the political reality of Palestine, but justified a great deal of colonial realpolitik.

Second, and more specific, are Ghandour's accounts of the rebel courts in Palestine and the Arab Rebellion of 1936–39, both of which are notable for their originality. The former, the rebel courts – which offer a fascinating parallel to the more formal Zionist legal system described by Ronen Shamir in *The Colonies of Law* (2000) – are not the subject of an exhaustive study; the object here is primarily to describe what went on in them in order to illuminate everyday life in contemporary Palestine. Still, these descriptions, nicely supported by verbatim oral texts, afford glimpses into an altogether unusual set of dispute processes; legal anthropology simply does not have much of an archive or a literature on rebel courts, anywhere. Similarly, the Arab Rebellion, which is rewritten anew here from the Palestinian perspective. Perhaps the most striking thing about this re(or 'un')writing is the introduction of the vernacular testimonies mentioned earlier. This archive is almost worth a dissertation on its own: finding really good eyewitness informants for critical events of the 1930s – informants still able to recall those events articulately, informants widely dispersed by the exigencies of a violent, troubled history, informants dying out quickly of natural attrition (if of nothing else) – is difficult enough. To elicit from them the high-quality texts that Ghandour has collected is little short of remarkable. The same is true of H.F.K's diary. We are not told much about its provenance, but its significance as an historical text is unquestionable.

Third, *A Discourse on Domination in Mandate Palestine* adds a great deal, hitherto missing for Palestine and the Middle East, to the growing literature on comparative colonialisms: such things as the importance of map-making – of cartographies of absence, emptiness, possibility, progress – to the founding of colonies; the workings of so-called indirect rule in reconstructing relations of power and authority between ruler and ruled, and between various factious of subordinate populations; the significance of the law in establishing the hegemony of empire, not least, to paraphrase Fanon, by means of the colonization of consciousness; the importance of the politics of representation in the creation of the truth-regimes on which modernity and its political economies were founded, including the truth-regimes that cast non-European 'others' as the savage foil – Michel-Rolph Trouillot's famous 'savage slot' – to the presumptive civility of the West; the centrality of land as material resource, moral ground, patrimony, territory, real estate, and economic basis of overrule. And so on.

In sum, Zeina B. Ghandour has produced a highly original, highly impressive work of scholarship, one that commends itself to a very broad audience. And, most of all, one that cannot but change forever our understanding of the history of Palestine.

Acknowledgements

I am deeply indebted, indebted beyond measure, to those who have stood beside me over the years.

First and foremost, I would like to thank Professor Simon Roberts, my supervisor when this project was a PhD. I was tremendously lucky to be given the opportunity to work with him and there is no doubt about it: there would have been no thesis, no book, without his encouragement and his belief in me. Thank you to Professor John Comaroff for his exigent critiquing of my work. I am so honoured to have had his stimulating engagement and moral support in the stages leading to publication.

Diana Kewon Allen and Mahmoud Zeidan, who founded Al Nakba Archives, a non-governmental organization collecting and video-recording Palestinian oral histories, led me into and around the shocking, shameful, Palestinian refugee camps of Lebanon. They found the people I was looking for and arranged interviews for me. I was humbled by the refugees themselves: the elderly men and women who were kind enough to allow me into their homes and treat me as lovingly and as casually as one of their own, who were generous enough to share and recite the tender and disturbing contents of their heart with me. We are linked by an invisible thread.

Leila and Tima Husseini in Amman, Jordan, sat with me and painstakingly translated family papers for me into English.

My family have provided extraordinary support over the years. Their love and humour are a constant harbour and refuge. Every writer needs a muse and mine is my unusually clever and deliciously cynical grandmother, Amira, who has been my inspiration throughout this project.

On a practical level, many thanks to Munizha Ahmad-Cooke for her formatting and getting my manuscript into shape. Finally, this project would have been impossible without funding from the Arts and Humanities Research Board, LSE Studentships, the Morris Finer Scholarship, the Wedderburn Grant and the Authors' Foundation. I hope I have done justice to those investments.

Zeina B. Ghandour
London, September 2008

'As must be eminently clear, I am no historian.'
Gayatri C. Spivak, *Towards a History of the Vanishing Present*

Introduction

This is not ethnography

Unwriting Palestine

The story of Mandate Palestine is plagued by ambiguities: double (triple, quadruple) deals, irreconcilable promises, an indeterminate moral compass, improvisational strategy, intense diplomacy but no real implementation plan, the chaotic introduction and suspension of laws, regulations and customs, the classification (eradication?) of native culture. Amidst all of which, as a result of an ideological, political, economic and linguistic blitz, the multi-ethnic, multi-religious and multi-cultural region was gradually transformed to replicate, and is now fully reminiscent of, an ancient struggle between two Abrahamic tribes: the sons of Isaac, and those of Ishmael, his brother from another mother.

There is a major body of literature on Mandate Palestine in the tradition of linear historical narrative. In this tradition, each account will typically rely on its own accumulation of facts to support a particular political incline – be it pro-Arab, pro-Zionist, or apologist for empire. But this literature is more homogeneous than might appear at first glance. Its component parts have become embroiled, helplessly drawn into the compelling catastrophe as it unfolded, and routinely fall back on the adversarial antagonism which developed between Palestine natives and immigrants – or 'Arabs' and 'Jews' as they have come to be known – in order to tell and counter-tell how a homeland was 'lost' and 'won'.

But what those types of historical accounts of Mandate Palestine habitually and persistently disregard, in favour of the drama of the escalating nationalist conflict, of mounting Zionist desperation in the face of Jewish persecution in Europe, of mounting Arab desperation in the face of disfranchisement and Zionist encroachment, is the nature of British colonial aspirations, which loomed larger than, whilst alternately prodding and suppressing both Zionist and Palestinian national ambitions (in relation to the latter, make that asphyxiate). This is manifest in the official British discourse of the period, and to an even greater extent within unofficial discourse (conversation?) which focused always on the consolidation, rather than on the devolution of power

over there. The ambitions and character of British rule were clearly and
explicitly enunciated at the onset of the occupation of Palestine – in relation,
for instance, to the best techniques with which to rule natives in the generic
sense/Easterners/Muslims, to the historical place of Great Britain in the bib-
lically inspired restoration of the Jews to Palestine, and to the fundamental
rights and responsibilities of the worldwide imperial enterprise. Yet they have
gradually faded into the background and out of the frame of historical studies
of Mandate Palestine. That the empire existed before and beyond native or
settler, is a stubborn but dimly lit fact.

British discourse during the Mandate then, with its unremitting convergence
on the problematic of the 'native question', and which rested on racial and
cultural theories and presumptions, as well as on certain givens drawn from
the British class system, has been taken for granted by subsequent historians.
The validity of cultural representations as pronounced within official correspondence and colonial laws and regulations, as well as within the private
papers of colonial officials, survives more or less intact. There are features of
colonialism additional to economic and political power. There are features of
colonial rule in Palestine which are glaring yet have escaped examination,
which carried cultural weight and had cultural implications and which nega-
tively transformed native society. This was inevitable. But what is less inevitable is the subsequent collusion of historians in this, a (neo-) colonial
dynamic. The continued collusion of modern historians with racial and cultural notions concerning the rationale of European rule over there has postcolonial implications. It drags these old notions into the present where their
iniquitous barbarity continues to manifest.

Histories of Mandate Palestine written by historians, even if they are well-
meaning ones, even if they seem impartial, focus on big events and rely on
certain preconceived notions. These notions are themselves drawn from explicit
musings within the official documents of the national archives of Britain and
Israel, and they lend themselves to crude and sketchy summarization: Palestinians rioted regularly. Their farming methods were primitive and inefficient
and were in dire need of improvement and modernization. Their land law, a
scenic Ottoman relic, was a mess – nothing an overhaul could not fix. Anti-
British activity was the work of criminals, armed resistance was banditry,
guerrillas were desperados. Peasants lacked a coherent political consciousness
and were incapable of political action beyond a knee-jerk defence of their own
little patch of land. They were only worth discussing when they posed a threat
to law and order. They were clannish and volatile. Religion (one in particular),
could really get them going. Political leaders from the towns and cities were
parochial and motivated by kinship ties rather than ideas.

A Biblical backdrop, a primordial people. The rest is history?

In this work, I hope not so much to rewrite Mandate Palestine, or any
aspect of it, as to undo or dismantle the scaffolding on which Mandate histories are mounted (awkwardly, to 'unwrite'). The Palestinian–Zionist

conflict, though central in every other way, is deliberately marginalized in my exercise of dismantling. I did not want to interpret Palestinian culture or to lament its demise under colonial rule. As I progressed with my own research, I also quickly lost interest in any sort of fact finding. I was bored with the prospect of exploring whether the Palestinian élite had responded appropriately to the opportunities presented by the Mandatory Government. I dreaded agonizing over the inferiority of the resources and institutions offered to Palestinians as opposed to immigrants. I did not want to ask whether land reforms and legislation had contributed to dispossessing the peasantry, or to puzzle over the ineffectiveness of various commissions of inquiry that had come to Palestine in the wake of yet another 'disturbance'. I was struck by the mantra-like repetition of value-laden linguistic constructs imposed by the Palestine and Home Governments on Palestinian (geographic, economic, legal, political and cultural) ground. I became despondent at the prospect of joining in with my own whining litany of the many ways in which the British failed us (failed to emancipate us, failed to protect us) and of the ways in which the 'Jews' overpowered us. As familiar as the fragments of the Palestine story are, a story is more than the sum of its parts. Historians have been helplessly and collectively gripped by the unfolding and colourful drama, telling it and retelling it: a story of many opportunities presented, fought over and lost, of attempts to introduce a modicum of 'self-government' with 'autonomous' Arab institutions, of ill-conceived rebellion, of a pre-modern, pre-capitalist, underdeveloped native culture overrun by a sophisticated and wealthy migrant one, of Arab familial infighting which counteracted efforts of resistant political unity, of Arab land sales by desperate, short-sighted, naïve peasants and amoral, louche landowners, of illegal immigration from Europe, of intensifying competition over cultivable land between natives and migrants, of a criminalized peasantry and a humiliated local élite. And finally, bearing but witness to all this, of a hand-wringing British arbitrator despairing over his hot-headed Semitic clients.

The empire struck with discourse and it is possible to discourse directly back. Discourse sugarcoats violence. It is discourse rather than the big events and as a prerequisite to the big events, which influenced, moulded and manipulated political reality in Mandate Palestine. A discourse appealing to the desirability of uplifting social evolution via the technology of benevolent colonial rule and industrial capitalism was deployed mercilessly and aggressively. British rule was justified based on an organization and enunciation of culturally nuanced knowledge. For British cultural domination comprises more than the obvious inferiorizing, exoticizing and reifying aspects of Oriental culture. It is a phenomenon which manifests in seemingly benign and innocuous language. The introduction of conceptual basics such as 'Jews' and 'non-Jews', 'Moslems' and 'migrants', 'communities' and 'development', 'National Home' and 'Nation State', 'self-determination' and 'autonomy', 'extremists' and 'moderates', 'private' and 'public', 'religious' and 'secular', is one which has been taken for granted by historians as simply grasping and reflecting cultural realities but which, on the contrary, is deeply suggestive, fundamentally flawed, irrecuperably partial, and has contributed to the creation of novel/foreign binary oppositions and ditto cultural realities. The linguistic domination of Mandate Palestine is an acceptable fact which has somehow been achieved outside time and outside history – and what remains at stake amongst waylaid historians, is the physical manifestation of this domination and the techniques with which it was implemented. So histories which at first might seem to diverge irreconcilably in terms of style, allegiances and focus, nonetheless conspire in two crucial ways: first, by uncritically prioritizing the methodology of the discipline of history and second by adopting, again uncritically, the weighted language of the British Mandatory. We know that the colonial archive is a deeply tinged source which taints scholarship that draws on it when its contents are taken as comprehensive and absolute. However, it is also a rich, multi-layered source, which contains indicators and markers and glimpses of an alternative history. The colonial archive is capable of generating an entirely dissident reading and writing of history. For the mischievous like me, it really can be the gift that keeps on giving.

British control of natives alternated between direct and indirect rule. The latter method, which purported to preserve native structures, laws and customs whilst subjecting them to British supervision, was favoured. The widespread practice of indirect rule in British colonies between the two world wars may serve as a lens to magnify the colonial mindset. It helps me to situate Mandate Palestine within British colonialism's wider project of cultural control. (Dirks 1992: 3) The practice of ruling societies/communities/tribes through their own leaders meant that British colonial governments deployed a two-pronged strategy: they harnessed existing peremptory potential in native culture by consolidating its conservative elements, and they institutionalized the 'customary' by writing it down the best way they knew how. The result was that '[t]he notion of the customary was part of the continuity in British colonial thinking in its transcontinental sweep, from Asia to Africa'. (Mamdani 1996: 22)

Although Palestine was ostensibly ruled directly, it is still possible to ask: what existing state apparatus did the British make use of in their support of the 'customary' and what apparatus did they impose where none existed? How did the method of rule traditionally favoured in the colonies – indirect rule – adapt to the circumstances of the Palestine Mandate and feed into the mindsets of high commissioners and other high-ranking colonial officials? This is a secondary question. I am not interested in a disinterested examination of the techniques of rule deployed by the British Mandatory, but wish to address the values and judgements which motivated them. I even resolved, initially, not to attempt to recuperate or restore authenticity to the story of Mandate Palestine. I wanted instead simply to strain against accepted ways of referring to events during the period of British rule there until 1939 and to do that by using as many narrative accounts as I could obtain (native, official, semi-official), to contest/derange the well-trodden historical terrain.

In the course of my research however, I came across some deeply moving material from native sources. I deliberately avoided interpreting or explaining or subjecting this material to analytic commentary, because it would have been overbearing to the narratives and would have diminished from their sensational impact and might even have drowned out their low, laboured whispers entirely. These narratives were initially to be introduced purely to mirror colonial language, to dislodge accepted linguistic and cultural constructs, and hopefully to make the reader feel slightly sick and uncomfortable when faced with them. The prime motivation for collecting them and presenting them was a strategic one: they were to be used solely to assist me in the exercise of unhinging. Arguably though, I undertook the endeavour with such enthusiasm that another story managed to seep through and the result was a satisfying ethnographic tableau. I had recovered the native voice, tape-recorded it, transcribed and translated it and the result was a due correction of perspective. For that I am grateful, since the alternative might have remained a purely nihilistic, ironic exercise. Even though Western domination of the history of Palestine continues, let there be, to use the phrase coined by the historian Ranajit Guha,[1] 'Dominance without Hegemony'. (Guha 1989b: 231)

Inspirations

There is a rich body of critical literature which chronicles the historiography, ethnography and sociology of colonialism, which has not been written by historians and which challenges and undermines the reliance on colonial and neo-colonial discourse across disciplines.[2] This literature is quite simply fortifying and provides a nourishing antidote to the malaise brought on by too much history. Bernard Cohn demonstrates how empirical and ethnographic representations made by the colonial state came to pass for knowledge about India. Edward Said argues that European knowledge of the Orient was gravely tainted by the European's own cultural, political, economic and military exigencies.[3] I became particularly inspired in the course of my research by the work of the Subaltern Studies Group (who, incidentally, pay great homage to Bernard Cohn), for their declamatory stance, and for their explicit and unremitting anti-colonial commitment. The Subaltern Studies Group draw on postcolonial theory and they particularly challenge the Anglocentric Cambridge school of history, which has focused on the activity and creativity of the imperial state, its policies and administration, all seemingly undertaken and chronicled whilst the natives did what natives do best: sleep (and riot).[4] The main aim of the Subaltern Studies Group was articulated thus: to address the question of restoring the subaltern (a term lifted from Gramsci to indicate a non-élite group[5]), to history. Their premise was that the absence of the subaltern from what we accept as history is itself revelatory. They asked whether it was possible to discover subaltern consciousness beyond that which has been attributed to it by external leadership. They also asked, more controversially, whether a critique of the West could extend beyond the colonial record of double-dealing and false promises, of exploitation, collaboration and oppression, to reach into the discipline of history itself. It is a question of validity: the tentative but unmistakable suggestion being that it was possible to draw on knowledge which has been communicated away from the official/public sphere. Knowledge, that is to say, drawn from immediate, organic and spontaneous sources of information, and which is not easily contorted to satisfy colonial categories. Subaltern studies draws attention to neo-colonialism as a continuing European grip on the third world in the form of language. Postcolonial theory is radical because it dares to critique discourses of modernity, liberalism and even humanism.[6] It enables us to contest the domination not only of one group by another, but of one mode of knowledge by another. It implores a clash of discourses. It can be revolutionary, inventive and unwaveringly dissident in both the theories it pursues and the subjects it chooses.

Until now, although a gradual shift is inevitably occurring, postcolonial theory remained largely the domain of scholars of literature. But since they meddle in history, they have been criticized by historians: for their apparent free-styling, their relaxed approach to the basic rules of chronology and context, and for their apparent lack of methodological focus. One accusation routinely levelled at postcolonial theorists is their 'theoretical promiscuity' (Kennedy 1996: 348) or generous intellectual expansiveness. In turn, the knee-jerk distaste that historians might feel for postcolonial theorists is reciprocated. Some, such as Gayatri C. Spivak (who is responsible for introducing post-structuralist theories into the postcolonial debate) and Homi K. Bhabha (who throws psychoanalysis into the mix), significantly undermine the value of history. They question whether it has any innate usefulness at all, and suggest it is primarily a (barely-concealed) complement to Western domination. So Bhabha reduces history to a 'grand narrative', a vast arena distinguished by its discursive value alone, whilst Spivak writes of the need to chip away at 'hegemonic historiography'(cited in ibid.: 350). Ashis Nandy's essays provide 'an alternative mythography of history which denies and defies the values of history'. (Nandy 1988: xv)[7]

Things are fraught, it is a face-off.

Another criticism levelled at postcolonial theorists is that they regularly draw on a coterie of largely French, but in any event Eurocentric scholarship to deconstruct Western domination of the third world.[8] That may be so, but it is understandable, as the disruptive energy of postmodernism and post-structuralism is too seductive, too useful to be left alone, even if it is blond and blue-eyed. Jacques Derrida's deconstruction is a profoundly anti-hierarchical and anti-authoritarian mode of seeing, understanding and explaining. Derridean deconstruction (or rather, our observation of the state of deconstruction of things, their deconstructability), is not negative or nullifying. On the contrary, it can be life-giving: 'For me, it always accompanies an affirmative exigency, I would even say that it never proceeds without love' (Weber 1995: 83) – and it may even be indistinguishable from reconstruction. Also irresistible is Jean-François Lyotard, who famously wrote: 'I define *postmodern* as an incredulity towards metanarratives'. (Lyotard 1997: xxiii–iv) Lyotard's metanarratives comprise discourses that inaugurate, establish and legitimate the status of knowledge. Michel Foucault is so ubiquitous in postcolonial critiques that one could be excused for doing Foucault without knowing it. It is difficult to imagine making incursions into history without his 'archaeology' (digging around the historical archive in order to uncover the processes which formed a particular field of 'knowledge'), 'discourse' (language associated with a particular institution which reflects the institution's values), 'epistemes' (periods of history associated with certain world-views, disciplines and 'knowledge'), 'games of truth' (when public institutions legitimize their actions by resort to claims of eternal truths, whilst in reality it is these 'truths' which are dependent on institutional practices), and 'genealogy' (following Nietzsche, this involves constructing a sort of family tree of what passes for knowledge or truth in a society, the suggestion being that these are produced as the result of institutional power struggles).[9]

Is there such a thing as colonialism anyway? What to do with assertions that it is not one monolithic construct, but that it is made up of a bunch of shifting, irregular variables and fragile paradigms, that it is full of tensions as well as triumphs, that it is full of incoherence and inchoateness, complexities and contortions? (see Comaroff and Comaroff 1992.: 183). Is any endeavour to talk about colonialism in a generic rather than technical sense therefore doomed to be unsophisticated and reductive? Are we, in effect, precluded from attaching adjectives to the word because its manifestations are so complex and intricate? Colonialism is based on coercion and it is based on conflict (an initial invasion or simply an intimidating show of force), inequality and brutality (see Mbembe 2001).[10] Where there are negotiations, treaties or agreements between colonialist and native, they invariably legitimize the colonizer's ultimate authority. The colonial world is divided and divisive and it rests on a central doctrine of power, where the subject and object of command is inevitably the native (ibid.: 34).

They are emboldened in their method by the postmodernists, but the Subaltern Studies Group may owe their unflinchingly anti-colonial moral legacy to a small but powerful body of work.[11] The stunning, self-righteous eloquence of Frantz Fanon, Aimé Césaire and Albert Memmi, their unreconstructed denunciations of colonialism as mental sickness, thievery, savagery and sadism, their warning that it dehumanizes and degrades the colonizer as much as he dehumanizes and degrades his colonial subject, provide irreversible and incontrovertible landmarks for any honest examination of European rule in Africa or the East. Fanon was a psychiatrist from Martinique, radicalized during his work in Algeria. Césaire was a poet, playwright and politician, also from Martinique, and one of the progenitors of the Negritude/Black Pride cultural movement. Memmi was a Tunisian Jew and a novelist who called himself 'a half breed of colonization' – as a Jew in a predominantly Muslim society, and as a man of colour under the auspices of a white colony. All three wrote in revolt against the economic and psycho-social dynamics of French colonial domination. Their first-hand experience of colonialism is their field-work and observation. They write down (savagely), the ethnos, the culture of the social group of colonialists in their midst. These men were inflamed by France, but the dynamics they illuminate are common to the project of domination that colonialism is. I adopt them as my ancestral pedigree.

These writers also made room in which it became possible to engage with the weaknesses and moral squalor of the colonialist subject of observation. Césaire writes that claims linking colonization with civilization are outright lies, and that colonialism is, contrary to such outright and widespread lies, 'neither evangelization, nor a philanthropic enterprise, nor a desire to push back the frontiers of ignorance, disease, and tyranny, nor a project undertaken for the glory of God, nor an attempt to extend the rule of law'. (Césaire 1972: 10) Colonialism is a mission undertaken with contempt. Naivety, senti-mentality or blundering good will are irrelevant to his analysis. Contact between cultures and individuals is not human contact as we know it, but characterized by 'relations of domination and submission which turn the colonizing man into a classroom monitor, an army sergeant, a prison guard, a slave driver, and the indigenous man into an instrument of production'. (ibid.: 21) By virtue of his brief, the colonialist cannot prioritize the interests of the native over his own, or the interests of the miserable nation where he finds himself at the expense of his own. His priority is not the well-being of the local. As much as he may find himself bewitched or seduced by or empathic to his subject, he did not disembark from his ship in an altruistic state of mind, looking for people to love or serve or gift. One way or another, it is safe to say he came to dominate. The culmination of this domination is manifest in the disciplines of history and ethnography, which are European/white disciplines. Ethnography is traditionally associated with the study not only of another group, but of another group which is perceived to be inferior by the observer. Why is it, Césaire asks rhetorically, that it is the West which studies the ethnography of others and not others the ethnography of the West? (ibid.: 54).

Under these conditions, is it possible to undertake a study of British colonialism as a historical ethnography of the Palestine Mandate? This is theoretically possible insofar as ethnography is the act/art of describing a group or a cul-ture, and insofar as that group or culture is often different from that of the observer's. The tribe consists of the extended family of British colonial officials. The colonial archive is the field. However, a real ethnography of colonialism would require/imply 'the provincialization of Europe',[12] and that will never happen. Still, although my tentative project is doomed to failure, I have to at least try: to question the authority which bolsters history and to contribute to its decolonization (see Young 1996: 11). Everything is, after all, subject to the impetus of time and universal cycles: according to the rules of evolution, power is defined by its susceptibility to challenge.[13]

In this study then, I would like to identify the symbolism of British officials' discourse. In order to do this, I intertwine them with the symbolism and imagery of the natives' own discourse (from oral interviews and private family papers). I wonder how the two might mesh, how they interconnect. At all times, I remain allied to those writers, philosophers and chroniclers whose central preoccupation is to agitate and challenge authority. I will adopt Memmi's, Fanon's and Césaire's unforgiving starting point: the assumption that nothing valid, acceptable or authentic can flow from the arrival of the colonialist, that his situation is therefore irredeemably illegitimate and that his persona (not necessarily his personality) is forged by his urge for profit, privilege and appropriation (or any combination of these). He cannot help it: his prescribed role is first and foremost that of a usurper and his remit is to disturb the local order and to substitute his own. He accords himself advantages at the expense of the native's, whose rights are innate. I will focus on the weighted language of the colonialist to ask what it reveals about the British justifications for colonization and how it manipulates and contributes to the dehumanization (in history, let alone in Mandatory reality) of the Palestine natives.

For beyond economic and political domination, lies mythology. It is a familiar and not particularly contentious protest but one I wish to raise and emphasize in this context: what we take as value-free, transparent language, should alternatively be read as audacious, exotically patterned myth-making. This myth-making is part of a world-view and is present at every turn of British colonial consciousness, in every reference to Great Britain, the King, civilization, progress and law. It is also part of an attempt to claim and impose that world-view as universal. The colonialist's priority is not to represent the place he loots and pillages, but to write/glorify the history of his own country, to engrave his white, modern, civilized, developed Word on an ahistorical, pre-historical, subhuman, archaic, ignorant, superstitious, empty-in-every-sense-of-the-word, amenable place:

> The settler makes history; his life is an Epoch, an Odyssey. He is the absolute beginning: 'This land was created by us'; he is the unceasing cause: 'If we leave, all is lost, and the country will go back to the Middle Ages.' (Fanon 1963: 51)

This, then, is a return to the Old School, a revisit of the optimistic, vibrant rhetoric of these radicals, who continue to inspire post- and anti-colonial thinking. In order to dismantle and undo and unwrite, I hold a mirror up to the language of the Mandatory by counteracting with an integrally oppositional discourse and a provocative rhetoric of my own. My style is confrontational as I am essentially calling time on the use of language invented during the Mandate and drawing attention to its vicious, contorting linguistics.

The Palestine Mandate is dead but its spirit is alive and haunting Jerusalem, where it has been seen roaming the cobbled streets of the Old City on a new, full and quarter moon, muttering to itself incomprehensibly.

Chapters

What, then, about this colonial vocabulary?

In Chapter 1, 'Through their chiefs', I look at British colonial narratives from Africa and the East. The writings of colonial agents/adventurers/administrators provide the seeds for legitimating narratives of Progress, and we consign them to the novelty section of the history file at our peril. How have they contributed to establishing the legitimacy of political discourse regarding the empire's Dependencies – most recently, the discourse around the League of Nations Mandates? (see Lyotard op. cit.: 34). The Mandates emerged out of the tradition of nineteenth-century colonialism, which hankered after order by inventing and imposing binary polarities and they amounted to an attack on non-modern cultures. It is sufficient to refer to their language to demonstrate this, which espoused a straightforward juxtaposition of old and new, useful and useless, the verifiable and the superstitious and so on.[14] Something in them, a trace, continues to haunt and resonate. They have shaped current cultural and political norms. In Lyotard's terms, their utterances are therefore not merely 'denotative', but 'prescriptive'. They are the imperceptible components of accepted, time-honoured, political, historical and cultural Western knowledge structures. This chapter also contextualizes Britain's interest in the Middle East. The spirit of evangelism and Christian Zionism ascribed cultural meaning to the British domination of Palestine, and it provides rich common ground, a cultural setting shared between colonialist and colonized.

In Chapter 2, 'Unmarked and undivided', I examine the language of development as it related to the issue of land and land law in Palestine. Again acknowledging and bolstered by Césaire, Memmi and Fanon, I ask whether what we read as history (both primary texts and historic interpretation of those texts), is interchangeable with fiction, where the rewriting of texts and reinscription of memory have imperceptibly stood in for truths. It is quite predictable: in order to introduce changes with conviction, with some peace of mind, the colonialist must inflate his own merits and those of his culture, as well as highlight the demerits of his subject. According to Memmi (1966: 90–91), it is therefore part of the psychology of colonization that, to be at peace with himself, the colonial agent must exalt himself and diminish the native and so justify the latter's subjugation. The language used by colonial officials to describe native systems of cultivation and tenure burnt new realities onto old texts, ones that were more consonant with their own world-view. So the passive, senile, idle, unbelievable indolence of the East is exemplified/echoed in these primitive land systems. Moreover, this exquisite dilapidation conveniently contrasts with the colonialist's taste for action, technology and advancement, and justifies his presence and interventions. As Fanon explains, the colonialist is not satisfied with simple delimitation of the space allocated to the native or appropriated for himself. The delimitation of physical dimensions is accompanied by psychological and cultural ones. (Fanon op. cit.: 41) So the underdeveloped, derelict agricultural landscape of the native is explicitly identified as corresponding with his decrepit and decaying moral and intellectual landscape. It is as though the native exists in a gigantic crack, a dearth of morals, resources, motivation and thought. The land is empty, the native a spectre who knows how to hover but not to cultivate. Conveniently, its 'ownership' cannot be readily ascertained or determined. It is screaming out to be exorcised and repossessed, inseminated and revitalized, dominated and owned.

In the third chapter, 'Between the bazaar and the bungalow', I use the 1936–39 rebellion to expose the flawed historiography which relies on exclusively élite (foreign and local) and official sources and values/vocabulary to account for local political developments. The nationwide strike of 1936 which became a fully fledged peasant rebellion is commonly recounted as an outburst of disorganized, primitive violence, which turned predictably inwards and eventually self-imploded. Rather, I will take the stand alongside Fanon and Memmi, and declare the colonial situation as a stranglehold to which there can only be one authentic reaction if one is a native from a non-élite (i.e. a subaltern) social group. This is not so much a claim for the necessity of violence on the part of the native in a colonial situation, as for its inevitability. The native has to do something with what Fanon calls his 'muscular tension' (ibid.: 54) since there is no demand for his vocal chords. Neither is the value of violence/rebellion therefore assessed according to whether it achieves its stated aim of ejecting the colonialist. Rather, violence is seen as reclamation of the self. The revolutionary instincts of the native stem from the discovery of his humanity and of his equality with the colonialist/settler (ibid.). In a colonial context, the chief qualities of violence are cleansing and redemptive. It is only once his rage boils over that the native recuperates his dignity. Violence represents rediscovered innocence and is an essential prerequisite to his self-love. (Memmi op. cit.: 164; Sartre 1963: 21–22) In the words of Memmi (op. cit.: 183): '*Pour vivre le colonisé doit supprimer la colonisation. Mais pour devenir un homme, il doit supprimer le colonisé qu'il est devenu.*'

The 1936 strike/rebellion may be used to show how the language of law, security, order and respect, is claimed by the colonialist to dissimulate and obfuscate the sins he cheerfully commits on the shore where he has landed, and the physical, economic and political violence he perpetrates against the natives he finds there, until 'the same violence is thrown back upon us as when our reflection comes forward to meet us when we go toward a mirror'. (Fanon op. cit.: 17)

In Chapter 4, 'Raising of the religious cry', I look at the psychological, class and political needs of the British élite, and at how those needs were projected onto local culture, to create 'Muslims', 'moderates', and 'extremists' out of the Palestinian aristocracy. I will use Memmi's starting point that the social status of the local bourgeoisie/aristocracy is begrudgingly accepted by the colonialist, for he knows that in the end, the power is in his hands and they are his subjects. The behaviour and attitude of the native élite in the colonies are traditionally characterized by a willingness to compromise, to adopt the language imposed by the usurpers and to accept its limitations. It is symptomatic of their class that they are conciliatory, reluctant to break off dialogue, and given to discussion and debate. According to Fanon though, that is not because the native intellectual/aristocracy/élite is at peace with what is happening to them, but simply because they have sublimated their aggression and hostility to their master: 'The native intellectual has clothed his aggressiveness in his barely veiled desire to assimilate himself to the colonial world.'(ibid.: 60) This ambivalence is never resolved as long as the colonialist is present. The native intellectuals/aristocrats/élites, who initially succumbed to Western corruption and domination at the onset of the colonial enterprise, will eventually turn away from the mindset imposed on them. The colonialist is aghast as he realises that there has, in fact, been no 'colonisation of consciousness' (see Comaroff and Comaroff: Ch. 9) – especially with regard to the Jewish National Home in Palestine, which remained equally unpalatable to the élite as it was to the peasants. It is this rejection of the colonialist's way of thinking and talking that is recounted as intransigence, extremism and rejectionist negativism. Instead of weighing up the constricted (re)actions of the élite I will also suggest that it may be more interesting to turn the tables and to ask how the British colonialist bore his impossible psychological burden, how he came to terms with his appropriative illegitimacy, and whether, in a surge of narcissism, he was driven to seek his reflection in his subject. I will ask whether it is not a pathology of colonialism and a dangerous self-exaltation of the colonialist which degrades adult native men into the status of children and which assumes that, like children, they must be trained, taught and socialised (cf. Nandy op. cit.: 14–16).

The final chapter, 'The last word', is a surprise.

The bias against Palestine (the root of the bias is a Western one, but insidious, and has penetrated the modern Arab world) is heavy because it relies on a manipulation of language. It is dominated by split-level thinking which distinguishes tradition from modernity, science from superstition, discipline from indolence and a few good men from the swarming masses. It is for this reason that I have congregated my thoughts and efforts around the use and manipulation of political idiom, that I choose to write/strike back rather than rewrite an alternative history of Mandate Palestine in which my own Negritude is exalted: 'Whosoever exalts himself shall be abased'. Or on a more worldly level, '*Ma vie ne doit pas être consacrée à faire le bilan des valeurs nègres.*' (Fanon op. cit.: 16)

In this exercise of undoing, if a concept seems obscure or unfeasible, then I appeal to its subliminal potential. Fanon told Sartre that in writing *The*

Wretched of the Earth, he wanted to reach the reader non-rationally, or even 'sensually'. He wanted his reader to remain susceptible to the magic of words, to their electric charge and kinetic energy. He wanted his reader to experience authentic, undeniable *'surgissements'*, (visceral realizations, intuitions or experiences of literal clair-voyance). For even as Fanon sometimes appears to dynamite his own discourse or explode his own arguments, he does so in order to shake the reader out of intellectual complacency. (Sartre op. cit.: 12) I similarly seek refuge in the suggestive, rather than literal power of words. Finally, I am aware that I am intimately implicated in the structures I claim to want to subvert, that my style is tangled with the styles of those structures, and that I am therefore indebted to those structures. In the words of Spivak: 'In the third world, no one gets off on being third world.' (Cited by Afzal-Khan and Sheshadri-Crooks 2000: 3.)

But enough about structures: we have circled the temple sufficiently. Let us go inside.

Notes

1 Ranajit Guha has led the work of the Subaltern Studies Group.
2 I cannot hope to do justice to this comprehensive literature here but with regard to Africa and Asia for instance, Bernard Cohn's *An Anthropologist Among the Historians* (1987), John and Jean Comaroff's *Ethnography and the Historical Imagination* (1992) and Mahmoud Mamdani's *Citizen and Subject* (1996) stand out. Other important exertions towards the decolonization of knowledge are also found in Adam Ashforth's *The Politics of Official Discourse in Twentieth-century South Africa* (1990), Mary Louise Pratt's *Imperial Eyes* (2000), Frederick Cooper's 'Conflict and connection: rethinking colonial African history' (1994). With regard to the Middle East, we have, just as examples, Edward Said's breakthrough masterpiece, *Orientalism* (1978), Timothy Mitchell's *Colonising Egypt* (1991), Nadia Abu El-Haj's *Facts on the Ground* (2001), Abdesalam Maghraoui's *Liberalism Without Democracy* (2006), Ella Shohat's *Taboo Memories, Diasporic Voices* (2006), Scott Atran's 'The surrogate colonization of Palestine, 1917–39' (1989), Ronen Shamir's *The Colonies of Law* (2000) and Ted Swedenburg's *Memories of Revolt* (1995).
3 It might be noted at this juncture that despite Said's breakthrough *Orientalism* (op. cit.), postcolonial theory and Middle East studies are still only occasional bedfellows.
4 For a short chronicle of the Cambridge movement and its significance, see Ronald Robinson (1982) 'Oxford in imperial historiography'.
5 The definition and notion of the subaltern are explored in more detail in Chapter 3.
6 See Sheshadri-Crooks (2000:7).
7 Nandy is not part of the Subaltern Studies Group but his work on colonial India is of the most significant.
8 Ethnocentric post-structuralism is not the only way to go, and we have Frantz Fanon, Aimé Césaire and Albert Memmi as models. I discuss them later in this Introduction. See Larsen (2000:142). Also, Derrida is a French–Algerian Jew and perhaps not exactly Eurocentric.
9 See Foucault (1991, 2001 and 1995). The latter marks Foucault's transition from his 'archaeological' to 'genealogical' period. For 'games of truth', see Herman (1998). See also Danaher *et al.* (2000; ix–xi, 29–40).

10 Mbembe (2001: 25) distinguishes three types of violence (founding, legitimating and institutional) which are all features of a state sovereignty in a colony.
11 This includes, for instance, the work of W. E. B. Dubois, C. L. R. James, Amilcar Cabral, Aimé Césaire, Frantz Fanon, Leopold Senghor, Albert Memmi. Walter Mignolo (2000: 90) writes:

> Subaltern rationality ... nourishes and is nourished by a theoretical practice that was prompted by the movements of decolonization after WWII and that at its inception had little to do with academic enterprises ... and had at its core the question of race.

12 Dipesh Chakrabarty, cited by Prakash (1994: 1485).
13 Cf. Guha (1989: 231), there is 'no Nazi fantasy of total force that is not disturbed by nightmares of dissent'.
14 Nandy (op. cit.: x) argues for a critique of universalism to be combined with a defence of non-modern cultures.

Chapter 1

'Through their chiefs':[1]

The metanarrative of imperial rule in Africa and the East

This is not an overview or summary of the external strategic/economic forces which drove the British Empire: its trajectory is self-explanatory from a historicist point of view and the strategic and economic motives which drove it are well known. The story of the British Empire is one that has been told many times, by many different people and in many different ways. Tackling this story was a potentially complicated exercise, since the British Empire was very busy, very large, and quite old. But there is one aspect of the British Empire which has not been written about as many times as it could have. This is the aspect of its poetics and lyricism, of the exquisite, soulful pain behind the official rhetoric.

A matter of style: what is the flavour of British imperialism?

A popular starting point for an excursion into British imperialism is to ask whether it is possible to identify any ideological progenies that were perpetuated between one Dependency[2] and the next – whether that Dependency was a Protectorate, a Crown Colony, or a Mandated Territory. To do this, alternative routes may be taken: in a chronological exercise, British thinking about India is not only implicated in British thinking about Africa, which itself is implicated in British thinking about the Middle East, but such thinking is demonstratively sequential.[3] This is a case of grabbing a thread in order to, say, follow the development of the idea that colonial rule was akin to a Trust. Another possibility would be to start with the assumption that even though a continuum appears to be at play, it is close to impossible to trace a straight line from, for instance, mid-nineteenth century Punjab, where the seeds of a certain governing ethos of ruling indirectly first germinated, and according to which thorough political control was achieved and maintained with minimal physical and financial exertion, to turn of twentieth-century Nigeria, where a certain Captain Lugard elevated indirect rule into an administrative principle.[4] The two approaches overlap considerably.

Either way, British imperial policy[5] – and there was never such a thing if by policy we mean policies devised in London, and if there were it was characterized by its adaptability – amounted to allowing the men on the spot, in that unenviable field, to get on with it. But we can still ask: is there a detectable trend across the geographic and historical expanse of British colonial rule? Can we trace one or two identifiable phenomena common to countries with a history of British rule? Can we stop examining the political, economic, legal or administrative measures instituted for the purpose of domination and modernization or for the drive behind them, and ask instead about Britain's own cultural legacy from her contact with those countries? For instance, British rule was chiefly characterized by a (relative, purported) ambivalence to the use of force – not because of any ultimate moral objections but, more interestingly, because British officers availed themselves of certain attributes – manly qualities which, they claimed, allowed them to function without resort to it: their command was flawless, the order around them like a dream.[6] Under these circumstances, invasion/domination and peacekeeping are indistinguishable. Even though initial power over a nation/people/community would have been established through the use, threat or display of force, this alone did not account for the implementation of day-to-day control over royal courts in their entirety, key ruling clans and influential élite classes, native subordinates in their hundreds, thousands and hundreds of thousands. For this, the imperial trailblazers could not count on London. In the British colonial fairy tale, they primarily relied on their wits as they forged new paths of war (indistinguishable from peace), commerce and government. In this fairy tale they ruled through example, persuasion, and little else. They relied on their intelligence and flexibility, and were driven by their conviction that they were good, and that what they were doing was good. Here is an indication: they advertised, and wrote about their missions in terms of devotion and sacrifice, progress and humanity, honour and bravery. A veil of benevolence and self-effacement sheathed the individual actions of these imperial agents. They saw themselves as servants to a higher cause, and their master was not only the British Government, or the King, or God, but humanity and civilization. Even as they sloshed about in African swamps, dehydrated in Arabian deserts, or heroically battled against the sensual corruption of Eastern administrations, the average awe-inspiring imperial agent also appeared selfless and sought and often received love from the natives. At least, this is the hard-earned 'mystique',[7] the aura of British colonial rule.

How did they do it? How did they make political domination look like devotion and selflessness? It was inevitably accompanied by something more robust, but the notion of benevolent, compassionate and ethical imperial government was common to India, Africa and the Middle and Far East. Even as battles raged and renegades were executed, tribes co-opted and territories annexed, all this was accomplished under an enduring veneer of progress, regeneration and service. Imperial agents overstepped the mark of duty, in a positive way and to a positive end; it was not mere prosaic economic and military advantage they were after, but palpable personal influence over local leaders, and their and the rest of the subject nation's moral uplift. The fate of British honour was in their hands. It was not enough for them to be powerful: they had to be admirable for their personal qualities too – loveable even. Foreign imperial rule was seen as ultimately ennobling: for the native, who could not resist the pull of moral improvement, and for the colonial representative, whose exemplary behaviour reflected on his own race and culture. The opportunity presented to them in the field was not limited to achieving the results set by London's agenda; they were set to prove themselves as men of the highest order.

The method of colonial government that became known as Indirect Rule (with capital letters) thanks to Captain Lugard and his work in Northern Nigeria, became especially popular in Africa between the two world wars. Indirect rule (without capital letters) is not necessarily associated with Africa; it was practised before Lugard and simply entailed rule through a façade of native institutions/leaders. It (both with or without capital letters) provided the perfect opportunity for the display of moral, intellectual and spiritual excellence. Where rule is indirect, the colonial agent had to be self-effacing enough to insist on the paramount preservation of the native leader's prestige, and canny and confident enough to strategically avoid the use of unnecessary violence without compromising his own, all-powerful position. Where there were native institutions (courts, councils, treasuries), which satisfied British institutional requirements, they were left intact but subject to British supervision. Variations on this basic model were practised in the opulent Princely States of India, in the ceremonial Emirates of Northern Nigeria, in an Egypt collapsing under the weight of the Turks, in Fiji and in the Malay States.[8] Indirect Rule made it possible to rule countless natives with nothing but a few (very) good men, who protected imperial interests thanks to their individual qualities of fearlessness, inventiveness, charm, intelligence, resilience, determination and compassion, without ever relinquishing a hyper-awareness of their superior status, and without hesitating to periodically (and literally) crack the whip to remind everyone of who was in charge. They needed those qualities and that awareness to see them through their arduous missions. As Lugard (1959: 59) wrote with hindsight, whilst tropical Africa was not a place for 'mean whites', nor was it appropriate to lower one's status and risk one's reputation by degrading one's self to the level of the uncivilized races.

Even though British colonial rule was not heterogeneous or centrally coordinated and London had little to say about the precise mechanics of British authority overseas, this does not preclude an enquiry into colonial culture. We are in a position to intercept their communications. We are in a position to infiltrate the writings of colonial agents and out of them weave the texture and fabric of British imperial domination. It may or it may not be that the texture and fabric of this domination, of this way of doing business, are emblematic of an 'English character'.[9] However those imperial officials did come with heavy cultural and emotional baggage: a belief in the superiority of their own world, that no other man on earth could sustain what they were sustaining and accomplish the miracles they were accomplishing, that without them the natives would self-destruct, that they were doing what they were doing not for any self-aggrandisement but on the contrary, selflessly – for God, for the King, for England, without a doubt for the unsuspecting natives themselves as well as for the rest of the world. Although domination, it was enlightened, benevolent, progressive domination.

Why should those men and their cultural and emotional baggage matter to us? Why bother to poke around their personal motivations, their insatiable emotional needs, their fixation with honour and fairness or the pain behind their wanderlust? First, it is because they coincidentally wrote about those things. Lugard of Africa, Cromer of Egypt and Lawrence of Arabia wrote more than official despatches to the metropolis; they wrote diaries and memoirs that seem dated to the contemporary reader. But it would be a mistake to dismiss them as the atavistic and inconsequential ravings of irredeemably suspect characters, of interest only for their antique or retro value. The narratives are of those men, who, after all, formed the empire's backbone. Secondly, theirs are metanarratives and they reflect the metanarrative of British colonialism which has since emerged.

Three men who wrote about themselves: the genealogy of a metanarrative

The narratives of the agents/diplomats/soldiers/adventurers of the empire do more than provide informative/entertaining glimpses into their lives and work. They represent the beginnings of a grand narrative which has since become inscribed onto our culture and world-view and they have contributed to the construction of a historical discourse which has since proved immovable.

What is the relationship between the private narratives of colonial agents, and colonial discourse/the discourse of the discipline of colonial history? What can the individual voices of colonial agents teach us about what passes for knowledge about Britain's Dependencies? What is their place in the legitimating public narratives of Progress and Freedom? Lyotard (1997: 36) writes:

> The important thing is not, or not only, to legitimate denotative utterances pertaining to the truth, such as 'the earth revolves around the sun', but rather to legitimate prescriptive utterances pertaining to justice, such as 'Carthage must be destroyed', or 'the minimum wage must be set at x Dollars'.

In other words, it is the prescriptive potential of these texts that is interesting. These men *wrote* the empire and in doing so they exposed their own moral and physical limitations, highlighting their triumphs all the more vividly. They wrote the empire in its ramshackle, dishevelled, feverish glory. Their narratives stand as cultural pillars for the empire. They tell us that it is not easy being a colonial agent, it is hard graft, but the personal rewards are nothing short of magnificent. The three men – Evelyn Baring in Egypt who became Lord Cromer; T.E. Lawrence (afterwards Shaw, afterwards Ross), who turned down the Companionship of the Bath and the Distinguished Service Orders in 1918, and sought obscurity once his mission was accomplished; Captain Frederick Lugard in darkest Africa who became the international statesman Lord Lugard – were very different one from the other: a racist and bilious Cromer, T.E. is as genuinely melancholic as the Bedouins he befriends, and Lugard's sanguine diaries reveal stoical poise in the face of devastating loneliness and heartache. We do not know what they were really like, or what they were really up to in the grisly field. Occasionally there are hints of a dark side, of momentary madness. They were basically unaccountable, untouchable. Donald Cameron, in charge of Tanganyika and then Northern Nigeria between 1925 and 1935, claimed Lugard was 'blood-stained to the collar stud'. (Tidrick 1990: 124) There had also been a question mark over Lugard's political career and future in the 1890s, when various accusations were made regarding his behaviour in Africa, to the effect that it was oppressive and inhumane.[10] And it is in the men's literary contributions, in their diaries and despatches, that the full depth and complexity of their experiences and characters are revealed. There we can leaf through their strategies for survival and control, their hopes and dreams and nightmares, their illnesses and fears and disappointments, their scandalous, edgy excesses. It is all here: sin and redemption, punishment and forgiveness, work and service, power and love. There is no way around it: whatever they were doing, it was risky, beautiful and worthwhile. They describe in detail the leaps of faith and imagination they made to fulfil their hazy mission. If they had to flog a few, shoot a few along the way, it was not out of old-fashioned sadism – they did it regretfully, with a heavy heart, and we forgive them, for it was on themselves that they were hardest. But beneath the luminous beauty of their texts lurk the shadows. As well as everything else, these were unbreakable men, unshakable. There is something steely in their eyes, carefully dissimulating the unprovoked cultural violence behind imperial action as it claims to wage war primarily against barbarity, as it claims to be guided by a higher purpose, as it launches control of native space, and as it throws a veil of benevolence and good will (or at the very least of reason, logic and objectivity) on acts of coercion, invasion and manipulation, as it shores up colonial hierarchies, and as it finally obliterates from history (because it is inferior and weak and begging for obliteration) the native world-view and the entire native experience.[11]

Certainly, it is not the history of those foreign peoples and foreign places which is either written or read, but the history of how influential individuals saw the empire which they served. There is a common assumption in the writings of Cromer, Lugard and Lawrence: the British will conquer because it

is indubitably in their nature, and the people in question have allowed themselves to be conquered because it is indubitably in theirs. Imperialism does not
need any more rationale than that, such as being the result of capitalist
expansion or of the ambitions of individual explorers and adventurers (see
Memmi 1966: 150–51). How have these men shaped what passes for knowledge
about the natives they fraternized with? Their writings might tell us.

Love, humility, prudence: some surprising characteristics of the colonial agent

East Africa, December 1890. A young Captain Lugard, 32 years old, arrives at
Buganda (Bantu for the Swahili 'Uganda'), north-west of Lake Victoria. There
the rain is regular, the land is green, the soil is rich and extensively cultivated.
The food supply is plentiful, the people have been able to devote their time to
other pursuits besides survival such as leisure and government, and they have
developed a high material culture. A centralized monarchy oversees a highly
organized administration. The court functions according to elaborate ceremony
and the King's entourage is formally titled, in a way 'reminiscent of the
entourage at Versailles'. (Lugard 1959, vol. 2: 13) Two rival missionary
groups, one French and the other English, have been conducting their work in
the area since 1877. There are also Muslims in the region competing for souls.
Party organization by the ruling class and 'intrigue' inevitably begin to fracture
along religious lines. When the King dies his son, Mwanga, inherits the throne.
This new king is not so friendly as his father and he is suspicious of foreigners:
a few years before Captain Lugard's arrival, Mwanga murdered an Anglican
bishop as he was approaching along a route to the north of Lake Victoria –
coincidentally, a route allegedly regarded with some superstition and dread by
the locals (ibid.: 15) – and Mwanga made sure the bishop was killed before he
could cross the Nile. By the late 1880s, the position of all Europeans in
Buganda had become precarious, and reports reaching the coast were full of
the new king's atrocities, of his 'cruelties, vices and unrestrained behaviour'.
(ibid.) Eventually the King became so impatient with foreigners, he tried to
maroon the leaders of their parties on an island on the Lake. More intrigue
ensued. Tensions between Catholics and Protestants escalated, and it was
probably only because of the threat from Muslims on the frontier that civil
war did not break out. (ibid.: 17)

This was the tense and complicated situation awaiting the young officer
Lugard on mission from a British company, and this volatile king the man he
set out to befriend. His brief, from the Imperial British East Africa Company,
was to take Buganda – with its rich commercial and political possibilities – for
Britain, before it fell to Germany. Lugard had marched from Mombasa on the
coast to Buganda through plains, mountains and forest. He arrived with his
sleeves rolled up (as it was in his habit to march, and this must have made him
look quite confident and laid-back), with a continually seeping wound in his

arm (where he had been shot whilst storming a slaver's stockade two years previously, and which was so severe Lugard was still periodically pulling out splinters of bone), and a no less serious wound in his heart (a romantic betrayal which 'nearly destroyed his mind'. (Lugard 1959, vol. 4: 19)[12]

Lugard's diaries cover those years in Buganda, as well as the early years in Nigeria, where he was employed by the Royal Niger Company to gain as many treaties as he could with as many kings as he could. The treaties would grant extensive and practically unlimited power to the respective British companies in exchange for protection and trade.[13] The man who emerges from the diaries covering those years in the early 1890s is quite different from the confident international statesman (he would sit as a member of the Permanent Mandates Commission at the League of Nations between 1922 and 1936) who wrote *The Dual Mandate* (1965) some 30 years later. He was a sensitive man labouring under extreme conditions: politically isolated as the only representative of his company in the area, physically exhausted (variously with toothache, dizziness, opthalmia, a persistent cyst on his lip, regular fevers and the chronic wound left by a bullet that had pierced him in seven places), resolutely committed to his standards and ideals.

Lugard came to Buganda then, to get a treaty signed between the King, the bigger chiefs and himself on behalf of the company. To do this he needed to win the trust of both Protestant and Catholic missionaries as well as that of the tribal chiefs. He had to keep quarrelsome, raiding Muslims at bay, deflect other European interests, and win the total submission of the King. He had to be authoritative without appearing arrogant, fair but firm with his native soldiers and porters, endlessly tactful with other Europeans and Englishmen. He told the chiefs he had come to bring peace not war, to help them resolve all their disputes. (ibid., vol 2: 30–31) To prove this, he presided over '*Shauris*' (Councils?), mediating between Catholics and Protestants. He hated to socialize, but dined with missionaries. He found the time to worry and write about the state of health of fellow officers, dispensing opium tablets, recommending bleeding, purgatives and a blanket around the stomach depending on the ailment. When his men expressed loyalty to him, he was touched. One morning, having slept away from camp the night before, one of his porters complained that they had slept like orphans without a father. (ibid., vol. 4: 258–59) When he was accused of bias towards the Catholics, he was piqued and did not deny his hurt in his diary: 'A miserable night – fever and great depression. I am so very cut up about this.' (ibid., vol. 3: 181) When the King sought to intimidate him, he stood firm: 'it is better to shew Mwanga that ... we come like men who are not afraid'. (ibid., vol. 2: 28) To assert his independence, he also rose from royal company before being dismissed and sometimes even kept the King waiting to drive the point home: 'This was a final assertion that I was my own master ... and do not mean to be ordered about, and treated as an inferior at the beck and call of Mwanga.' (ibid.: 30)

Lugard was a skilled diplomat and he achieved his aim within a week of his arrival. The Treaty signed between himself and Mwanga granted large powers

to the British East Africa Company. The company promised to protect
Uganda, to promote its prosperity, commerce and civilization, as well as to
introduce an administration towards that end. (see Treaty in ibid.: 42)
Mwanga also agreed to acknowledge the suzerainty of the company, and
undertook to make no treaties with, or grant any concessions to, or allow to settle
in his Kingdom, or to acquire lands, or hold offices of State, any European of
whatever nationality without the consent of the company's Resident. In
exchange, the company assured the King that it would uphold his power and
authority, and would allow him to maintain the 'pomp and display' of his
court. (ibid.: 42–44) This was a lot more than trade, and it made sense of all of
Lugard's personal sacrifices.[14] He had started by treading gently but once he
realized that he had checkmated the King and neutralized his influence by
empowering the big chiefs, Lugard quietly relished his behind-the-scenes glory:

> It appears as though the King were now quite superseded ... a little judicious
> handling of affairs, and there will be little need of a Sultan in Uganda at
> all, though for some years it may be useful to keep up the face of one
> (ibid., vol. 3: 198).

Where he had been careful not to offend Mwanga, Lugard began to express his
true feelings. He became impatient with the King who was now, by formal
agreement, his subordinate. 'I *detest* both having him here and going to him'
he wrote. He found it increasingly difficult to tolerate the slave/king, to whom
he started to refer in small bursts of contempt ('he is a murderer, and a public and
open sodomite – a mean despicable brute, and a notorious coward'(ibid.: 234),
and whose authority in the country he had all but replaced.

A talent for unobtrusiveness was also a trait which allowed T.E. Lawrence
(T.E.) to enslave the King, or in his case, the Emir. Until World War I, Britain
had supported the Ottoman Empire to protect her land route to India, and the
borders of her own empire against the desires of other foreign powers. Britain
also kept her eye on political developments across Afghanistan, Persia, Mesopotamia, Syria and the Gulf with the help of formal and informal intelligence
mechanisms. The Arab Bureau in Cairo was part of these mechanisms and T.E.
worked there making maps, interviewing prisoners and drawing information
from agents behind enemy lines. When Turkey joined Germany and Austria in
the war, Britain decided to increase the likelihood of Ottoman defeat by supporting Arab secession against the Turks. An Arab Movement across Ottoman
territory was conceived, funded and controlled by the British government in
Cairo to galvanize the sluggish Arabs into action. T.E. explained that the term
Arab Movement itself was invented in Cairo, 'as a common denomination for
all the vague discontents against Turkey which before 1916 existed in the Arab
provinces' (Lawrence 1939: 158). T.E. was working for the Arab Bureau when
the Military and Political Intelligence department of the government sent him
down to Arabia in 1916. The Sherif Hussein had been given his title by the

Ottoman Sultan but he was growing tired of his master. The Sherif was a religious figurehead and had some influence in and around Mecca, but thanks to Britain's designs, the Arab Movement and the revolt that followed transformed him and his four sons into a dynastic leadership for the entire Middle East. T.E.'s desert escapade contributed significantly to the fulfilment of this plan. Britain bestowed money and arms on the Sherif and his sons so that they could 'lead' the Arab Revolt. This was primarily for the maintenance of a facade.[15]

The British then, hoped to pick one of the Sherif's four sons as Commander-in-Chief of an anti-Turkish Arab uprising. It was T.E.'s mission when he was first sent into the desert to choose the warrior amongst them most likely to lead the Arabs to freedom from Turkish rule. T.E. assessed them carefully. He found one boyish and effeminate, one consumptive and weak, the third too keen on sensual pleasures. This last was Abdullah, who, wrote Lawrence, would ride a little, shoot a little, then return to his tent for a massage. Abdullah's easy, open charm weighed against him. He had a twinkle in his eye and he seemed to be a bit of a playboy. His tent was too luxuriously carpeted, his table too well supplied. Feisal on the other hand, the fourth brother, was measured, skinny and grave. T.E. commented on Feisal's 'rich tenor voice', on his austere demeanour, and on the way he played with his food absent-mindedly until his guests had had their fill. The fact that Feisal did not seem to eat, or rest, or rush, or play, showed discipline, character and focus. All in all, he was heart-stoppingly commanding: 'Looks like a European, and very like the monument of Richard I, at Fontevraud ... Hot tempered, proud and impatient ... Personal magnetism ... very clever'. (ibid.: 37) Whilst Abdullah had been dismissed as a no-good prankster, phlegmatic when it came to field action, T.E. thought he could rely on Feisal for war-mongering and dynamiting Turks. T. E. never looked back. If the moment of decision making is, as Derrida proposes, a moment of madness, of 'non-knowledge' that marks the suspension of deliberation and reason,[16] then it was in a moment of madness that T.E., guided by a vision of Feisal as avatar, threw on full Arab mufti and launched himself into guerrilla warfare against the Turks. A spectacular desert adventure ensued over two years and the two photogenic men in matching attire famously galloped the Turks out of Wejh, Medina, Aqaba and finally, gloriously, Damascus. However, with the war behind them, as immersed in Feisal's voice, movements, stature and real or projected magnetism as he had been in the desert, and in the same way that Lugard abruptly lost interest in Mwanga, T.E. inexplicably wrote of his former protégé and brother-in-arms: 'Faisal was a brave, weak, ignorant spirit, trying to do work for which only a genius, a prophet or a great criminal was fitted. I served him out of pity, a motive which degraded us both.' (Lawrence 1966: 517)

Feisal might have been gutted to read that.

T.E.'s unassuming manner, something which dated back to his days at Oxford, equipped him to deal with the prickly, guarded Bedouin.[17] His

'Twenty-Seven Articles', published in the confidential *Arab Bulletin* in August 1917, was meant to serve as a guide to new army recruits on how to handle Arabs. In this article, he explained that his guidelines (and they are only that, since 'handling Hejaz Arabs is an art, not a science') should only be applied to the Bedouin and not to the townspeople of Syria, who require completely different treatment. He reminds his readers that Britain is lucky to have won over King Hussein, who had also been pursued by Germany, and that great tact was required to maintain his devotion. The first step towards this end is to 'win the confidence of your leader' which you do by bolstering his prestige even at the expense of your own. (Article 4) The ideal position is when one is present and not noticed. (Article 8) The idea of the Sheriffian family as the aristocracy of the Arabs should be magnified and developed. (Article 9) You could do worse than 'wave a Sherif in front of you like a banner and hide your own mind and person'. (Article 11) Finally, the Bedouin are sensitive and the more discreet /self-effacing you are, the more influence you will wield. (Article 14) (See Lawrence 1939: 126.)

In order to wield power then, one had to grit one's teeth and perform regular obeisance before the barbarians. Cromer is not as sympathetic as the other two, but he also did this well. Britain occupied Egypt in 1882 and in 1883 Cromer, then Sir Evelyn Baring, was appointed Consul-General. Britain did not want to annex Egypt, but she did not want to leave her alone either. It was in Britain's interest for Egypt to be stable and free from the danger of other foreign encroachment which might prejudice Britain's own imperial interests/ communications. The Ottoman Empire had left a mountain of potential administrative reform to Britain, and she could not turn her back on Egypt. This was Britain's declared interest in Egypt: to reform, then retreat. It was claimed that Egypt needed Britain to foster democratic institutions and remove Turkish tyranny. Despite the presence of its garrison (= coercion), British discourse persisted along the lines of selfless service. To remain a spectator whilst the country fell once again under the crushing weight of incomprehensible Eastern ideas would be irresponsible. They could not overstress the point: if Britain left, the old barbaric habits would once again find their way into the structures of government. The old Turkish families would swoop down like vultures and finish off Egyptian society. Without Britain, there would be anarchy, bankruptcy. Despite the reality of a British military occupation primarily intended to repel other foreign powers coveting the place, the Consul-General saturated his speech with the idea of British presence in Egypt being primarily for the good of the people. The discourse was careful, since Egypt had not been annexed and, in concert with public opinion at home, would not be annexed. Cromer insisted Egypt's natural wealth had been depleted by debt and corruption. Britain would take whichever replenishing measures were deemed necessary. Similarly for the maintenance of law and order. Britain was the trustee and the beneficiaries were the Egyptian masses – all of them children. Britain would remain until they came of age and their education was complete. This, seeing their utter primitiveness and the hopeless state of affairs, would take some time. The Consul-General was not given any clear instructions about how to do this, and neither did he ask for any. Yet, he explained, 'I had to maintain British authority and, at the same time, to hide as much as possible the fact that I was maintaining it.' (Cromer 1908, vol. 1: 324)

Cromer specialized in bizarre, convoluted and simplistic cultural and racial equations, which make his memoirs excruciating and exhausting reading. For instance: 'the peculiar characteristic of the typical Turco-Egyptian is his Catholic capacity for impotent hatred'. (ibid.:172) Nonetheless, his administration of Egypt is legendary and whilst no one doubted that he ran Egypt, he did it and especially enjoyed doing it, without appearing to.[18] Cromer is said to have institutionalized the idea of mortifying the ego in service to a higher purpose.[19] Sensitivity is not a trait we immediately associate with the abrasive tone of his memoirs, yet he must have possessed enough flexibility and skill to intervene from the highest to the lowest of Egyptian affairs. Cromer *was* Egyptian government. As he put it, he had to uphold the Khedive's[20] prestige and at once oppose Turkish interference in government; he had to encourage reforms without appearing to be himself a reformer; he had to keep the Egyptian question simmering in Britain without forcing it as an issue. At the same time, he was accessible to the cross-section of Egyptian society, and they came to him for help: if a slave girl wanted to marry, if a game of cards turned sour, if a village was unhappy with their Sheikh, if a peasant was looking for his faithless wife, if a car was needed to take a 'lunatic' to the asylum, if a Jewish sect wanted government recognition – it was to Cromer they all turned. (ibid., vol. 2: 323–26)

Preach and proselytize: 'our task'

The men who wrote about themselves were messianic as well as martial. They were proselytizing apostles. They were bringing some good news to the uncivilized world and that good news was Britain. A religious vapour infused the atmosphere around them. They were prophetic and visionary and they pursued their worldly mission in response to a divine/spiritual command.

As Lugard's confidence in his position grew, so did his private rhetoric gain momentum and breadth. To consolidate his Boxing Day triumph of the signing of the treaty with Mwanga, he held 'a big flogging parade'. (Lugard 1959, vol. 2: 54) In January, two weeks following the signing of the treaty and 17 days after the flogging parade, he sent a messenger to the Mahommedans 'to tell them to cease from war, for we had come to the country'. (ibid.: 55) It was that simple. Mwanga was on his knees and the exchanges between him and Lugard, as well as between Lugard and others took on a curious turn. A few weeks after the signing of the treaty, the King summoned him:

> He said that in every single thing he would consult me. Said I had saved the country from imminent war. That if war came the Mahommedans would eat up all the country, and what would become of him; … That I

was his bed, his food, his house and his power, and he should do nothing without me. (ibid.: 98–99)

A preternatural aura had developed around Lugard. His task exceeded the immediate task at hand of company business. He talked of saving tribes from extinction, of creating a peaceful Uganda, and of himself as deliverer. (ibid.: vol. 3: 180) The Protestants look upon him as their saviour, his work is seen as God's work, and, quite simply and literally, he was a Godsend. (ibid.: vol. 2: 105)

Cromer threw words around even more freely than Lugard. He relied on totalizing, unqualified concepts, and assumed that they reflected universal, eternal, quasi-religious truths. The Englishman landed in Egypt, wrote Cromer, focused on the mission ahead of him. He encountered a poor, ignorant, credulous nation crushed by hundreds of years of oppression and mismanagement. It was the civilized man's (more specifically, the Englishman's) inexorable duty to extend the hand of fellowship to this nation and raise it morally and materially. Should his resolution waver or any doubts engulf him as to whether he is up to the task, he simply has to look to India,

> and he says to himself, with all the confidence of an imperial race, – I can perform this task; I have done it before now; I have poured numberless blessings on the heads of the Ryots of Bengal and Madras, who are cousins to the Egyptian fellaheen; these latter shall also have water in their fields, justice in their law courts, and immunity from the tyranny under which they have for so long groaned. (Cromer op. cit., vol. 2: 130)

This is a mission of biblical significance, but one which the Englishman should not fear for he is enabled, 'indeed, guided divinely by the lights'. (ibid.: 132) According to the rules of this discourse, the enslavement of natives is obstinately paraded as their emancipation. It, their enslavement paraded (but not parading) as their emancipating education, is the necessary result of a clash between the backward East and advanced Britain. The grand totalizing vision deployed here relies on a teleological/progressive understanding of history, on claims to absolute and eternal truths.[21] In Cromer's bedtime story, just as the world is gradually evolving towards an ideal Utopia, so was Egyptian society destined to flourish under British guidance.

T.E.'s desert mission was distinguishable by a more immediate, ecstatic fervour than either Lugard's or Cromer's. This is manifest both in his ardent descriptions of the saviour/Prophet Feisal, as well as in his own experience of desert life. Like a true mystic, T.E. learnt to dispense with the mediation of a priest and was humbled by his direct experience of God. The desert, as the scene of a politico-spiritual uprising, had a transformative effect on T.E., who felt that he was following in the footsteps of all the prophets who had trodden the same sands that he was treading. To be like them, he mortified his body and renounced physical comforts. Later on, he explained:

The empty space of the deserts, irresistibly drive their inhabitants to a belief in the oneness and omnipotence of God ... Arab movements begin in the desert, and usually travel up the shortest way into Syria ... it is the Semitic townsmen or villager who receives the revelation. For this reason, ... this present Arab movement, the craving for national independence and self-government, was started in the desert. (Lawrence 1939: 88)

T.E.'s asceticism found full expression in Arabia, and he turned renunciation (of all bodily comforts, essentially of control) into a political tool. There was messianic zeal behind the Arab Revolt, and the messianic zeal was entirely his.

Describe and dominate: savage this, savage that, savage 'the Other'

Sensuality, corruption, intrigue, indolence, mindlessness, debility – float across the surface of our colonial agents' narratives. They are part of the current of Occidental thinking about unpredictable, unreformed, Africa and the Orient. The dark propensities of their rulers present a potential menace to all that is light, all that is order. They are of the past, and Britain/Europe are the future. Should we try to recuperate his original identity, or has the native drowned in a sea of ink? Who/what are these creatures our colonial agents have taken so much trouble to describe? Their essence *cannot* be captured /written in English. The native evaporates in translation. The discourse is at its most racist here, most stereotyped, most reliant on binary opposites. White supremacy was not a myth: it was confirmed by their so-called observations, it emerged out of their steady anthropological gaze, out of the picturesque tableau they described. The inert object of their observations, enslaved forever by a pen. When Lugard wrote about savages and half savages ('I know the savage forgets excessively quickly' (Lugard 1959, vol. 2: 50), 'to agree to the position that mere half savages shall be allowed to ... ' (ibid., vol. 3: 190), he was simply reflecting the Western ordering of the world. From a native perspective, their descriptions were acts of cultural transgression, conducted under circumstances of political transgression. They were also, very often, wrong. So for instance, Margery Perham, introducing the Nigeria volume of Lugard's diaries, writes about the scene of French-British conflict: a place called Borgu. It is difficult, she explains, to define either the character or size of this place, as these constantly changed according to the shifting military and diplomatic positions of the interested parties (i.e. the French and British). It is even impossible to tell if Borgu was a Kingdom, a state, or a group of independent chieftainships. The very name had been given by Europeans to cover a complex of people, who were called the Borgu or the Borgawa or the Bariva, but who called *themselves* (my emphasis) Batomba. What Perham does feel able to describe with some certainty though, is the fierceness of these people (whoever they are), the potency of their poison arrows, and the formidable character of their witchcraft. (ibid., vol. 4: 35)

Lugard, Cromer, Lawrence: the three men are very different, but all three were particularly scathing and fearful of sensuality, and guarded vigilantly against it. The perceived sensuality of the natives was a fixation. Of Mwanga, Lugard writes: 'He is a young man with good features, but a face which shews irresolution, a weak character, and a good deal of sensuality.' (ibid., vol. 2: 9) Yet at the same time, they could not take their enraptured eyes off this revolting sensuality. The savages, semi-savages, noble savages or educated savages were at once mesmerising and repulsive. Lugard writes of 'the organised despotism and barbaric display of a negro kingdom'. (Lugard 1965: 72) He describes the awesome spectacle in his diaries, recounting the 'pomp and glitter of savage king-dom'. (Lugard 1959, vol. 4: 244–45)

Acts of mindless barbarity or of shameless licentiousness are described – not for their value as sordid entertainment – but to confirm the natives' urgent need to be ushered out of their darkness. Meticulous stocktaking. The inventory of a treasure (Pandora's?) box. Listed and catalogued. There is no domination without surveillance and description. Observations explain why they must colonize and govern. They explain why, demanding as the task may be, unpleasant and risky as the venture may be, they are bound (for it is the fate of Britain) to carry the burning torch of culture and progress to the darkest corners of the earth. The act of observation and description also has a practical function: it designates potential sources of trouble, it helps to explain who amongst the natives is fit for training in the art of government, and who is most definitely not. It identifies which groups are more docile or more servile than the rest. It often subdivides natives into aboriginal races and later, migrant ones so that their power struggle/political relationship may be monitored. In *The Dual Mandate*, Lugard is meticulous in his description of African races. Africa, he writes, is inhabited by widely divergent races. Knowledge/information are crucial to an understanding of the natives, to better know how to rule them. He divides the races broadly into those of Asiatic origin who came to the continent through the east and north-east with their 'Negroid descendants', and then the pure negro tribes who occupy the rest of Africa. The immigrant races are called Hamites, and this includes the Abyssinians, Somalis, Galas, Masai, Wahima, Nandi, and Fulani. One can tell who is a negro and who is not by the amount of hair on the face and head. There are innumerable tribes of negroes and negroids. The Hamites are quite talented at social organization, the Bantus are physically a fine specimen of the human race, and they are happy, excitable and thriftless. They have no sense of veracity, they love music and weapons as an Oriental loves jewellery. Islam has been embraced because it suits the savage character: it sanctions polygamy for instance, which is popular in the tropics, and its social code is easy to follow. (Lugard 1965: 67–78) Lugard seems to think that Christianity only became Christianity once it reached Europe, and puzzlingly refers to it as 'the religion of the temperate climates'. (ibid.: 78) Finally he writes, the educated African should be treated with caution: an overeducated native is an ungrateful native, who might turn against his mentors whilst remaining incapable of ruling either his own community, or the backward people of his own race. (ibid.: 89)

Cromer dedicates several chapters to the science of describing natives in multiracial, multicultural Egypt. He begins by warning his readers that there is no 'true Egyptian' – which, he points out, incidentally makes a policy of 'Egypt for the true Egyptian', as some amateur politicians have advocated, redundant. (Cromer op. cit., vol. 2: 128) Walking down any Cairo street, writes Cromer, you might encounter a peasant, a Bedouin, a Copt, a Turco-Egyptian Pasha, a Circassian, a Syrian money lender, a Jew, or 'a Levantine non-descript whose ethnological status defies diagnosis'. (ibid.) Despite this amalgam of races and religions, of these textures and hues, fair-skinned European is cast against dark-skinned Easterner in Cromer's two-toned, two-dimensional world. The two are 'poles asunder' in every moral and intellectual attribute, in every aspect of their culture. Under any given circumstance, the Easterner would do the exact opposite as the Westerner. It is in the Easterner's nature to lie: the Eastern mind is so inaccurate it automatically 'degenerates into untruthfulness'. The Occidental expresses himself logically and clearly, the Other rambles on, contradicting himself. The Occidental is energetic, inquisitive, the Other grave, silent, lethargic. Even an apparently positive trait, such as the Other's generosity, is judged immoderate, too lavish. Where the Egyptian attempts to do as his master does, he is a good imitator, although he does not understand the thing he is imitating. He is an automaton. Western literature is refined, the Other's is coarse. European punishments are mild, the Other's are cruel. At most, this was a 'pseudo civilisation'. (ibid.: 322) This is a population, writes Cromer, which is 'walking on its head' and if we do not understand this, it will be impossible to govern them – whereupon the need for his astonishing catalogue. (ibid.: 144–65)

Cromer is predictably derisive of Islam: it is a complete failure as a social system and it is barbaric – in its treatment of women/in its penal code etc. He writes both that Islam tends to have a civilizing effect on the more primitive societies which adopt it ('*L'Islam est un progrés pour le nègre qui l'adopte*' (Renan, cited in ibid.: 134)), and that it is dangerous in the hands of converts as most of them tend to be war-like savages and semi-savages. (ibid.: 139) The Eastern Christians do not fare any better, since they are Oriental and governed by their racial instincts. The Copt practises a 'debased' form of Christianity. He is as immovable and immutable, and as full of 'bigotry, ignorance, dissimulation, deceit, faithlessness, the pursuit of worldly gain, and indulgence in sensual pleasures' as the next Moslem. (ibid.: 201–10) The Syrian Christian and the Armenian are in turn just as servile as the Copt. Finally, like Lugard and T.E., he reserves a special contempt for the class of educated/Europeanized natives, these 'de-Moslemised Moslems and invertebrate Europeans' who are alienated from their own people, and yet who will never be equal to a true European who is on the contrary, upstanding. (ibid.: 228–31)

T.E. then, is also dismissive of the 'intelligentsia', the tinctured townsfolk of Beirut, Damascus, Cairo and Jerusalem, with their reliance on half-baked Western ideas. T.E. preferred and appreciated authenticity in a native (he was particularly fond of 'street Arabs' and 'ruffians' (Graves and Liddell Hart 1963: 80)). These semi-educated urbanites on the other hand, are defined by their dangerous amorphousness, having 'bared themselves to the semi-Levantine, semi-European fashions of the renegade Moslem – the Moslem who had lost his traditional faith – and with it all belief in all faiths'. (Lawrence *War Diaries*)

T.E. published an arresting description of the inhabitants of a region referred to as 'Syria' in the *Arab Bulletin* called 'Syria, the Raw Material'.[22] However the term 'Syria' itself was dubious. As he explains, it was a Turkish term with no Arabic equivalent for the province of Damascus. The fact that the 'inhabitant of these parts' has no word to describe his own 'country' (?) at once reflects his 'verbal poverty' and his (equally impoverished?) 'political condition'. (Lawrence 1939: 77) Never mind. T.E. follows with a masterful, detailed and authoritative description of this place and of its inhabitants. But what, precisely, is he describing, and for whom, and for what purpose?

The interior, he begins, is divided longitudinally. The peasants of the Jordan, Litani and Orontes rivers are quite stable, and beyond them is a 'strange shifting population of the border lands'. The Ansariyya are 'disciples of a strange cult of fertility'. Amongst them are colonies of Christians, Armenians, Druses and Circassians. North-east of them are the Kurds, who hate Christians most, followed by Turks and then Europeans. Beyond the Kurds are Yezidis, who worship to placate an evil spirit, and who are mesmerized by a bronze bird. Christians, Jews and Moslems unite to spit on these Yezidis. In Aleppo, a quarter million people of all races and religions live and mix freely. South of there, quarrelsome Mohammedan Circassians live by the sea. Inland of them are the Ismaliyya who look miserable, worship the Agha Khan, and hate Arabs and orthodox Moslems. Beyond them are semi-nomadic tribal Christian Arabs, sturdy and 'most unlike their snivelling brethren in the hills'. East of them are semi-nomadic Moslem peasants, then some more Ismaliyya outcasts, and 'Beyond them only Bedouins'. As we approach Tripoli and Beirut we start to come across Maronites and Greek Christians, who both slander Mohammedans. The Sunnis are very similar to them although their dialect is 'less mincing'. Higher up are some Shias who migrated from Persia, 'dirty, ignorant, surly and fanatical'. Approaching Acre, there are more Sunnis, then Druses, then Metawal near the Jordan Valley, then Algerian colonies, then native Palestinian Jews, who are 'interesting', although T.E. does not say why (perhaps because he was not expecting them?). Then across the eastern plains, where, amidst a labyrinth of lava, 'all the loose and broken men of Syria have foregathered for unnumbered generations'. Going further down there are German Zionist Jews, who are 'unable to endure near them anyone not of their race'. Beyond them is their designated enemy, 'the Palestine peasant, more stupid than the peasant of north Syria, materialist and bankrupt'. This evocative tableau would be incomplete without the towns. Jerusalem is a dirty place, and 'its people, with the rarest exception, are characterless as hotel servants'. Beirut is basically 'bastard French'. It provides 'a Levantine screen through which shop-soiled influences flow into Syria. It is as representative of Syria as Soho of the Home Counties'. In Beirut, there is a nucleus of people, 'Mohammedans, talking and writing and thinking like the doctrinaire cyclopaedists who paved the way for revolution in France, and whose words permeated to parts of the interior where action is in favour.' Lawrence concludes that this wide divergence of race, religion and culture has common characteristics. These people, he writes, are quick-witted, self-satisfied, not incapable of grasping abstract ideas (unlike Egyptians), whilst also being lazy and superficial. They have no respect for the law, but they are obedient when they fear being beaten. They are as passionate as they are ignorant about politics. The coast is devoid of Arab[23] feeling and the moral of the story seems to be that there is an argument for putting the littoral under one government and the interior under another (see ibid.: 70–78). Finally, for all his love of the Bedouin lifestyle and despite his dedication to the Bedouin above the half-educated townsfolk and the half-witted peasantry, Lawrence could be bitingly derisive about them too. The universal native trait of undisciplined, mindless sensuality resurfaces. One has to have patience as wide and deep as the sea to travel with the Bedouin writes T.E., for they are very odd people:

> slaves of their appetites, with no stamina of mind, drunkards for coffee, milk or water, gluttons for stewed meat, shameless beggars for tobacco … They dream for weeks before and after their rare sexual exercises, and spend their days titillating themselves and their friends with bawdy tales … They will follow us, if we can endure them, and play their game.' (ibid.: 108–9)

'How do you like my treaty?': the metanarrative emerges

When the League of Nations placed former enemy possessions under the administration of one or the other of the victorious Allies as Mandates, the unguarded talk regarding savages, half-educated savages and gluttons for sensuality was refined to suit the political moment, post-war idealism and the new principle of self-determination for all nations. Whilst self-determination had become a watchword since President Woodrow Wilson entered the war,[24] it could also be a euphemism for anything but. The spirit of Derrida complicates the seemingly straightforward concept of self-determination. Derrida warns against selective critical thinking. Critical thinking should be extensive, far-reaching and indiscriminate. To demonstrate this, he engaged in some light wordplay and questions the meaning of 'Jewish': 'what is at stake, what is implied, when someone is identified in terms of his Hebrew descent or religion? Imagine if 'Christian' were applied in the same way'. (Royle 2003: 2) Derrida is not really asking what it means to *be* Jewish. He is asking us to question what it means to *use* the word 'Jewish'. He is asking us to look at who is using the term and the circumstances under which it is being used. Similarly, everybody knows what self-determination means. The concept itself is simple enough; but *what is at stake, what is implied, when a nation is told it is entitled to self-determination?*

Wordplay aside, it is clear that the concept of self-determination, as well as the use of the term in this context is not an absolute, unqualified or self-sufficient one (in which case there would have been no need for it at all), but one which is dependent on the word which must precede it, the concept of *entitlement* to it: I (war victor), am not pronouncing you (ex-enemy territory) self-determining, but I am willing to concede that you are *entitled* to self-determination. So what? In terms of actual self-determination, this is beginning to sound like its antithesis. For instance, T.E. wrote in 1920 in conjunction with the new, popular ideas that the Arabs 'lack system, endurance, organization. They are incurably slaves of the idea, men of spasms'. (Lawrence 1939: 87) Nonetheless, even they are entitled to self-determination, as well as to that British bestowed blessing, self-respect:

> This new Imperialism ... involves an active side of imposing responsibility on the local peoples. It is what they clamour for, but an unpopular gift when given. We have to demand from them provision for their own defence. This is the first stage towards self-respect in peoples. (ibid.: 95)

Lugard's heart-rending diaries also contain the seeds of the serious (and to this day lasting) political theory which emerges in *The Dual Mandate*. This mandate[25] was based on the premise that neither did the sovereign power in a foreign land have an exclusive right over its natural resources, nor, astonishingly, did the natives have the right to deny it to them because it was the legacy of the whole of mankind. The interests of natives and those of the sovereign were dependent on each other. Trusteeship was the ideal which provided the opportunity for Britain to guide the natives (casually: the 'backward races'). Despite references to democracy and the construction of reliable institutions, independence for them was not imagined 'within any period of time now visible on the horizon'. (Lugard 1965: 201) For the time being though, the imperial power was a trustee[26] for their welfare.

How to discharge the responsibility of being a sovereign power? How to stay true to God, to the civilized world, to one's own culture and nature whilst guiding and controlling entire nations? This is the conundrum of imperialism that may have caused Lugard, Cromer and T.E. some angst but they were steadfast and of its absolute, fixed value they were sure. Trusteeship, writes Lugard, was an unassailable principle, whether in a Crown Colony, Protectorate or in a Mandated Territory.[27] It was a grave task, one which entailed teaching the natives self-respect, self-control and responsibility. (Lugard 1928: 10)

The specific powers of Britain as a sovereign power in foreign lands have varied according to the type of responsibility Britain took on. Colony,

Protectorate and Mandate were subjected to varying techniques of control, depending on the size of the territory, the perceived developmental stage of native civilization, as well as on public opinion at home. In a Crown Colony, government was centralized and conducted according to British institutional structures: a Governor was assisted by an Executive and a Legislative Council. The latter would consist of official and unofficial members. A Chief Justice with other judges formed a Supreme Court. Gradually, the colonial government would increase the number of 'unofficials' in the Legislative Council, a secret ballot would follow, perhaps leading to an actual majority of 'unofficials' in government. This system was applied to small islands (in the Caribbean, in Hong Kong, Mauritius, and off the coast of West Africa), to small enclaves such as British Honduras, British Guiana, etc., and more or less to British India (see ibid.: 7–9). It was also the system the Mandate government wanted and tried and failed to implement in Palestine. In a Protectorate, it is technically the natives who are placed under the control and protection of the imperial country, whilst ownership of the land remains, in principle, unaffected. In theory then, Protectorates were subjected to a lesser degree of interference. Egypt, coastal Kenya, parts of Bechuanaland, Swaziland, Tanganyika, Aden and Kuwait were placed under this kind of protection and partial control. Formal control was less conspicuous than in the Colonies and indirect rule flourished in those places, as dozens of native administrations and institutions continued to function under the supervision of talented and terminally patient British officers. Mandated territories were placed under the administration of one of the victorious Allies after World War I, subject to supervision by the League of Nations. Article 22 of the Covenant of the League of Nations embodied no less than the 'conscience of Europe' regarding entire helpless nations, marked by their inability to stand for themselves. (Lugard 1965: 55)

The Mandates then, were supposed to indicate a new era; but the attack on vulnerable cultures continued behind an appeal to universal values, as did the siphoning of their natural resources, the manipulation of their boundaries, the restriction of the political rights of their native population. By claiming that some nations were unable to stand alone, the Covenant institutionalized their political/cultural inferiority. It sealed those nations' inferior status in relation to the new international community.

In this insurmountable circular dialectic, the ruler is unable to overcome the fact that he has accorded himself privileges at the expense of the trapped (indistinguishable from liberated) and humiliated native. The most the latter can hope for is that his new teacher will recognise his potential. The Mandates institutionalized and regenerated the inner conflicts of the wandering explorer/adventurer, the well-meaning colonial agent who had befriended natives so warmly (Lugard, T.E., and even Cromer, who said that some of his best friends were natives – we have to take his word for it). By charging him with beneficent over-rule, they revived the demons of self-doubt and the obsession with fairness, leading him to balk when he is forced to use violence, to end-lessly justify himself in more diaries and letters and in despatches to the Metropolis, to excruciate over his resort to coercion and constraint. Even though he is repulsed or at best amused by the natives and their inertia, by their incompetence, by their unfathomable morality and unpredictable impul-ses, nonetheless he shoulders his task with the patience of a parent. The Mandates embodied the dilemmas of the tragic, poignant, colonial agent of good will,[28] marked by his own ambivalence to his job, unable to see or accept that he is a usurper, unfulfilled and ultimately torn apart by this inner conflict (see Memmi op. cit.: 90). He claims to want to liberate the native, but he cannot shake off a discourse centred around words which might not mean anything to the native, or which mean something else to the native, or which, in any event, the colonialist does not *really* mean. So whilst relying on the repetition of terms such as democracy, progress and justice, he also qualifies the universality of these values for the sake of political expedience as well as with an allusion to the exceptional circumstances of this particular eco-system of rights.[29] A chasm slowly forms and widens between the rhetoric of democracy/progress/ justice/freedom, and actual practice; and it is in this gaping black hole, in this whirling magnetic field of meaninglessness that the psycho-drama is enacted, that the colonialist and native are fated to endlessly recite their formulaic lyrics.

Yet the colonial agent persists in his discourse, despite his own discrepant and uneven application of the vaunted, supposedly universal principles that he adores so much. He persists in perpetuating the myths of a civilizing mission, the myths of progress, and the myths found in native stereotyping. Racism, writes Memmi, is an essential and inevitable element of colonialism. (ibid.: 108) The Mandates are racism manifest. They are racism watered down so that everybody (the conscientious colonialist, the English speaking native, the Powers, the Allies) can swallow. The background to the Palestine Mandate in particular is one of lies, greed, double-dealing, bribery and impertinent diplo-macy. Britain competed with her wartime allies over the nations that were eventually handed out as Mandates. This competition was famously referred to by Woodrow Wilson as the 'disgusting scramble' for the Middle East. Britain wanted to preserve her supremacy and exclusivity over the Persian Gulf, but did not necessarily want to accumulate more formal responsibility. The shambolic preparations regarding ex-enemy territory in Asiatic Turkey, a sort of feasting on the corpse, must have been ugly to watch. Britain concluded agreements with several parties over Palestine as World War I progressed and occupied and ruled the territory a few years before it was granted a Mandate by the League of Nations. In other words, the upshot of any negotiations was that Britain was never, ever, not going to have Palestine. Nonetheless, Palestine was 'promised' to third parties left, right, and centre in a literally vomit-inducing and very British intrigue.

In 1915 (a year before the spectacular Arab Revolt was launched with the spellbinding, matinee worthy Lawrence/Feisal duo at the helm), McMahon, the British High Commissioner in Egypt 'promised' to the Sherif Hussein of Mecca (Prince Feisal's father) that Britain would grant the 'Arabs' 'independence' in the aftermath of war. The preponderance of inverted commas here indicates that the famous and wonderfully vague promise of independence to the Arabs meant different things to different people, that it was a somewhat fluid promise, based on an unspecified definition of independence, and a flexible, variable idea of who was an Arab for its purposes. Nevertheless, this 'promise' is contained in the Sherif/MacMahon correspondence.[30] The Sherif Hussein was held in some esteem in Mecca and its environs. He was also a religious figurehead, and he was probably picked as the 'Chief' of the Arabs as their representative to appease Britain's millions of potentially volatile Muslims elsewhere.[31] At the same time, Britain entered into another agreement, incompatible with McMahon's private undertakings to the Sherif, in anticipation of Ottoman defeat in the spring of 1916. This time, it was a tripartite understanding between France, Britain and Czarist Russia. This is the Sykes-Picot Agreement, named after the French and British agents who concluded it (although the Russian agent's name has inexplicably slunk away from history). Whilst McMahon was writing to the Sherif, the peripatetic diplomatic advisor Mark Sykes was holding his own negotiations about the same territory with Paris and Moscow for the Foreign Office. This agreement divided future ex-enemy territory three ways into states and rebuffed France from the Suez Canal. McMahon and Sykes apparently did not know what the other was doing. According to T.E., McMahon did not find out until Sykes got back to Cairo and the two men met, possibly over tea in the lobby of a hotel. According to T.E., Sykes then pulled out a map: 'Sykes told him – Sykes saying casually: "haven't you heard of my treaty?" others nearly threw up.' (Cited in Liddell Hart 1934: 60.)[32]

But it is the Balfour Declaration of 2 November 1917 which captured the full flavour of British imperialism. The War Cabinet agreed its terms and wording during a meeting on 31 October (CAB 23/4/261), and two days later, Arthur James Balfour, Lloyd George's Foreign Secretary, wrote to Lord Rothschild, a prominent British Jew:

> His Majesty's Government view with favour the establishment in Palestine of a national home for the Jewish people, and will use their best endeavours to facilitate the achievement of that object, it being clearly understood that nothing shall be done which may prejudice the civil and religious rights of existing non-Jewish communities in Palestine, or the rights and political status enjoyed by Jews in any other country.

In this Declaration, the natives are barely mentioned. They are not anything in particular, apart from being non-Jews. There is allusion to their civil and religious rights but the Declaration carefully avoids any reference to their political rights. With the Balfour Declaration, British imperialism reaches a literally celestial zenith. Notwithstanding the Zionist movement's exhortations for such a declaration after the Basel Conference of 1897, and the energetic mobilizing of government by prominent Jews in the UK, the Declaration so authentically captured the spirit and drive behind British imperialism, it has led one writer to comment that if there had been no Zionists in 1917, Britain 'would have had to invent them'. (Vereté 1970: 50) For the Declaration did not fulfil Britain's strategic needs alone, it had something quite mystical, even weird, about it.

The credentials of some of its architects are somewhat controversial. The Declaration was made under the Liberal government of David Lloyd George. His Sunday school days had had a deep impact on Lloyd George. He loved the Old Testament, apparently could not forget his childhood readings of Prophets and Psalms and said he knew the Kings of Israel better than he knew the kings of England. He was excited at the idea of playing a role in the restoration of the Jews to Palestine, and at the same time made anti-Semitic (that is to say, anti-Jewish) remarks.[33] Then there was the committed Catholic Mark Sykes, the itinerant diplomatic advisor for the Foreign Office, who had actively promoted his brand of spiritual salvation for the East. Sykes was suspicious of international finance, which he associated with organized international Jewry and believed that the existence of the European Jew was one of tragic 'root ess cosmopolitanism'. This urban, assimilated, corrupt European Jew however, could redeem himself by returning to his origins, and by a lifetime of tilling the soil.[34] Finally Balfour himself was lukewarm in his defence of Jews against allegations made by anti-Semites. He believed that their dignity and self-respect were lost but salvageable, and Britain would help in this by giving them a territorial centre. (Sykes 1965: 18)[35] The profound sense of mission, the unwavering conviction that Britain was an instrument in the hands of God, became literally manifest in the Balfour Declaration. If the hand of God was visible in Britain's mission in India and Africa, imagine the almighty force with which it came down on their mission in Palestine. With the Balfour Declaration, the salvation of souls and races and cultures found institutional expression. A month after the Declaration was made, the editorial in *The Times* newspaper stated that Britain's support of Zionism would save the entire region:

> [T]he approaching fulfilment of ancient prophecy was being celebrated ... yet it was not only the coming re-establishment of a National Home in Palestine for the Children of Israel that the meeting portended ... Colonel Mark Sykes did well to insist upon the need that Jew, Arab and Armenian should go hand in hand in working for national redemption. Thus only can they be, jointly and severally, secure, and make Asia Minor an intellectual and spiritual bridge between West and East. (*The Times*: 3 Dec. 1917)[36]

The co-operation of Jew, Arab and Armenian then, is desirable not merely for practical purposes, but is essential for their redemption. Britain was on a political-spiritual mission of global proportions, with Biblical implications. How could the natives not acquiesce, not *want* this?

The fact that a considerable part of Anglo-Jewry (some even suggesting that it was, at one point, 'most' (Samuel 1945: 145)) were either hostile or indifferent to Zionism was a cumbersome detail. Until recently, it was amongst certain Evangelical circles, amongst millenarianists[37] and eschatologists[38] that an apocalypse was anticipated, and the suggestion that British Jews were waiting to return to Palestine to till the land may not have sat well with the British Jews themselves. (L. Stein 1961: 9)[39] Lucien Wolf, an anti-Zionist Jew and something of a celebrity wrote that until recently, the most enthusiastic proponents of a Jewish restoration in Palestine had been Christians and that Jews themselves were indifferent to this plan (Wolf 1919: 102–3). It is possible that Wolf was over-generalizing. However, what can be said with certainty is that the Balfour Declaration did not have the same support from British born Jews as it had from Jews in other countries, such as Russia or Eastern Europe, and that a significant number of wealthy Jews in Britain were opposed to it. Edwin Montagu, the Secretary of State for India and the only Jew in Lloyd George's Cabinet, actively campaigned against the Declaration and wrote to Lord Cecil (Acting Secretary for Foreign Affairs), insisting,

> [n]ow you will forgive me for saying that if I am right in thinking that Jews of British birth are in the main anti-Zionist, if I am right in thinking that anti-Zionism is a belief held by at least half of the Jews of this country, what can be the motive for our Government, in the midst of its great preoccupations and perplexities, doing anything in this matter? (CAB 24/27, 14 Sept. 1917)

Finally, when the representatives of Anglo-Jewry did face each other on the Conjoint Committee, which was made up of the representatives of the Anglo-Jewish Association and the Board of Deputies, the Zionists secured a narrow majority of 56 to 51. Again, a distinction was made by Montagu at a War Cabinet meeting between English-born Jews, most of whom were against Zionism, and foreign-born Jews, who were for it. (CAB 23/4, Minutes, 4 Oct. 1917)

They argued fruitlessly. The Covenant of the League of Nations was signed in June 1919 in Versailles. Article 22 recognized the provisional independence of former Turkish possessions, which were to be prepared for full independence with the help of a Mandatory, and which were to be chosen in consideration with the wishes of the community in question. The Balfour Declaration found its way into the Preamble to the Palestine Mandate, which was endorsed at the conference of San Remo in April 1920, then formally approved by the League of Nations in July 1922, and technically operative as of 29 September 1923. Lord Balfour, as Secretary of State for Foreign Affairs, spoke plainly about the provisions of the Covenant, pointing out the wide divergence between fact and wishful thinking:

The contradiction between the letter of the Covenant and the policy of the Allies is even more flagrant in the case of the 'independent nation' of Palestine. For in Palestine, we do not even propose to go through the form of consulting the wishes of the present inhabitants of the country ... The four Great Powers are committed to Zionism, and Zionism, be it right or wrong, good or bad, is rooted in age-long tradition, in present needs, in future hopes, of far profounder import than the desires and prejudices of the 700 000 Arabs who now inhabit that ancient land. (Internal Memoranda by Balfour, dated 11 Aug. 1919, in Woodward and Butler 1952: 242 at 345)

The inference, in Balfour's statement, is that the Arabs are impostors in that ancient land, a mishap of history that Britain was in the fortunate position to be able to correct.

A Miasma had settled over Palestine.

Notes

1 The general principle that subject races should be ruled 'through their chiefs' was declared by Lord Milner. See Lugard (1965: 194, 215).
2 'Dependency' is a general term which describes a country under the political control of another.
3 See for instance Low's (1973) examination of British imperial power.
4 In *The English Utilitarians and India* (1959), Eric Stokes links British colonial culture as we know it to a militant evangelical Christianity advocated by the radical, reformist and rather aggressive Clapham Sect and which flourished in India in the nineteenth century. According to Stokes, by the late nineteenth century, the governing ethos for India combined an evangelical sense of mission with a zeal for administrative efficiency. K. Tidrick's *Empire and the English Character* (1990) picks up from Stokes and explores why a certain style of colonial rule comes so naturally to a certain (prototype) of Englishman.
5 I use the terms 'imperial' and 'colonial' interchangeably for Britain's relationship with its Dependencies.
6 See Stokes op. cit. Stokes lays bare the nineteenth-century English political mind in India. Tidrick (op. cit.) draws on Stokes: benevolent imperial domination can be detected in the 1840s.
7 This is Tidrick's (op. cit.) term.
8 Indirect Rule became very popular in Africa and propagated across British territory: Southern Nigeria, the Cameroons, Tanganyika followed Northern Nigeria. In the Sudan power was devolved to the regions first to the judicial and then financial spheres. In Northern Rhodesia, the system was introduced to native courts and authorities, followed by Nyasaland, Gold Coast, Gambia and Sierra Leone. In 1931, the system of Indirect Rule was approved by an all-party Joint Committee of both Houses of Parliament. See Margery Perham's 'Our Task in Africa' in her *Colonial Sequence 1930 to 1949* (1967). For a sketch of the different strategies which were applied in the government of local peoples across the British Empire, see J.W. Cell (1999). The Indian Princely States were granted nominal autonomy within a framework of British supremacy, with Resident advisors reporting to the Government of India's Political Department. The Residents had to be careful to save face for the Princes at every opportunity. In Malaya, a Residency system was also in place,

although the Resident's powers were extensive. One Resident is quoted: 'we must first create the government to be advised'. (ibid.: 238) In the Ugandan Kingdoms, chiefs were sometimes removed by British over-rulers. In Southern Nigeria, Kenya and Tanganyika, Warrant Chiefs were created; this was not traditional indirect rule, since it did not rely on pre-existing local hierarchies and it was based on a misunderstanding of how local communities were organized. Classic Lugardian Indirect Rule, where chiefs were granted financial autonomy and native courts left to apply native custom, was practised in Northern Nigeria, Northern Gold Coast, Mandate Tanganyika, Southern Sudan, Barotseland, Matabeland, Basutoland, Bechuanaland, Swaziland, Zululand and Transkei. For studies on the relationship between indirect rule and law/justice, see H.F. Morris and J.S. Read (1972). On the other hand two-thirds of India, Hong Kong, Singapore, Cyprus and Gibraltar were ruled directly.

9 Stokes (op. cit.: vii) writes that British rule in India 'holds a mirror up to nature, reflecting the English character and mind'. This is also the basis of Tidrick's *Empire and the English Character* (op. cit.).

10 Apparently, most of these accusations were made by the French. An inquiry into his behaviour resulted in a report to the Cabinet in 1893. The report was unpublished but the French were paid some compensation. See Perham's 'Introduction' in Lugard (1959: 25).

11 I am not alone: see Christopher Tomlins (2003) and Mignolo (2000) for a discussion of the legitimating grand narratives of colonialism, along the same lines.

12 Following his heartbreak in 1888, the promising soldier decided that he could most usefully throw away his life by fighting the slave trade and travelled to Africa with 50 Sovereigns. He joined the battle against the slave trade without permission of the War Office. He returned to England a year later and there built himself a reputation as something of a firebrand, passionately lecturing the British public and lobbying Parliament on the subject.

13 Lugard's treaty with the King of Nikki in 1894 in West Africa granted similar privileges to that signed with the King of Buganda. (Lugard 1959, vol. 4: 185–86)

14 The treaty was renewed in March 1892 and made the agreement between the two parties binding in perpetuity. (Lugard 1959, (ed), vol. 3: 165)

15 In the minutes of a War Cabinet Eastern Committee meeting in 1918, two pages are devoted to the question of which title should be accorded, by Britain, to King Hussein of Arabia. This was important as it would affect his standing in the Arab world, and would therefore directly affect what use Britain could make of him. At first, he was to be King of the Hejaz. The Foreign Office thought it more appropriate that he be known as King of the Arabs. The India Office opposed this because it might insult other chiefs in the Persian Gulf and in Central Arabia. The chairman of the committee agreed with this view because whilst calling him the King of the Arabs

> might assist us in dealing with the problem of Syria, the grant of such a title might compromise our position in Mesopotamia, where King Hussein's claims were shadowy, to say the least of it, might be repudiated by the local population, and might prejudice our case before the Peace Conference as regards main-tenance of the political regime which had been set up in Mesopotamia.

It was crucial to bestow the correct title on the Sherif Hussein: if he was called King, then his sons would be princes, and that would assist the wider picture in the imperial frame of mind:

> Col. Lawrence took the view that the recognition of this title might help us at the Peace Conference if we desired the assistance of Feisal in regard to our

Mesopotamia policy ... Col. Lawrence took the view that just as we have a nominal Albanian ruler in Egypt, so it was desirable that we should have an Arab Prince as nominal ruler in Mesopotamia. (See CAB/27/24, War Cabinet Eastern Committee Meeting, 21 Nov. 1918.)

16 Derrida often refers to Kierkegaard's 'non-knowledge', or the recognition that a decision and actual knowledge are heterogeneous to each other. See Royle (2003 5).

17 Lawrence was equally self-effacing at home, and sought anonymity, in particular after his return from Arabia. In England, he refused the Order of the Bath and the D.S.O. from the King. He changed his name to Ross and then to Shaw, and joined the RAF. There is also a rumour that he applied for a job as a bank security guard in London rather than accept a government post.

18 'Cromer cherished the thought that he "remained more or less hidden and pulled the strings".' (Tidrick op. cit.: 210)

19 D. Bivona (1997) writes that Cromer also demanded complete self-effacement from his British subordinates, and that he may even have helped to create this ideal of self-effacement as 'the prime characterological qualification for would-be administrators of the Empire'. (Bivona 1997: 92)

20 The Khedive was the Turkish Viceroy in charge of Egypt.

21 cf. Foucault, following Nietzsche: history does not unfold rationally according to the development of 'reason'. See Danaher et al. (2000: 9–10).

22 A secret document printed in Cairo at the Arab Bureau for the Foreign Office, the War Office and the Admiralty in London.

23 I.e. the authentic Arab is the Bedouin.

24 See CAB , War Cabinet Eastern Committee meeting of 24 April 1918. President Woodrow Wilson's Fourteen Points, presented in a speech in January 1918, stated that there would be no annexation of conquered territory, and that all peoples have a right to self-determination.

25 Lugard uses the word generically, not in relation to the League of Nations Mandates.

26 Again, the term is used generically.

27 He relied for this statement on a British State Paper in 1923, which laid down the Government's guiding principles regarding policy in Africa. (Lugard 1928: 6–7)

28 This is a reference to Memmi's (1966: 58) 'colonisateur de bonne volonté'.

29 Prakash (1995: 3) calls this 'contortions of the discourse'.

30 The correspondence between the two parties is controversial. The central debate is whether or not Palestine was included in the 'promise' – the implication being that if so, Britain did not honour her word to the Sherif. Antonius (1938: 180) writes that no one who has read the original correspondence can sustainably hold the view that Palestine was excluded from the 'promise'. The argument has not been settled.

31 The Sherif was a Hashemite of Bedouin origin and Arab nationalists in the cities did not necessarily want him and his sons ruling the Middle East. An anonymous appeal was made by 'Seven Syrians' living in Cairo to the Foreign Office, in which they expressed their concern that the Anglo-Sheriffian understanding would install the Sheriffian family as overlords in Palestine, Mesopotamia and Syria. HMG responded in June 1917 with what became known as 'The Declaration to the Seven', in which the Seven were assured that HMG would recognize the 'complete and sovereign independence' of those territories which were free before the war, or which were liberated from the Turks by the efforts of the Arabs themselves. Territories liberated by the efforts of the Allies would be governed on the basis of consent.

32 Also reported by Liddell Hart in his biography of Lawrence as 'What do you think of my treaty?' (1934: 48–49). Lawrence was not exaggerating. Lord Curzon told the Eastern Committee of the War Cabinet:

> As the Committee will remember, Sir Henry McMahon, who knew nothing of the pourparlers already going on, which culminated later in the Sykes Picot Agreement, while negotiating with Hussein, who also knew nothing of what was in contemplation, gave certain undertakings by which we have been a good deal embarrassed ever since. (CAB 27/24, 27 Nov. 1918)

Hussein himself did not hear about the Sykes-Picot Agreement until the Bolsheviks seized power in Russia, raided the Ministry of Foreign Affairs and disclosed its secret documents. Despite the betrayal, and an offer of compromise by Jamal Pasha, the Turkish military commander in Syria, Hussein remained loyal to Britain.

33 Leonard Stein (1961: 140–46) explores Lloyd George's complex attraction to Zionism.
34 For Sykes's complex views on Jewish salvation, see ibid.: 273–81.
35 Sykes touches on Balfour's ambivalent views on Jews.
36 From miscellaneous papers relating to the Balfour Declaration, assembled by E. Monroe.
37 Millenarianists such as Mormons, Jehovah's Witnesses and Adventists believe in the Second Coming of Christ.
38 Christian eschatology is concerned with final revelations, the destiny of the soul, and the end of the world. It anticipates the imminent return of Christ.
39 Stein gives a full discussion of gentile Zionism.

Chapter 2

'Unmarked and undivided':[1]

Language, law and myth – how to transform aboriginal landscape

---

Some bloodless tools of imperial ascendancy

Laws, maps and surveys: these are the ideological and ostensibly non-violent tools of imperial ascendancy in Palestine through land control.

The role of law

Land developments in Palestine can be traced through court cases, ordinances, regulations and other pronouncements emanating from the Mandate government and excavated from the colonial archive. But a focus on law can only tell us *what* the Mandate government did, and *how* they did it. It does not tell us *why* they *really* did it, and consequently the importance of law (even where it is accessorized with government appointed committee findings and the results of political and economic enquiries) within this narrative has assumed disproportionate importance.[2] Without it, we would be lacking an unproblematic and normative methodological baseline (see Jones 2002: 174). The terrain is treacherous but law punctuates and synthesizes apparently disparate and contradictory principles and approaches. A discussion of land developments as the development of property rights provides a sterile sanctuary for a historian of Mandate Palestine. The impoverishment of the peasant, caught between a determined Zionist movement, a faltering Mandatory and an indifferent land-owning class, recurs across the literature as a foreseeable but inevitable tragedy – one which was achieved *despite* the Mandatory's best efforts to guard against it. This is a familiar and weighted narrative and it rests on two principal presumptions: first that the Mandatory government was a legitimate legislator (and '*why do we think that governments can legislate property rights?*' (ibid.: 174–75, my emphasis)), and secondly that law is a precursor to progress and that reform of native systems of land tenure/cultivation was commensurate with the improvement of society. Rather, I will suggest that it was advantageous for the Mandatory to propagate the legend that prior to the advent of British domination, there reigned a lack of order, meaning and functionality.

In this chapter, besides providing an overview of what the Mandate government did with regard to land and how they did it, I will avoid the temptation to attempt to pin down customary tenure in Mandate Palestine. I will suggest instead that Mandatory measures regarding land were appropriative, that the Mandatory came to Palestine with sticky fingers, and that the native system of landholding and agriculture became endangered by the *mere fact* of British occupation. European concepts were not introduced, as is often suggested, because Mandatory officials were enslaved by their European mindset and could conceive of no other systems of land tenure. As we will see, a perfectly feasible reading of the documentary record is that rather, these concepts were applied to Palestine quite simply to facilitate the commandeering of native land.

Law officiates landholding and use. It has ultimate declaratory value. In a colonial context, it is used to nullify, nuance or conditionally proclaim indigenous land rights. The acknowledgement of certain, lesser, indigenous rights to land was usually commensurate with less than total political domination (see Klug 1995: 125). In other words, the definition of the property rights of colonial subjects did not seek to reflect, and was essentially indifferent to the actual rights residing in those subjects. Instead, it reflected the designs of the colonial regime and its own structures of rule.

Law is one of the fundamental coercive tools of empire and it is deployed to subordinate the native and his social structures to those of his civilized master.[3] Here, in the colonial torture chamber, law is sublimated violence. It is 'lawfare'[4] despite claims to the contrary: that it is an integral part of the enlightened and benevolent venture to export progress and order worldwide. Imperial laws that oversee native systems of landholding are an ode to power relations. When conflicts arise, as they are wont to, they are mediated as legal confrontations according to a colonial rationale (see Forman and Kedar 2003: 492). The priority of colonial land systems was either to facilitate and institutionalize the transfer of land from native to settler/colonialist, or to set down the limits and conditions of native access to land. Colonial land systems and their attending institutions (land registries, surveying and mapping departments, land courts, etc.) categorically transform the social order in a dependency. (ibid.: 494–95) Palestine was no different.

'Why do we think that governments can legislate property rights?'

This question was posed by legal geographer Gareth Jones in relation to national governments and under colonial conditions, we ought to pause even longer (indefinitely) before coming up with any answer. Property rights in a colonial context compound issues of class with those of race. Fanon writes that the delineation of native space, the attempt on the part of the colonizer to define, confine and exclude the native and all his nativism, far from gearing societal progress as claimed, were exercises in offensive political and economic warfare. Here are the seeds for future rivalry, conflict and struggle. By the mid-1930s in Palestine, as traditional Arab villages began to stand apart from modern Jewish towns and settlements, the bleak scenario projected by Fanon was manifest:

> The native town is a crouching village, a town on its knees, a town wallowing in the mire. It is a town of niggers and dirty Arabs. ... The colonised man is an envious man ... for there is no native who does not dream at least once a day of setting himself up in the settler's place. (Fanon 1963: 39)

How does the settler's place come to be? How does the native's patrimony slip from his hands? Which ideological devices are deployed by the settler and the colonialist to justify their stomping all over native land with the help of police, army, tribunals, courts, ordinances, foreign experts and even local agents? Should the colonialist notice that he is a usurper, that his actions are making the native uncomfortable, that his incursions into every aspect of his life are stifling the native, he simply absolves himself by imagining that he is destined to rule, and that the native is destined to servitude. In the words of Memmi, 'Aux délices de la vertu recompensée, il ajoute la necessité des lois naturelles.' (Memmi 1966: 112)

The colonialist must be thorough if he wants to detox his psyche. He must negate the essence of both the native and his land. He pretends they are respectively absent and empty. The land is dormant and the native is not even on it. The land is unproductive and the native is barely human. The native and his land are chiefly characterized by their lack. The Director of Surveys in Palestine spoke of 'the featureless nature' of the Maritime Plain, the Valley of Kishon, the Plain of Esdraelon, the Beisan Ghor Plateau, and the Jordan Valley – which had interfered with their survey and settlement. (Le Ray Hugh Granville Papers (LRHG), box 1, file 2, Director of Surveys, 4 April 1929) It is as though they had accidentally come across a gigantic physical, moral and spiritual crevice. And it gets worse: emptiness and lack are not neutral qualities, but ones which attract wickedness. Gazing upon the measly native and his worthless land, the colonizer and settler see nothing but a vast gravitational black hole of maleficent energies. The colonialist/settler conceptually dominates the native's world by falling back on the old dualism of black and white, good and evil, human and inhuman, normal and abnormal, pre-modern and modern. The misfortune of the colonizer, the cause of his inevitable psychological seizure, is that he becomes trapped in this dialectic of his own making. (Memmi op. cit.: 92) In order to sustain the fraudulent justification for his rule, he is fated to endlessly proclaim his own worth, at the expense of that of the native's and in contrast to the latter's worthlessness.

Nandy (1983: ix) writes that in the Judeo-Christian tradition, ageing is seen as the consequence of man's sinfulness, and the decomposing body as a reflection of his moral deterioration. Only a healthy and vigorous adult male offers a glimpse of the potential for salvation (ibid.). The debilitated state of native agriculture, the frailty and infirmity of the land itself, reflect in the eye of the colonizer the moral and intellectual degeneration of local culture. They are both desolate and redundant. It becomes acceptable to speak interchangeably in terms of the frozen morality of the native, and of his underdeveloped techniques of agriculture. (Memmi op. cit.: 60) Youth, vigour, rigour, action, willpower, discipline, incisiveness – these are the things that heroes are made of. The rejuvenation of the land, more than for the sake of mere material productivity, is *equated* with the moral/spiritual rejuvenation of the nation. Once he has convinced himself of this, and in a surge of what Memmi calls 'charitable racism', the colonialist can charge ahead with his programme of reform, convinced that it will earn him the gratitude of the natives. The colonialist can then sleep soundly at night, glad to have been chosen as the conductor of a natural moral order. (ibid.: 111–12)

Fanon (op. cit.: 53) calls the colonialist 'an exhibitionist', (if he was not one at the outset, he is destined to become one), who must display his physical/mental prowess on a regular basis in order to remind the native that he is his superior. For Nandy, reform is manifest with the introduction of 'secular hierarchies' preaching secular salvation through the ideologies of 'progress, normality and hyper-masculinity'. (Nandy op. cit.: x) So the concept of evolution is crucial to this production, and it is specifically brought into play to universalize the dominating discourse. Lugard pronounced with regard to native systems of land tenure:

> [I]n the earliest stage the land and its produce is shared by the community as a whole; later the produce is the property of the family or individuals by whose toil it is won, and the control of the land is vested in the head of the family. When the tribal stage is reached, the control passes to the chief, who allots unoccupied lands at will, but is not justified in dispossessing any family or person who is using the land. Later still, especially when the pressure of population has given to the land an exchange value, the conception of property rights in it emerges, and sale, mortgage and lease of the land, apart from its user, is recognised. ... These processes of natural evolution, leading up to individual ownership, may, I believe, be traced to every civilization known to history. (Lugard 1965: 280)

The 'secular hierarchies' include law, and science. The veneer of law is flawless: it is incontestably objective, beneficial and progressive. It is a necessary step on the road to 'civilisation' and enhanced social 'development'. (Forman and Kedar op.cit.: 495) It often comes as a surprise to the natives in question then, when, despite law (this slick, convincing institution), they end up destitute, dispossessed and displaced. Literature on land in Mandate Palestine may be critical of the British administration's legislative approaches, or it may be in favour. It may note that an Order/Ordinance favoured the *fellah*[5]/local nobility/ Jewish settlers. It may record the discrepancies between Ottoman practice and Mandate interpretation of that practice. In the main though, it leaves intact the aura of illegitimacy – obscured by jargon, disguised by majestic claims, but indispensable to any thorough critique of legal structures founded on compulsion and intimidation. The structures – the paraphernalia of law – which bolstered and legitimized the discriminatory colonial regime, have been seamlessly absorbed into the historical literature without any significant challenge to their moral validity or the acceptability of their premise. Kedar raises this issue with regard to Mandate Palestine, as well as modern day Israel as an ethnocratic state. In 'On the legal geography of ethnocratic settler states' (2002), he focuses on the role of law and the courts in establishing settler societies' 'geographies of power' and asks a simple but neglected question when it comes to Mandate Palestine/Israel: how does law serve ethnocratic land regimes? Legalism is deployed to conceal the political/economic/cultural violence undertaken in its name.[6] It is no longer considered too scandalous or subversive to claim that legalism is a major element of domination, hegemony and legitimization, and that the more abstract a legal discourse, the more it is able to lay claim to neutrality in both process and outcome, and to depoliticize inequalities based on class and race. (ibid.: 410–11) Yet when it comes to Palestine, the claim is still slightly unthinkable, taboo. The mention of Palestine is guaranteed to raise the stakes – but why? There is no exclusive response as to whether law can be equated with violence – it depends on one's rank/status according to that law. Law is particularly cruel because it requires that we keep on smiling, even as we are beaten to the floor.

By promising to match dearth with cornucopia, laziness with technology, amorphousness with boundaries, the colonialist claims moral, spiritual, intellectual and cultural superiority over the native. He reinforces this with wholesale references to treaties, covenants and agreements, to legal education and training, to regard for the principles of equity and respect for local custom. Together, these form an artificial moral headquarters or base camp. Various versions of this refrain, this hypnotic chant, must be reiterated at every public opportunity for full effect, and they were pivotal to the booming discourse which adorned British presence in Palestine. The execution of the entire colonial enterprise, the implementation of the colonizer's separatist ideology, would have been inconceivable without them.[7] There could be no claim of sovereignty without incursion into and seizing control of the landscape, and no incursion into or seizing control of the landscape without survey and map-making.

The mysterious sciences of map-making and surveying[8]

The cultural influence of maps

As well as being part of the active discourse of early explorers and the geographic mission, map-making is a primary and essential technological tool of the military wing of imperialism. Maps identify and lay claim over boundaries.

They embody a political perspective and reflect the interests of the mapper (the state) and as such they may misrepresent the real world.[9] Maps carry significant symbolic force and claim conclusive knowledge of a foreign territory, of its human and botanical specimens:

> [T]he ineluctable necessities of conquest and government are to understand (or to believe that one understands) the physical space that one occupies or that one hopes to dominate, to overcome the obstacle of distance and to establish regular contact with the peoples and their territories (by enumerating the former and by measuring the dimensions, the surfaces and the capacities of the latter). (Nicolet 1991: 2)

Cartography promises to deliver a systematic representation of landscape. It is a tool of modernity, of advancement and of cultural momentum. Cultural domination is contingent on geographic domination and there can be no subjugation of an individual without the prior appropriation of his physical space, of the area of his jurisdiction and traditional sway, by another. The work of surveyors, cartographers, mathematicians and other data collectors is therefore potentially highly contentious. For as well as being scientists, they are agents of empire, and the figures and sketches buried in the pages of their notebooks have been collected in the service of their own definition of a higher cause. Their aim is not, as we can imagine, to helpfully supply the natives with maps so that they may hunt and gather and plant and herd better – but to organize the entry into and control of the desirable territory with the aid of convenient and accessible cartographic representations of it. The science of cartography is only one, but an important manifestation of the mind of British imperialism. It is an integral part of the British imperial élite version of what constitutes knowledge.[10] It contributes to the British conceptual construction of a territory. The symbolic significance of a map is indisputable, and it might as well be written all over it: 'this is British territory; if it is not, then it could be British territory; this is an imperial space to be governed by us'. (Edney 1997: 325) Maps amount to a visual declaration of the orbit of colonial authority. Their psychological impact on both native and colonialist is at once intense and subliminal. They decide, depict and confirm boundaries – not according to local folklore of major events such as a famous fight, or to distinctive physical characteristics such as a rock, river or tree – but in line with the imperial penchant for fixed marks circumscribed according to mathematical abstractions. The landscape is delineated according to British interpretation and understanding of it. Edney goes as far as saying that it is the British élite cultural perception of native space which is turned into any given map, and that an imagined empirical space is projected and transposed onto the real, the actual one, the native's. The dynamics which Edney exposes were duplicated in Palestine. There the necessity for surveys was promoted under the guise of agricultural improvement, and the initiative to settle title in Palestine was declared a necessary precursor which would herald the improvement of the countryside. The discourse of progress, rationality and dynamism persisted, and reinforced the claim of European technical and moral superiority over the native.

So the definition or declaration of native property rights by an imperial regime, far from capturing their essence or even semblance, simply reveals the colonialists' designs on them. The objective of map-making was to identify the actual or hoped for orbit of colonial governance, to visually announce to the natives and to confirm in their own minds their capacity for spatial domination – rather than to benignly illustrate territory. Land as target.

The fallibility of cartography and survey

This knowledge then, its nature and its quality, which is accumulated and filed into the colonial archive via the science of map-making, is culturally and politically inclined. To complicate things further, the methodologies which were applied may have been scientifically inexact. For example circumstances did not always permit the required sequence of triangulation, followed by topographic survey.[11] This meant that the strict hierarchical requirement of succession from one type of survey to another was not adhered to and in these cases the likelihood of errors was significantly increased. In Palestine, logistical obstacles were myriad: the self-funding British colonies were habitually strapped for cash, expert personnel was sometimes scarce, the climate could be over-whelming and officers were exposed to a series of exotic illnesses. For all the excessively scientific claims made with regard to survey/settlement of title, the procedure in Palestine was a little slapdash. There was ample scope for blunders when it came to cutting up a preliminary map into 'fiscal blocks', demarcating newly claimed parcels of land, surveying them on 'large-scale Registration Block-Plans', and passing these Block-Plans to Settlement Officers for Investigation of Rights. The Settlement Officers would then revise rights, adjudicate disputes and return plans for final revision in the case of divided lands, and in the cases of 'communally owned' land they would form parcellation schemes with a view to ultimate demarcation. (LRHG op. cit.) The geographical knowledge collected by agents of the British Empire and injected into the colonial archive was no different from other knowledge claimed by the colonialist (relating to law, religion, cus-toms etc.) – it was saturated with political interest and complicated by technical, cultural and linguistic gaps and ambiguities. The result was that representations of the local law and geography, enshrined as they were in technical legalistic and scientistic language, were in reality imprecise, tenuous, or just wrong.

Maps are the site of struggle

Still, the collected knowledge was good enough to be functional. It was precise enough and adequate enough to fulfil its one honest-to-God aim: conquest and control. Maps yield and seal influence and authority by virtue of their absolutist depictions of space. There are no grey areas on any particular colonial map to betray the questionable scientific method, logistical difficulties, linguistic barriers, cultural struggles or any other conceivable margin of error which may have been encountered in its creation. For information, agents of empire had to rely on informants, and the process of information gathering would have entailed (as in the case of the initiative to settle title in Palestine for instance), protracted negotiation, mediation and contestation between families, groups, village leaders, native and British colonial officers. The final results are sworn to secrecy: definitively noted down in English ink, fossilized and classified according to the ethos of the colonial archive, they dissimulate those malleable dynamics and never betray the volatile conditions under which they were recorded.

Yet despite these contingencies, the British fortified themselves with the insistence that they were conducting a scientific exercise based on cold observation. The rituals involved in surveying communities, calculating space, laying down fixtures and renaming areas contributed to the aura of power and mystery carefully developed around the white man, to his clear superiority exemplified in the rigour, coherence, discipline and order which he claimed to selflessly launch to combat the languor, chaos, ineptitude and corruption of the olive one.

Where might I seek authority to suggest that the government was indifferent with regard to whether their maps reflected native perception of their territory? The priority of any survey/mapping exercise abroad was the control of territory, and the fact that natives were aware of this became apparent when they resisted probes for information or were less than exuberant about the master plan. This occurred in Palestine, when locals posed obstacles for instance with regard to the government's settlement initiative, by refusing to point out the boundaries of their land to the government appointed Settlement Officers. Vexed by their non-cooperation, criminal sanctions were imposed (see 'On the ground' below). Even if the administration had not been aware of the political and economic controversy their settlement exercise would stimulate amongst the rural population at the outset of the mapping, survey and settlement exercise, they certainly became aware of it during the course of the ultimately failed attempt at implementation.

The official narrative: verisimilitude

Going back to the top: Ottoman-influenced Arab models of land tenure are not my focus, and I will not seek a more authentic knowledge of these models than the ones advanced by Mandatory authorities and subsequent historians. I also avoid pinning down the factors during British rule which contributed to the dispossession of the farmer. My enquiry stubbornly focuses instead on the Mandatory's *intentions*. I will focus on the process through which native models of land tenure were interpreted by the Mandate authorities, and challenge the language and dictates of 'land reform' in Palestine. I will focus my investigation on the British ethos and in doing so, I will rely on an implicit assumption that Palestinians' relationship with land and experience of their rural environment were deeply incongruent with the ones of their European rulers. They were deeply and fatally incongruent with one another first because of a cultural and philosophical schism, and secondly because the relationship of political domination and subjugation in which the two sides were locked ensured that that schism widened, grew stubborn roots and glossy leaves and fragrant flowers. I also assume that the Palestine peasantry would have readily refuted their European rulers' assessment of the value and quality of their rural existence, as well as for their need for 'reform'. In other words, the natives were not convinced of the European assessment of the worthlessness of their ways, nor of the Balfour Declaration, which provided the highly contentious context in which their 'rights' came to be discussed.

It is not what the Mandatory authorities *did* to Palestinian land through legal measures, but rather how they dictated the vocabulary of land tenure and ownership. On a private discourse of white cultural superiority and entitlement, they imposed the neutral legal jargon of 'freehold, leasehold, rent, individual, communal, co-ownership, usufruct, possession, trusteeship equity, legal and customary'. Wound together, these two strands of public and private discourse form a mesmerizing, if ultimately unconvincing tale of colonial trusteeship and failed local autonomy, colonial advice and local improvidence, colonial reform and local resistance, colonial good will and local suspicion, colonial restraint and local stubbornness, colonial rationality and local ignorance.

A legal basis

Article 6 of the Palestine Mandate of July 1922 placed an obligation on the Mandatory to facilitate and encourage 'close settlement by Jews on the land, including State lands and waste lands not required for public purposes'. Article 11 provided for Britain to 'introduce a land system appropriate to the needs of the country, having regard, among other things, to the desirability of promoting the close settlement and intensive cultivation of the land'. Article 12 (1) of the Palestine Order in Council of August 1922 (POIC), the document which provided a constitutional framework for British rule, granted complete sovereignty to the government over 'public' lands, stating '[a]ll rights in relation to any public lands shall vest in and may be exercised by the High Commissioner for the time being in trust for the government of Palestine.' Article 13 POIC allowed the High Commissioner (HC) to make grants and leases of Public lands for the purpose of implementing the provisions and obligations of the Mandate. Article 17 POIC enabled the High Commissioner to pass ordinances in consultation with an Advisory Council. Article 46 POIC conforms to international law[12] in relation to the preservation of the status quo in occupied territory:

'The jurisdiction of the Civil Courts shall be exercised in conformity with the Ottoman law in force in Palestine on 1st November 1914.' It also provided that the jurisdiction of the courts would be exercised 'in conformity with the substance of the common law and the doctrines of equity in force in England.'

Ottoman law – in English

The land system in Palestine prior to the advent of the British administration was, to put it delicately, complicated. It has been described as an indecipherable amalgamation of laws, orders and judgements of the civil and religious courts, a condition compounded by an incompetent or even corrupt administration. Ernest Dowson, the Government's Chief Advisor on Survey and Land Settlement just called it 'rubbish'. (LRHG, box 1, file, 2: Dowson to Clayton, 'Notes on Land Tax, Cadastral Survey, and Land Settlement in Palestine' 7 Dec. 1923) A more subtle assessment was made by contemporary historians of Ottoman land tenure, the Slugletts, who describe its 'elusive' and 'ambiguous' character.[13]

The main provisions of the Ottoman land regime are contained in the Ottoman Land Code 1858 (OLC). The OLC was supplemented by the *Tapu* (Title) Law 1858 and the Civil Code 1869 (known as the *Mejelle*). The former related to *Miri* property, and the latter to *Mulk* (these are explained below). The following categories of land tenure in Palestine broadly follow the labels of the OLC. I largely draw (unless otherwise stated) on a study prepared by Goadby and Doukhan as part of a government initiative in 1927, with a view to assisting officers engaged in the Land Settlement effort.

<u>Mulk:</u> This is roughly translated as freehold, or private ownership. An owner of *Mulk* property exercised extensive ownership rights. These were not complete though, since testamentary disposition is prescribed by *Sharia*, and article 1 OLC provided that *Mulk* was outside its scope, and subject to *Sharia* and the *Mejelle*. Under the Ottoman regime, *Miri* land could become *Mulk* by special order of the Sultan alone. The Palestine Government eventually claimed this Sultanic privilege for itself and in 1933 declared that

> The High Commissioner may, if he thinks fit, by order under his hand to be published in the Gazette, convert such land in Palestine of the category termed *Miri*, as may be described in such order, into land of the category of *Mulk*.[14]

<u>Miri:</u> This is similar to the usufruct, and described a heritable right to possession of land and its profits, in turn providing the government with revenue. Goadby and Doukhan (1935) translate the concept into English in an attempt to pin it down:

> The Ottoman commentators speak of the *Miri* holder (*Mutessarif*) as holding land from the State under a lease of indefinite duration at a double rent of which one consists in the *Tapu* payments (*Bedl Misl*)

and fees payable upon transfer and succession, and the other takes the form of tithe or taxes, or analogous periodical payments (*Ijara Zemin*). (ibid.: 17)

The OLC was an attempt to bring all *Miri* land into its scope. It enabled legal rights to be sold or mortgaged, subject to the consent of the state.

Miri Mahlul: Where *Miri* land remained unused for three consecutive years, or if its 'owner' died without an heir, it became *Miri Mahlul.*

Waqf: This is a religious charitable endowment and therefore outside the scope of Ottoman statute. *Waqf* (plural: *Awqaf*), is sometimes classified as 'true' (where it is held on *Mulk* land) or 'untrue' (where it is held on *Miri*). Goadby and Doukhan (ibid.: 76) translate the distinction between true and untrue in this way:

An Untrue dedication of *Miri* leaves the *Raqabe* [legal ownership] vested in the State and does not, therefore, change the category of the land. It is merely a dedication of the interests which the State has in the produce of the land and in the fees arising therefrom. The land does not really become *Waqf.*

Mawat: This is land which is unoccupied and unheld, although it may be cultivated with authorisation from the Sultan. This category of land was neither used for grazing nor for collecting firewood. It accounted for about 50–60 per cent of Palestine, and according to Article 6 OLC, it must lie at a minimum distance from a village so that a loud human voice cannot be heard calling from its periphery.

Cultivators of *Mawat* could, in theory, obtain title. Whether it could be converted into *Mulk* however, was debatable. Goadby and Doukhan thought it could not:

Comparing the terms of the *Mejelle* Article 1272 and Land Code Article 103, we infer that in the usual case permission to cultivate *Mewat* will be subject to the condition that, when cultivated, the land will be *Miri* and the *Raqabe* will still be vested in the State. It would appear that this condition must always be imposed by the official. (ibid.: 46)

Matruka: This category is subdivided into land left for public use such as a highway, and land assigned for use by a village or town such as pasture, woodland, threshing floor and places of worship. Goadby and Doukhan interpret *Matruka* as a category that might as well be *Miri/Mulk*, and subject to public or communal rights.

In addition the following two categories have been described as customary systems of landholding:

Mudawara/Jiftlik: This is land which was once privately owned, but which was 'turned over' to become government land. In addition to the tithe, cultivators on this category of land were required to pay an additional 10 per cent of their gross production as rent. Tenants on this land were not liable to eviction.

Musha': This is a system of cultivation whereby shares of land are periodically allotted on a rotational basis to each cultivator within a community. It is commonly described as 'collective' or 'communal' tenure in the literature. It has been debated by writers on the subject, whether this form of tenure evolved from the tribal system of common grazing rights over one territory. A Commission set up in 1923 to look into the possible partition of *Musha'* concluded that such land was subject to some form of corporate ownership. (ibid.: 206) Goadby and Doukhan on the other hand, thought it was more of a 'customary joint ownership' and approximated *Musha'* to an English Tenancy in Common. The critical distinction between the two interpretations relates to the ultimate potential alienability of each share.

A very brief description of the main land issues

One of the first problems faced by the British administration related to land registration. There had been no formal title deeds to land in Palestine prior to 1858. Registration was voluntary and most of the population was reluctant to register their land: poor villagers had little incentive to register, since this would make them liable to a registration fee, taxation and military conscription. Non-registration of title may have been the desperate peasant's way of keeping out of harm's way. In order to counter this, the 1858 *Tapu* law made title deeds obligatory. The system of registration related to the transfer alone, so that it was the transaction between individuals which was noted but not the piece of land in question. Villagers anxious to preserve a low profile continued to bypass the obligation to register and surrendered their formal tenure to an influential local, who registered it under his name. Land registers and records were also missing in the aftermath of war, carried away by the Turks.[15] These variables meant that the correct state of land ownership in Palestine was unclear from the land registers. The military administration closed the Land Registry in 1918 and prohibited all transactions in immovable property for the foreseeable future. The Department of Land Registries opened in July 1920 and resumed the functions of its Turkish predecessor, such as charging registration fees and investigating title. A month later a Land Commission was appointed by the High Commissioner, '1. to ascertain the area and nature of the various kinds of land which might be at the disposal of the government. 2. to report upon what lands in Palestine are available for closer settlement'. (CO 733: Shuckburgh to the Duke of Sutherland, 5 July 1921)

Another substantial hindrance to the imperial design was the *Musha'* system of cultivation. Kenneth Stein writes that '[t]he Musha' land system was described by every major authority on land in Palestine as the most debilitating factor affecting the economic betterment of the Palestinian fellaheen'.[16] (K.W. Stein 1985: 15) But 'every major authority on land in Palestine' was a biased one – as we will see, the main concern of the Mandatory government and its agents and experts was not the improvement of the natives' agricultural practices, but the requisition of as much land as possible. A *Musha'* Land Committee was established in 1923 to investigate. The aim of this committee was to 'determine and register existing rights in land; to facilitate dealings and reduce litigation; and to provide an accurate record of landholding, for the purpose of a fair and efficient distribution of land taxes'. (Israel State Archives cited in Atran 1989: 725) It was said that the division of communal plots into fixed parcels would improve the rural economy. Some 753 villages were visited as part of this effort, 56 per cent of which were found to operate according to the *Musha'* system. (Tyler 2001: 8) The committee recommended that the system stood in the way of initiative and investment, and should be controlled with legislation. The committee's recommendations were never implemented and *Musha'* partition was eventually conducted as part of the general Land Settlement initiative.

Large tracts of land were sold by the Sursok family. The Sursoks were absentee landlords and the sales they made guaranteed Jewish settler dominance over the Jezreel valley. Land sold by the Abd Al Hadi family linked Jewish lands in the valley to the coastal plain. The Tayyan family disposed of Wadi Hawareth, a coastal plain between Haifa and Jaffa. These purchases, although they amounted to a tiny percentage of Palestine, are considered strategically decisive, and provided Jewish immigrants with contiguous terrain, a core territory which separated the north of the country from the south, the east from the west. (see Atran, op. cit.: 727–33) After the 'Wailing Wall Riots' in the summer of 1929, a Special Commission was appointed under the chairmanship of Sir Walter Shaw to investigate the causes of Arab/Jewish grievances. In 1930, the commission recommended the suspension of land sales to Jews and the introduction of a Jewish immigration quota. Following the commission's recommendations, Sir John Hope-Simpson was appointed to inquire into land settlement and Jewish immigration. He concluded that the country had reached its absorptive capacity and that further land sales and immigration would lead to the dispossession of the *fellah*.

Legislation

Soon after he arrived in Palestine, the first HC Herbert Samuel made a point in French: '[n]e pas trop gouverner is a good maxim, particularly in an eastern country, and above all in the early years of a new regime'. (CO : Samuel to Churchill, 25 July 1921) But what he did was different from what he said. Bunton calculates that by the end of his term of service as High Commissioner in 1925, Samuel had enacted some 130 ordinances. Yet despite the overwhelming evidence Samuel continued to insist that 'it has been the policy of the government not to change the laws which closely touched the lives of the people and to which they were accustomed.' (cited in Bunton 1999: 32)

And yet ...

Land Transfer Ordinances (LTO) 1920, 1921. LTO 1920 reopened the Land Registries that had been closed upon British arrival in Palestine. The purpose of the LTO was to promote a market in land whilst protecting the status of tenants by avoiding land speculation and the aggregation of large estates. LTO provided for the administration to approve all land transactions, and S.6 stipulated that such consent be withheld where the Governor was not satisfied that the tenant in question retained the means to support himself and his family.[17] LTO 1921 lifted those restrictions, providing that the Director of Lands shall grant his consent provided he is satisfied only of the transferor's title. However S.2 confirmed the protection of cultivators' rights on leased land, providing that they must retain sufficient land so as to enable them to support themselves and their family. The Advisory Council[18] had unanimously approved the removal of the impediments to land transactions contained in LTO 1920. Samuel wrote to Churchill '[t]he Ordinance was passed with scarcely any comment and there is every reason to believe that the removal of the restrictions will be popular throughout the country.' (CO : Samuel to Churchill, 9 Dec. 1921) LTO 1921 allegedly made everyone happy, especially the landowning classes who, deprived of any real political clout, could at least concentrate on consolidating their capital – whilst the *fellaheen* were delighted to receive what seemed to them huge sums from their landlords to vacate the land. Arab-Jewish transactions conducted as a result of the amending ordinance were kept secret. By the time of the Shaw Commission inquiry in 1929, the Director of Lands reported that he had not come across one case of the administration's consent being sought prior to sale:

> A vendor would come along and make a contract for sale and purchase with the Jews. We would know nothing of this until 4, 5, or 6 months later when the transaction would come to the office. We then instructed the District Officer to report on the tenants. He would go out to the village and in some cases he would find that the whole population had already evacuated the village. They had taken certain sums of money and had gone, and we could not afford them any protection whatever. (Report of the Commission on the Palestine Disturbances of August 1929 (the Shaw Commission Report): 115)

Land Court Ordinance (LCO) 1921. This ordinance authorized the High Commissioner to set up Land Courts (presided over by a British judge and a Palestinian assistant) wherever they were needed, and to hear cases relating to settlement of title. The ordinance was intended to relieve some pressure off the District Courts. By 1924, the jurisdiction of the Land Courts was curtailed following Dowson's derisory verdict on their proficiency, and a new system for land settlement was introduced.

Mahlul Land Ordinance (MLO) 1920. This ordinance required cultivators of *Mahlul* to request a lease of the land from the government, which would be granted at the administration's discretion. The Peel Commission (appointed to investigate causes of unrest in the country following the nationwide strike in 1936) noted in 1937 that this was ignored. This ordinance appeared to copy Ottoman law –

which provided that a squatter on *Miri* land could apply for a grant on payment of its unimproved value. One way in which it did not copy Ottoman law was its requirement that village authorities/leaders report *Mahlul* land to the government. Where *Mahlul* land was unreported and remained undiscovered to the government, it joined the category of illegally occupied land. There was another important distinction between Ottoman practice and colonial innovation: whereas *Mahlul* land could not revert to the Ottoman state if the squatter was in a position to pay the tithe, the colonial government claimed wide discretion for itself to do this. (Goadby and Doukhan op.cit.: 26)

In 1933 the Land law Amendment Ordinance killed *Miri Mahlul*, pronouncing that such land may be declared 'Public' by the High Commissioner, in pursuance of Article 12 (1) of the Palestine Order-in-Council.[19]

Mewat Land Ordinance 1921. Article 103 OLC entitled anyone who had improved *Mawat* land to apply to the authorities for a title deed in exchange for payment of its unimproved value. This ordinance repealed the article, revoked the right, and declared cultivators of *Mawat* liable to prosecution for trespass. A conditional amnesty was written into the ordinance, which allowed cultivators to lease waste lands from the government as long as they applied for such lease within two months of the ordinance coming into effect.

Land Settlement Ordinance (LSO) 1928, 1930, 1932, 1933. This relates to the settlement of title and not to the close settlement of immigrants on the land required by Article 11 of the Mandate. The settlement of title was a chief aspect of the reorganization of native tenure in Palestine by the Mandate government. Land in Palestine had been little registered or inaccurately registered: the registers were directly linked to taxation and military conscription, which meant that the natives did what they could to avoid them. So land may have been registered under the name of a big landowner as a protective measure. Compounding this lack of certainty, the loss of land registers at the end of the war meant that most of the government records themselves were missing at the onset of the British occupation. In addition, land which was registered was not readily identifiable to British eyes: either a distinctive physical feature, a memorable event, or other local folklore was often sufficient to indicate a piece of land – a colourful and frustrating feature which begged the Mandate government for an overhaul.[20] At Ernest Dowson's behest, a new procedure for determining the size and ownership of parcels of land was introduced, with a view to conclusively settle and register title.

Land Law Amendment Ordinance (LLAO) 1928. This ordinance went straight for the essence of Ottoman law/practice. Attorney General Bentwich explained what it aimed to achieve: 'The Ordinance is concerned with changes in the Ottoman Land Code, as interpreted by the courts in Palestine, on points that have been found to be embarrassing.' (CO 733/159/1)

What could possibly constitute 'embarrassing'?

LLAO made several fundamental changes to the 'Ottoman law in force'. Where the OLC had prescribed that land which escheats to the State must be sold at auction, Bentwich advised (and his advice was taken) that since an auction cannot guarantee an adequate price, and alternatively, that since the government might want to reserve the land for its own use, it might be wise for the government to retain the right to dispose of *Mahlul* land by private sale. The ordinance also repealed Article 126 OLC, which had provided that the boundaries of towns and villages may only be delineated through the mediation of a religious authority or other 'trustworthy' person (is there irony in this?). Finally Articles 109, 110, 111, 112 OLC, which had limited the inheritance rights of non-Muslims and non-nationals, were simply repealed.

Protection of Cultivators Ordinance (PCO) 1929 (further amendments consolidated 1933–34). PCO 1929 provided for monetary compensation to a cultivating tenant who was served notice to quit. It repealed Section 2 LTO 1921, which had required a cultivating tenant to retain an adequate subsistence area for himself and his family. After the Shaw Commission criticized the government for facilitating the alienation of title, PCO 1933 was a reversal of policy, and made it a condition of sale that a cultivating tenant should be provided with an alternative, adequate subsistence area.

They acted like two faced, fork-tongued opportunists. The British, as Europeans, were bound to let their assumptions about private property or the reification of land rights influence their interpretation and reinscription of the native system of land tenure. But they also capitalized on the Ottoman system's weaknesses and ambiguities. Attorney General Norman Bentwich wrote in his private papers regarding the disappearance of the Land Registers by the Turks at the end of the war, '[a]gain the Turkish will to hamper has really assisted the Administration' (Bentwich Papers, 'The Legal Administration of Palestine under the British Military Occupation'). Similarly, the Land Commission's brief in 1920 to 'ascertain the area and nature of the various kinds of land which might be at the disposal of the government', betrays a similar preoccupation. They had a vision: to disentangle native rights in order to interlock them with the new system of political control. Government interest in the recuperation of the Ottoman legacy, and the interpretation of Ottoman/Islamic concepts were not part of a purely etymological exercise. For all the streams of ink and the despair over the chaos that was Ottoman government, the beauty of the native system lay in its malleability.

Faced with such 'rubbish', the only option was to clean up.

Behind the scenes: violence

Behind the cool legal categories lay a trail of verbal destruction. Congruent with the imaging of the native, the Palestinian legal legacy was represented as characterized by debris and a load of atrophied concepts and theories.

Native wrongs

Ernest Dowson[21] spent three or four days in Palestine in November 1923 on mission to advise the British administration on landholding and agriculture in Palestine, and on possible future measures or campaigns by the government. His resulting verbal onslaught on the 'evils' of the land system inherited from the Turks is a breathtaking tirade of ills and grumbles. Dowson's assessments regarding the sheer uselessness of Palestinian agriculture and system of tenure are dated and retrograde documents, and they read like the reveries of a traveller in the grips of culture shock.

At the end of a three- or four-day (mini) recce, Ernest Dowson felt he was able to pronounce on land tax, cadastral survey and land settlement in Palestine. His study had consisted of conversations with the government Chief Secretary, with the Attorney General and the Treasurer, with the Director of Agriculture and Fisheries, with the Director of Lands, the Director of Surveys, with the Governors of Samaria and the Southern Province and with the Assistant Governor of Jaffa. He had also inspected the work of the Survey of Palestine by making visits to both the office and the field (LRHG: Dowson to Clayton op.cit.). Dowson's documents are an invective against the confusing legal and cultural mess he came to unpack. It is all there: the listless aristocracy, the glum peasantry, the pointlessness of both their existences and the backwardness of their ways. His reports are spellbinding. Dowson launches into Palestine by relying on what he knew of Egypt, where he had served in various posts for 23 years: as Director-General of Surveys, Under-Secretary of State for Finance, Financial Advisor to the Government and Chairman of a land reform commission (Forman 2002: 62):

> When Mohammed Ali wrested Egypt from the Turk he took over a land which, allowing for the difference in natural advantages, was as agriculturally derelict as Palestine is to-day. A conglomeration of land tenures – the complicated heritage of ages – survived, the taxes are of the mediaeval Moslem type, the peasant was a starveling without incentive to improve the land and without hope of improving his own position. Mohammed Ali and his successors regarded Egypt simply as their personal estate, but they had the natural genius to appreciate that the clogging effect of obsolete survivals must be lifted from the land if enterprise was to replace apathy, and its ancient prosperity was to be restored. Although much that was evil and economically deadening persisted till the British Occupation, and even persists to-day, it was none the less the House of Mohammed Ali which cleared away the top layer of accumulated rubbish

and carried Egypt up the earlier rungs of the ladder leading to her economic establishment. (LRHG: Dowson to Clayton op. cit.)[22]

Moving on to Palestine, he couches his appraisal in the language of disease and degeneration: 'Agriculture is the one sure, and probably the only important national asset, and it is by universal admission in a very unhealthy state. The diagnosis of the causes of the sickness afflicting agriculture appear also to be universally admitted and indeed to be indisputable.' (ibid.) According to Dowson, the agricultural industry was collapsing beneath the weight of a crushing tax, and ailing because of 'uneconomic systems of land tenure and the prevailing uncertainty and insecurity of real rights'. (ibid.) Further on:

> The second important disability under which Palestinian agriculture suffers is a widespread uncertainty in regard to real rights and the prevalence of uneconomic systems of land tenure. Such merits as the Turkish system of record of land rights possessed, and they were from the point of view of the people negligible, were to a great extent annihilated by the destruction or removal of the registers by the retreating enemy when the country was occupied by H.M. Forces. An effort has since been made to initiate an improved system, but with the best will in the world it is impossible to do so without a thorough clearance of accumulated rubbish and a rebuilding de novo on simpler and better lines, which means on the basis of a national cadastral survey and settlement of real rights from one end of the country to the other. (ibid.)

How does Dowson know that the Turkish system possessed negligible merits 'from the point of view of the people', having gathered his information from the Attorney General, the Directors of Lands and Surveys, Governors and Assistant Governors, etc.? And how could he have reached such confident conclusions after four days in the country? Undaunted by his own sketchy familiarity with Palestine, and relying, as he does throughout the entire document, on his experience in Egypt, Dowson ploughed on with his outlandish claims, this time relating to the duplicity of the locals:

> It may not be without significance to Palestine that in writing of the defective registration system which is now being replaced in Egypt Judge Halton stated 'that quite a considerable number of the deeds registered in Egypt are believed to be forgeries' and that 'in fact, registration is usually resorted to by the forger, as it gives a spurious appearance of genuineness to a fabricated document' (ibid.).

The words 'derelict', 'lack', 'apathy', 'evil', 'deadening', 'rubbish', 'sickness', 'unhealthy', 'afflicting', 'disability', 'annihilated' and 'blighted', speckle his report. Ernest Dowson knows his own mind and has no time for paralyzing self-doubt or womanly wavering. He is a specimen sample of Memmi's '*Le colonisateur qui s'accepte*' (Memmi op. cit.: 90) as well as a perfect example of how, as Nandy writes, colonialism purports to offer salvation via the (illusory) ideologies of 'progress, normality and hyper-masculinity'. (op. cit. x) The pioneering Dowson is very 'masculine'. His tone is robust, commanding and sure-footed, even as he blunders over quite important things.[23] Dowson harbours no ambivalence or reservations regarding his superior status/heroic role. He is a potential saviour, if only his advice were heeded. Convinced of his and his nation's cultural and racial supremacy, he is arrogant, sneering and rude. Never mind reform, he has come to cleanse, or in his own words, to 'purge'. When he suggested a registration system for Palestine, it was one which would facilitate the dual role of the State: as custodian of Public land, and as steward of its exploitation.

Dowson's reports also rely on the other stereotype portrayed by Memmi (op. cit.: 117): that of a mythical universal native – as anticipated and projected by his master. The colonizer is not interested in who the native really is, and simply invents him. The native's legendary and universal passivity/debility/laziness occupy pride of place in the colonizer's self-ennobling monologue. This is asserted repeatedly and methodically, not as an objective, differentiated remark, but as one that has institutional implications. In the end, the colonizer makes the native lazy/passive/debilitated by the mere force of his assertions (see ibid.: 119–22).

'Improvement'

Law is one of the most comprehensive dialogic constructs, but it is not the only one, and others were established in the name of progress and improvement. In reality, these were institutions which were not merely incompatible with the native social order, but were hostile to it, and ultimately destructive. One such hierarchy superimposed on the local native order related to the mapping of Palestine: to the surveying, measuring, dividing, and labelling of native land supposedly as a sort of gracious kindness, for the sake of the benign enough sounding progress and improvement. Dowson's remarkable prejudice, parading as evaluation, set the tone for the British administration. Explicitly, Dowson referred to the Mandatory's role as one that would ensure the 'economic rescue' and 'economic salvation' of the country. The Mandatory was responsible for the 'establishment of healthy national economy'. Yet at the same time, he was open about the motivation behind the enterprise. Improvement of the economy equals the exploitation of natural resources, and the exploitation of natural resources is a bread-winner for the state. (LRHG: Dowson to Clayton op. cit.)[24] In order to be effective, one had to be ruthless, and what was needed was nothing short of 'a comprehensive attack on the country as a whole'. Dowson concluded the Preliminary Considerations section of his report with a cutting remark:

> The economic development of the country has been blighted initially by
> years of Turkish apathy and maladministration and subsequently by war,

and its removal has doubtless been postponed by the inevitable political pre-occupations engendered by racial rivalry and consequent unrest. The causes of the blight have been diagnosed and are removable, and it is sound business to see that they are removed with the least possible further delay. (ibid.)[25]

In his report, and as the first tentative steps towards 'improvement', Dowson proposed first the preparation of draft legislation that would 'simplify' and '*modify*' current land law as needed. Sometimes, this just meant 'dispensed with', as he emphasized the need for 'dead wood' to be 'lopped away'. Second, he suggested cadastral survey and settlement, to be followed by the intro-duction of compulsory registration of real rights. He suggested that the (Australian/ Swiss) Torrens system of recording real rights should be applied in Palestine, as well as the effective overhaul of local practice:

> The Torrens principle of basing record and passage of real rights on the indes-tructible, immovable, and readily definable unit of land instead of the ephem-eral, mobile and indifferently definable unit of humanity who temporarily enjoys rights over it is winning its way surely throughout the world, and neither its superiority nor its simplicity are seriously contested anywhere. (ibid.)

He ended his report by appealing to the universal mission in which he was a big player: now that they had 'set their hand to the plough as mandatories of the civilized world', the British government and people, he wrote, could not turn away from their grave responsibilities. He recommended that the nomads of the south and east of the country (through colonial remapping of the region, newly named 'frontier districts') ought to be included in the administration's programme of reform. There should be no differentiation in the government's approach between their system of land tenure and that of the rest of the country, and they should not be given any special privileges on the basis of their tribal customs. This is tough love: nomadism is, after all, 'a stage in the development of human communities' (one step away from vagabondage?) and he looked forward to its demise. Eventually, he wrote, the nomads' traditions and habits will pass 'with merely surface bubble from their old life as we ourselves have passed, into the stream of settled folk'. (ibid.) The exposed discourse of technical progress, global evolution, rationality and inevitability then, is supplemented with this submerged vocabulary of destruction and annihilation, entirely justifiable and likened to a quasi-religious sacrifice for the greater good. Dowson imagined and declared himself (and his country) to be the shepherds of a new era, the heroic combatants without frontiers against all things corrosive and the very repositories of meaning.

Cordoning off public domain

'Public lands' are defined in Article 2 POIC as 'all lands in Palestine which are subject to the control of the Government of Palestine by virtue of Treaty, convention, agreement, or succession, and all lands which are or shall be acquired for the public service or otherwise'.

To eject natives in your way, begin with the discovery and labelling of Public lands.[26] The discovery and labelling of Public lands was a priority for the Palestine government, and the pressure was on to define as much land as possible as 'public'. As corroboration, HC Chancellor wrote in 1929, in those words, that MLO 1920 had been passed in order to preserve the State Domain (CO 733/170/2, Chancellor to Passfield, 23 Dec. 1929). Public land was to be made available to new immigrants on long leases,[27] but there may have been an intention to dispose of it by sale. HC Samuel explained in 1921 why he thought the Land Department should be scaled down:

> [I]f it is proposed gradually to dispose of the state lands to private purchasers, and also, (as I imagine) to transfer the land registry to the Survey Department on its formation, I should not have thought this Department required so many senior appointments. (CO , 5 Dec. 1921)

In any case, a Land Commission was appointed by the High Commissioner immediately as the Civil Administration took over in the summer of 1920, to report, inter alia, on how to obtain an accurate record of State land and to advise on its best disposition in the interests of the country generally, as well as with regard to closer settlement[28]and increased production. The Land Commission recommended the creation of a new department (the Department of Lands), which would specifically 'ascertain, delimit, register and control all State properties'. (CO 733/170/2, Chancellor to Passfield op. cit.)

The Ottoman category of *Miri* lent itself to redefinition as State Domain. *Miri* comprised most of agricultural Palestine, and ultimate authority over this category was traditionally vested in the State. However, whereas under the Ottoman system, *Miri* cultivation and use were encouraged, the British administration claimed it as its own and proceeded to limit and condition and prevent native access to it. It is in that spirit that indiscreet remarks were made by senior officials to each other: 'Most of the land is Government land over which the occupiers have certain shadowy rights by virtue of their occupation; this should facilitate the work of 'resumption' by the authorities.' (Clauson, 2 Nov. 1929, cited in Bunton 2000: 126) Shadowy rights? Shadowy according to whom, to which spectrum of light? Did the occupiers themselves experience their rights as 'shadowy'? What does it mean, what is at stake when someone describes someone else's rights as 'shadowy'? Does it accidentally reveal the person describing as an opportunistic predator assessing the vulnerability of his prey?

There was also a sense of urgency in Dowson's 1923 recommendations, when he pressed the Government to 'salvage' as much Public Domain as possible and to do so as quickly as possible. Dowson later explained that his sense of panic arose from the fear that long-term use of Public Land would lead to the creation of *Mulk* title, whereas he understood, in retrospect, that it could at most lead to a prescriptive *Miri* claim. (ibid.) This from an expert in native/Ottoman/Islamic systems of land tenure with extensive experience in neighbouring Egypt? There had certainly been no suggestion of uncertainty in his blustering 1923 report:

> The discovery and definition of public domain throughout Palestine is a secondary object of systematic cadastral survey and settlement which alone appears to promise a return to the exchequer of the work, more direct, quicker, and possibly during the next critical decade even greater in amount, than that which will be indirectly derived from the gradual establishment of a healthy national economy. I was advised by a competent authority that the *'mewat'* land that would be discovered and thus defined as State Domain during the progress of cadastral survey was likely to comprise one-third of the area of Palestine, and in addition to this there are the categories of land known as *'matruka'* and *'mahlul'*. It therefore appears evident that, even if all the occupied and exploited *'mera'* [i.e. *Miri*] land is allowed to be inscribed as *'mulk'* and all *'mera'* land is allotted to village or other communities, a large and potentially very valuable public estate yet lies in Palestine both largely unlocated and undeveloped … and experience in Egypt emphasizes the need in the public interest to locate and define this potentially valuable national domain with as little delay as possible … While the permanent retention in the hands of the State of a considerable proportion of the land of the country is of questionable desirability, it is clearly a culpable neglect of national interests to allow hundreds of thousands of acres of public land to be simply stolen. (LRHG: Dowson to Clayton op. cit.)

Could Dowson really have been referring to native theft of their patrimony, with the victim of this theft being the Mandatory government? And which national interests does he mean? He really does seem to suggest that the (primary?) purpose of survey and settlement was to 'rescue' land from potential native theft of it. He is urging the government to resume control of as much land as possible and declare it Public, either for the purpose of leasing it to immigrants, or for the exploitation of its natural resources. He continues:

> My experience of what occurred in Egypt leads me confidently to hazard the anticipation that the promptest possible execution of cadastral survey and settlement in Palestine will be repaid by the much larger extent of public domain that will be salvaged alone, that if on the other hand survey and settlement pursue the leisurely course at present indicated the vast potential estate which justly belongs to the nation at large will shrink to a relatively petty measure. (ibid.)

The outbursts of colonial officials and experts provide an easy target for derision. More serious though, is the fact that expressions such as 'unlocated and undeveloped', 'stolen', 'salvage', 'potential' and 'justly belongs to the nation at large', have remained undetected and may have been allowed to seep, poisonously and uncritically, into historical accounts of land developments in Palestine.

Did the latent violence of the official record finally manifest on the ground? Through which legalistic and scientistic techniques was this frenzy of insults directed at local culture?

On The Ground

Difficulties

There were considerable logistical difficulties which affected the interpretation of Ottoman law, survey, and the initiative to settle title. The confident Dowson did not seem to mind, and he relied on a three- or four-day visit to make his assertive recommendations to Chief Secretary Clayton. The administration was impressed with him and he was invited back the following year and this time remained in Palestine from November 1924 to March 1925 for a second report. In January 1926, he was appointed to advise on the practical implementation of the recommendations in his reports. Dowson left Palestine in July 1926 and returned in November of that year, remaining for some eight months until July 1927.

Dowson's assessment of Ottoman law and practice – a conceptually challenging enterprise under the best conditions – was hindered by another two factors. We have seen that his task was complicated by the absence of reliable statistics regarding land ownership, and it seems that he may have also been deprived of the elementary tools necessary for the execution of his assignment: he neither had access to the full collection of all the orders-in-council, proclamations, ordinances and public orders passed since the British occupation of Palestine, nor adequate access to Ottoman laws in translation. He presented his 'Preliminary study of land tenure in Palestine' with the pre-emptive disclaimer that it was 'inaccurate and incomplete'. He explained:

> When I first visited Palestine in November 1923 a private copy of Ongley's translation of the Ottoman Land Code was temporarily borrowed for me and supplemented by a scratch collection of post-Occupation Proclamations, Ordinances, etc. When preparing for my second visit a precious copy of Young's *Corps de Droit Ottoman* was secured for a short time for me from the Foreign Office. During and since my second visit the same difficulty has been experienced in obtaining standard translations or a complete collection of Ottoman texts. (CO 733/109, 'Preliminary Study of Land Tenure in Palestine')

By the time of Dowson's first brief visit to Palestine in the winter of 1923, not one acre of cadastral survey had been achieved (LRHG: Dowson to Clayton op. cit.), even though the Survey Department, whose object was the production of cadastral plans and data of agricultural land with a view to settle title, had been engaged for three years. The Department enumerated the 'difficulties' which had, in effect, paralyzed its work:

(i)   Necessity for diversion of much energy during the first two years on Town Plans of Jerusalem, and some minor subsequent diversions.
(ii)   Difficulty in obtaining efficient supervising and instructional staff, and of training up a body of surveyors and draughtsmen from Palestinian elements.
(iii) Unavoidable delay in obtaining equipment.
(iv)   Diversity of terrain, climate, races and languages in Palestine.
(v)   Existing systems of tenure and cultivation, ignorance of holders and general absence of property marks, definition, or other evidence concerning boundaries.
(vi)   Failure of many Gaza owners to demarcate and point out their property boundaries.
(vii) Poor quality and high cost of labour.
(viii) Interference in certain areas by armed robbers and gangs (LRHG, box 1 (file unnumbered), Report on Work of Survey Department, Aug. 1920– Aug. 1923. Annual Reports of Director of Surveys, Palestine and other Departmental Reports, 1920–39).

Which 'minor diversions' could have been allowed to interfere with the urgent task of cadastral survey? Why were the lack of competent staff and the delay in obtaining equipment not anticipated? How could the 'diversity of terrain and climate' come as a surprise to a land department, and to which diversity of 'races and languages' could they have been referring? How could the diversity of races, languages, terrain and climate been so overwhelming to a colonial government and once again, unanticipated? Was absence of 'evidence concerning boundaries' not the reason for the survey anyway? Why do the enumerated 'difficulties' read like the hedging pretexts of amateurs? Why so many excuses, instead of understanding? Finally, how do these tremulous excuses square with the myth of competence, experience and skill projected by Mandate officials?

The necessity to 'secure' title via survey, settlement and registration was periodically declared a priority for the government. Yet by the time Dowson wrote his 'Land Tenure and Taxation in Palestine' (CO 733/136/8, 11 Jan. 1927) no progress had been made. He judged this to be due to a lack of strong leadership as well as some 'detachment' on the part of the administration. Dowson suggested the appointment of a Commissioner of Lands to push the reforms along. The Commissioner would be a senior officer of the administration, with an office in the building of central government and he would also be a member of the Advisory Council. He would have an intimate relationship with the government and his advice would be authoritative: 'Neither the responsibility nor the authority of the Commissioner of Lands should be watered down by enforced association with any standing council or committee.' (ibid.) Dowson suggested that Settlement Operations should be under the direct control of the Commissioner of Lands, and Settlement Officers would go out into the rural areas to investigate title. With such determination and expertise in place, the failure of the scheme to settle title may be one of the more interesting failures of the Palestine Government. A settlement survey finally commenced in 1928, with only five Settlement Officers. The quality of the work turned out lacked in care as officers in the field felt under pressure to present results. Salmon, the Commissioner for Lands and Surveys in 1936, thought that the system in place encouraged unnecessary disputes and gave rise to too many claims:

> The recording of claims by Assistant Settlement Officers was, in my opinion, and also, in the opinion of my predecessor, being carried out too fast. The main object of these officers was to show progress and in many cases the work was sketchily done and unnecessary disputes were recorded for later decision by Settlement Officers. (LRHG, box 1, file 3: 'Notes on the Progress of Survey and Settlement', 4 Dec. 1936)

Transactions in land and the 'improvidence' of the fellah. Problematizing land

In 1929, HC Chancellor wanted to enact immediate legislation to control dispositions of agricultural land. The Colonial Office responded: 'In the case of any other Dependency, the question as between local interest and outside clamour could be answered in only one way. Unfortunately Palestine is an exception to most rules.' (CO 733/185/3: Memo on Land Question, for P.M., from the Colonial Office, 20 June 1930)

Why?

Jewish settlers had two options if they wanted to live in Palestine: they could either buy land from Arabs, or obtain a lease from the government on State Land. In 1920, a Land Commission was appointed to identify how much 'State Land' was available and to suggest ways of increasing its productivity so as to make it fit for dense settlement. The commission's findings were published in 1921. 'Palestine' consisted of 26,158,000 *Dunams*,[29] approximately 11m of which was cultivable land.[30] This figure included the 12,398,000 *Dunams* making up tribal Beersheba. By 1929, 900,000 *Dunams* of cultivable land had been purchased by Jewish settlers, the greater part of which was land 'of the best quality'. (CO 733/185/2, Chancellor to the Colonial Office, Despatch of 27 January 1930 on 'The Land Question'):

Between 1921 and 1925, 236,000 *Dunams* were purchased from absentee landlords, most notably from the Christian Lebanese Sursok family.

By the time of the Shaw Commission Report, 116,000 *Dunams* were sold by notables and *fellaheen*. According to the Report, 10 per cent of these sales were made by *fellaheen* indebted at 'usurious rates', who sold land to discharge their liabilities. Where notables sold undivided shares in village lands, cultivators were allowed to remain on the land as tenants, pending partition. (ibid.)

In 1929, over 30,000 *Dunams* in Wadi Hawareth were sold to the Jewish National Fund by another absentee landlord. (ibid.)

The Shaw Commission Report was critical of the government's land policies because of their impact on the Arab cultivator. Hope-Simpson, who presented his findings shortly after, thought the commission had underestimated rather than exaggerated the problem, and that a landless and disgruntled underclass was already in existence. (CO 733/185/3, 1930, Memorandum on 'The Position of the Arab Cultivator') They wrung their hands and lamented: how could HMG protect the Arabs against their own 'improvidence'? (ibid.) This was the time of HC Chancellor's term in office and he was also anxious. It was not only land sales from Arabs to Jewish settlers which threatened to dispossess and displace the Arab *fellah*. With regard to State Lands, Chancellor wrote:

> If more land now in occupation of the indigenous population is sold for the purpose of Jewish settlement, either the existing cultivators will be dispossessed of their land and will cease to be cultivators, or their holdings must be reduced below what is now regarded as the average area sufficient to support an Arab agricultural family. (CO 733/185/2, Chancellor to the Colonial Office op. cit.)

Chancellor thought it was too convenient and easy to blame peasant dispossession on the peasants themselves, since it was the positive duty of the government to protect their interests. He had it in mind to create land reserves for them, and wrote home requesting copies of the Tanganyika Land Legislation and the Kenya Native Land Bill. (CO 733/185/2, Despatch, 23 Jan. 1930)

LTO 1920 and 1921 had been passed to promote a market in land whilst averting the crisis of a landless underclass. LTO 1920 provided for all transactions in land to be carried out with the consent of the administration and through the Land Registry. Consent would be withheld by the District Governor if he felt that the tenant on the land could not maintain the means of supporting himself and his family. The 1921 ordinance lifted that restriction. The government hesitated to take full-scale measures to prevent the eviction of cultivators: PCO 1929 introduced compensation and a notice period prior to the eviction of tenants. The Shaw Commission felt that this ordinance may have actually stimulated land sales due to the provision of cash compensation.

An amending ordinance in 1931 provided for a Court or Judge, as well as the High Commissioner, to be satisfied that all conditions had been met before issuing an eviction order. This ordinance was conceived as a temporary measure, pending the findings of Hope-Simpson, the government scientific/technical advisor on agricultural improvement. (CO 733/185/3: Memo on the Land Question op. cit.) It was not until two years later that the issue of dispossession was targeted, and the amending ordinance of 1933 prevented the eviction of a 'Statutory Tenant' who had cultivated a particular holding for at least a year, without the offer of an alternative, and local, subsistence area. The ordinance also forbade unreasonable rent increases. Owner-occupiers and waged labourers fell outside the definition of 'Statutory Tenant' and landowners sidestepped the government restrictions by offering leases of less than a year.

Jewish settlers purchased the core of what would eventually constitute their national territory by 1939.[31] The transactions were tactically significant in that they effectively made up a Jewish heartland, and probably enabled Zionist seizure of the country during the war of 1947–48, but the percentage of Palestine disposed of by Arab to settler sales was negligible: by 1948, Jewish settlers had purchased 6 per cent of the total area of historic Palestine, including 20 per cent of its cultivable land. Land sales from Arabs to Jewish settlers also preceded the Mandate.[32] Some writers suggest that land sales from Arabs to Jewish settlers did not become politicized until well into the Mandate.[33] Rashid Khalidi shows that Zionism, settler land purchases and the displacement of the cultivator were controversial issues prior to WWI, both amongst the *fellaheen* and the professional/notable classes. The press of that period testifies to the periodic and violent confrontations between natives and colonists in the countryside (see Khalidi 1988).

Why, as a 'first essay in dealing with State Lands' (CO , SSC Amery to HC Plumer, 'Disposal of Jiftlik Lands', 26 Aug. 1926) did the government grant the cultivators of Beisan, who held perpetual leases under Ottoman law, the option of buying (and potentially disposing of) their land? Amery made a candid remark to Plumer about this. The Colonial Secretary reminded the High Commissioner in 1926 that the interests of long-term tenants on State Lands were all well and good, but that the government was committed to pursuing 'agricultural development', 'with all the means at its disposal'. (ibid.)

How the wretched Palestinian peasant might have trembled, if only he had spoken English, every time he heard the words 'agricultural development'.

The Shaw Commission's findings were favourable to the Arabs. But its neutral tone maintains a fictitious balance and symmetry between all sides in the conflict, and belies the vulnerability of the natives to a legal, linguistic, political, economic and military offensive. The Commission concluded that even though the plight of dispossessed tenant farmers[34] was not unique to Palestine, some exceptions featured in this particular colonial scenario: there was no viable alternative for evictees to relocate to, and farmers had 'a strong moral claim' to remain on the land since they had only nominally relinquished their title to a local strongman for the sake of protection in the past. The *fellah* was an illiterate mute who was not in a position to voice his response to this generous concession. However if he were, might he not have wondered why these foreigners were so interested in the nature of his rights in the land of his birth, and of his ancestors? In other words, the issue of whether a tenant farmer had either a legal or moral claim, or whether his claim was strong or weak, had political significance irrespective of the result. The process of evaluation itself is one which symbolizes and signifies a certain dynamic. The assessment, description and outline of the nature and extent of the cultivators' rights by the government, or even by an independent government appointed commission, effectively amounted to their swansong.

So, at the risk of repetition, and simply because it does not bear ignoring: the Shaw Commission was empathetic to the Arabs when it tackled the land 'problem'/'question'. However, this empathy is distinct from the fact that the posing of the 'question' and the expert knowledge hauled in to solve it, immediately evoke a relationship in which the natives are subjects of power. Even though commissions of inquiry are independent of government, although they gather evidence, hear opinions from all sides, comb through government policies and are dedicated to objective fact finding, nonetheless the exercise takes place within the same discursive framework of the politics of the colonial state.[35] The terms of the discussion have been pre-prescribed and the proceedings are carefully ritualized. They are enshrined in the presupposition that the white man is good at finding solutions, but we, so many years later, ought not be distracted from the notion that the 'question' might not have arisen without the white man. Arguably then, the symbolic role of commissions of inquiry is more important than their investigative one. They demonstrate to the native that the government has noticed that he existed, engaged with his pitiful self, listened to his peevish complaints attentively and taken notes, generously paid for experts to deploy their expertise in order to solve the problem that he posed in the first place, worried about his 'community's well-being. In other words, commissions of inquiry ingeniously boost the government's claim to legitimacy and righteousness.

Was there an innate problem with land in Palestine? Rather, and once again prompted by Derrida, is it possible to turn the question on its head and ask what is meant, what is at stake, when the land 'question' is posed? What was the 'problem' with land? Was it that Arabs sold land to Jews? Was it that the government, an experienced colonial power, who was aware of the apparently universal tendency of the peasant to excitedly dispose of his land for (to him) seductive amounts of cash, failed to protect the peasant from his own improvidence? Was it that the British administration had to 'overhaul' a 'medieval' system, whilst dealing with hindrances such as 'the ingrained customs and prejudices of the people' and the notorious *Musha'* system? (LRHG, box 1, file 1, Director of Surveys, 4 April 1929) Or was it rather that Britain's very presence and her motives in Palestine were appropriative and dangerous to the locals? Was the problem not caused by the overbearing measures of the

Mandate government, exemplified in the imposition of English linguistic constructs which transformed the signifiers of the culture of land tenure and cultivation, plus a flurry of legislation which catered to the colonial regime's commitment to the Balfour Declaration? Was this not the 'problem'?

Division, illegitimacy, and the un-settlement of the fellah

The fellah's relationship with land becomes illicit

Claims regarding the inferiority of the quality of the soil, the inadequacy and primitiveness of methods of cultivation were routine. British officials denunciated the mess they were delegated to clear. The Director of Surveys expressed the general frustration in 1921:

> After full consideration of possible methods in a largely unmarked and undivided country it is concluded that a sufficient survey must first be made of all property boundaries claimed, whether marked or unmarked, so that the position and area of each claim is determined with reference to the controlling network. (LRHG, box 1, file unnumbered, Annual Reports of the Director of Surveys 1920–39)[36]

This pique with the lack of marks was central to British anxiety around land. The urge to fix demarcation lines was irresistible. As early as 1920, when Britain's Mandate had yet to be confirmed by the League of Nations and Britain administered Palestine without a constitution, it became an offence to interfere with government marks circumscribing new boundaries. These new marks were considered important enough for the government that collective punishment or other types of deterrent punishment, were urged in case of interference with them. The Director of Surveys wrote with regard to the production of cadastral plans that had begun in 1920:

> The vital importance of permanent fixed marks for the network is thus apparent. Ordinance 161 May 1920, extended by Public Notice 166 July 1920, gives protection to Marks. The case of interference with marks have occurred during the year and fines ... have been inflicted. If exemplary punishment on individual cases or communities can be meted out in a few initial cases it is not anticipated that serious trouble from interference will arise in the future. (LRHG, box 1, file unnumbered, Annual Report of the Director of Surveys 1921, op.cit.)

Locals may have found all this talk of settlement on the contrary, quite unsettling. They did not run to claim the boundaries of their paltry little patch of land. When they stayed home they were branded 'defaulters' and punished. The Report on Cadastral Survey for 1922–23 explained:

Considerable but anticipated delays due to default and inadvertence of owners both in demarcation and attendance to point out boundaries, have occurred. The list of defaulters includes 96 case of non-attendance reported to the District Governor, of which 32 appear to have been charged and 2 convicted. (LRHG box 1, file unnumbered)

The settlement initiative was contentious. The *fellah* was too primitive and ignorant to accept that his system of landholding and cultivation were insecure, 'an unintelligible compost' based on 'principal evils'. Land settlement had been slowed down 'when conflicting claims are stubbornly maintained'. (CO 733/221/4, 'Land Reforms Progress' report by Dowson) In 1931, as part of the Commissioner of Lands' proposal for accelerating and 'simplifying' land settlement, natives were requested to provide the government with proof of their entitlement to land:

> Claims to a category of land other than ordinary *Miri* or *Metruka* would have to be supported by documents, or by full statements in case documents are alleged to be missing, as to why the land is claimed as *Wakf Sahih*, *Miri Mauqufa* or *Mulk*. (CO 733/208/5, Lands Department, O'Donnell Recommendations 1931)

This requirement that the native prove his entitlement to his native land to a visiting foreigner, according to conditions set by the latter, did not seem at all pathological to the Mandatory or indeed, to subsequent chroniclers of this Mandate. Successive land experts sojourning in Palestine displayed the same confidence. A few years later, Salmon, the Commissioner for Lands and Surveys thought it was the greed and the 'litigiousness of the population' that was holding up a perfectly sensible exercise. He wrote in 1935: 'Since the value of the land has gone up the number of claims submitted and the amount of litigation has increased enormously.' Salmon had detected a 'growing tendency to dispute every claim where there is a shadow of a doubt' for slowing down the 'important work' of land settlement. (LRHG box 1, file unnumbered: Salmon's Annual Report for 1935, Annual Reports of the Director of Surveys, Palestine and other Departmental Reports 1920–39)

Excessive science

The abstract language of science veiled the ferocity involved in the dividing (dismembering) of Palestine. Science modified the way land was perceived. Triangulation interpreted the landscape as a series of angles connected by reference points. Science, like law, provided a refuge from any potential self-doubt in the colonialist. It presented a powerful psychological tool which bolstered the colonialist's self-confidence and expunged his anxieties. Equally, science takes us into the realm of magic and mysterious powers. Only the colonialist had access to the astral code of land measurement and survey. Resort to science turned the colonialist into destiny's helper, a tool in the hands of a grand design. The native was either completely excluded from the proscribed procedures of the new science, or his participation was carefully co-opted for the sake of training. The chroniclers of this movement were the scientists and technicians themselves. The elaborate complexity of their narratives was designed for the British expert ear. Science was as much a weapon of warfare as law, and just as bewitching. The cryptic, soothing beauty of the Annual Report of the Director of Surveys for 1921 is a good start:

> The main object was defined to be the production of large scale maps which would show the position, shape and area of all landowners' property with sufficient accuracy for Kushan. A military triangulation of doubtful use had been made in the war, and the decision had been made to start work in the south.

Headquarter Organisation:

A.   Administrative staff and clerical stores sections ...
M.   A computation office under a Cambridge Mathematician. This forms an entirely distinct and incontrovertible check upon every section of the work of the Survey, computes all sheet corners point coordinates and areas, is equipped with modern calculating machines, checks plotting, and trains computers.
D.   Under a British Chief Draughtsman this includes a plotting section and a Drawing Office for final tracings, and is equipped with a Coradi Coordinatograph. The section trains draughtsmen.
I.   A class of apprentices under a British Chief and an Egyptian Instructor, is trained in the elements of Survey. Equal numbers of Jews, Christians and Muslims are as far as possible selected.

The Cadastral Survey:

A reconnaissance Party started work in April with Camels only and completed reconnaissance of all the points of the old Military Triangulation in the Gaza and Beersheba Districts before May ...

Horses being available in June, reconnaissance of the coastal chain and a short extension to Beersheba was pushed forward, the former was carried as far North as Jenin. ...

A Beaconing Party started work in May and was occupied until middle of July in refixing old points of the Military Triangulation (LRHG, box 1, file unnumbered, Annual Report of Director of Surveys 1921).

A couple of years later, Dowson reported his disappointment with the way the survey of Palestine had been undertaken thus far: it was inefficient, inexact and uneconomic. The government needed to rethink its strategy. There were:

important measures that are required to enable the cadastral survey, settlement and assessment of Palestine to be attacked rapidly and effectively as a whole area:

(a)   The definite determination of the lengths of the northern and southern base lines, of their azimuths and of the geographical positions of their terminals ...

(b)   The laying down of a standard map sheet system of Palestine on the basis of the above primary positions and those of the second order (Principal) national triangulation deduced therefrom ...

(c)   Provision for economical reproduction and safe and orderly storage of all national map series. ... The safe and orderly storage of the maps – especially the original cadastral maps – is a matter of first class importance ...

(d)   ...

(e)   The extension of the survey framework of reference points throughout Palestine so that work can be taken up in any village at any moment. The advisability has already been urged of extending the framework of reference points so that parcels of land dealt with in advance of cadastral survey can be located ... the reference points primarily referred to are those of the second, third and fourth order triangulation, which I myself would like to see fortified by systematic traverse. It is no part of my intention here to discuss technical methods which cannot be pronounced ex cathedra as they depend on local conditions, the idiosyncrasies of local staff and the degree of accuracy needed ... If traverse work – observation, calculation and plotting alike – is reduced to routine its speed can be greatly increased and its cost lowered, while it has the outstanding advantage of being independently controllable, and if reasonable protection for marks is secured, is of permanent value. (LRHG, Dowson to Clayton op.cit.)

Distant, abstract and cold, the report extends to 53 repetitive pages. It reveals the extensive planning entailed in controlling land. It does not as readily reveal however, the failings of the method, or its imperfections.[37]

Division

In his annual report for 1921, the Director of Surveys suggested an administrative way for the government to decide and declare property boundaries:

As each block or sheet of this preliminary map is prepared a tracing is made for decision of all disputed claims and proposed divisions by the Land Court. The latter must decide these on the spot, if possible, while the surveying party is still in the immediate neighbourhood, so that one of the surveyors can correct the field sheets from the fixed points ...

An apparently possible simplification is that a Senior Survey Official should have the legal power of decision on the spot, subject to appeal, and apart from pure questions of ownership. The power would apply to all minor cases of overlapping claims, and to divisions of property among heirs, where agreement on the spot might be easy. Probably 2/3 of the work of the courts would thus be obviated, with much advantage to speed and economy. (LRHG, box 1, file unnumbered, Annual Report of the Director of Surveys 1921, op.cit.)

Dowson periodically reminded the government of its prerogative to permanently partition land, an exercise based on 'knowledge, consideration and judgement'. The division of 'communally held' land, as in the *Musha'* system, would be conducted via the land settlement/settlement of title initiative (see CO 733/109, Dowson, 'Preliminary Study of Land Tenure'). In other words, 'land settlement/settlement of title' meant land division.

It took a few years for the government to take Dowson's advice and organize a fully fledged initiative to settle title. Eventually, Abrahamson was appointed to the Office of Commissioner of Lands in November 1927 and the Land Settlement Ordinance (LSO) befell the rural population in 1928. A Settlement Survey commenced shortly thereafter. The LSO identified four operative stages to the survey. (CO 733/208/5, Lands Department, O'Donnell Recommendations 1931).

1. Villages would be divided into registration blocks and plans prepared on the basis of the new blocks. Individuals claim parcels.
2. Assistant Settlement Officers would conduct a Preliminary Investigation of claims and counter-claims.
3. The Final Investigation of claims takes place when the memoranda of claims prepared by a Settlement Officer are checked in the Settlement Office. Settlement Officers then proceed to the villages and decide which claims to admit.
4. Registration of title.

The Preliminary Investigation of claims and counter-claims carried out by the Assistant Settlement Officers consisted of a request for documents, the questioning of witnesses, and the preparation of a schedule of claims which was then posted in each village. The sleepy Palestinian backwater came face to face with English bureaucracy. Perhaps anticipating local reticence, Settlement Officers were allocated a bribe allowance of coffee and cigarettes to distribute amongst the locals, (Bunton 'Demarcating the British Colonial State' 139, fn62: 'A great deal of consideration was given throughout to the necesity of securing the cooperation of the village cultivators.') Villagers were to make a claim and supply supporting evidence of their right to a given piece of land. This hubbub continued in the countryside for about a decade. The intentions behind the settlement exercise and the extent to which it was disruptive to local rural order as well as to customary dealings with land are written all over the official documents. For instance, the 1927 draft Land Settlement Ordinance caused some worry – Clause 33, which compelled the owners of small fragments of land to transfer their share to a neighbour, was described as 'a high-handed provision with the sole object of simplifying registration.' (CO 733/142/11, Minute) Clause 56 (b) proposed to enable the Settlement Officer to partition undivided land on the application of the 2/3 of the registered holders. Secretary of State for the Colonies Ormsby-Gore had misgivings about what appeared to be the intention of the government to substitute individual holdings for land held in undivided ownership by compulsion. (ibid.) Eventually Settlement Officers, with the guidance of the High Commissioner, were given the power to partition any piece of land held in undivided ownership 'if such partition is deemed to be in the public interest.' (Goadby and Doukhan 1935: 280) The Ottoman law relating to partition was conveniently declared inapplicable.

Which 'public' are they talking about?

The Arabs expressed fear before the Shaw Commission proceedings (CO):[38] they were convinced that the settlement initiative would have them relegated to the inhospitable hills, whilst new immigrants enjoyed the fertile valleys and coastal plains. Dowson was relentless. In 1930, he reiterated his belief that *Musha'* was 'a common expedient of primitive communities', and remained the cause of much confusion and uncertainty. Best then, that it be terminated as part of an accelerated, advanced, 'land settlement' scheme. (CO 733/221/4, 'Land Reforms Progress' op. cit.)

Although it relied on technical and systematic methods, the partitioning of land itself was not strictly accurate. Clause 33 of the draft LSO 1927, which recommended the absorption of small shares of land into larger ones, was justified by dismissing both very large fractions of land as well as very small ones, as having no 'real' or 'substantial' value. Rights in land remained 'baffling' as long as they were not recorded in 'a definite figure of integral metres'. As for the very small fragments of land, why they were not even worthy of registration, and should instead be transferred to 'a neighbouring owner'. (CO 733/142/11, On Draft LSO, Explanatory Note) It is difficult to imagine a more random, capricious and irresponsible, basis for partition. Clause 22 (1) proposed that the Settlement Officer may, when demarcating boundaries, quite simply lay out a fresh boundary in place of the original: 'where the boundary between separate parcels of land is a curved or irregular line.' (ibid.) Clause 41 stated that no claim could be brought against the government, either with regard to title or with regard to boundaries, based on the records of the old Land Registry. The recommendations of the Commissioner of Lands in 1931 for making the settlement of title process more workable, continued along the same lines and were equally callous:

An additional improvement would be the provision of a clause for the elimination of shares of smaller value than a stated minimum to be prescribed by order, village by village. Or if a large number of heirs or co-owners held many shares of small value in a number of parcels, for the voluntary regrouping of owners in the different parcels or for their compulsory regrouping by the Settlement Officer in case of a disagreement, or for the elimination of shares of small value. (CO 733/208/5: Lands Department, op.cit.)

By the end of the Mandate, although only 20 per cent of the entire area of Palestine had been settled, a high proportion of this related to the cultivable land and rich citrus plantations coveted by Jewish settlements. The hills of the interior were relatively neglected (see W.P.N. Tyler 2001: 41, 173). How much of an objective and purely impartial exercise was the demarcation of Public Domain? How long before 'discovered' 'Public Domain' became inaccessible to the *real*, original, public?

Stranger than fiction

Some Palestinians today were alive during the British Mandate, and some of them are old enough to have memories of those Mandate days. Most of them are scattered around the Arab world in a ring of refugee camps. They live on dirt floors, beneath leaking roofs, by open sewage. They sit on lumpy sofas, in very old clothes, and bewail the blow fate has dealt them. They are classic victims. They have not overcome their victimhood. However, they recall days when they were not sufferers. They do not recall the evils of their system of agriculture, or their shambolic system of land-holding. Nor do they remember being hungry, wanting, or wretched. Being hungry, wanting and wretched are things they are now. They do not recall the British Mandate improving their lives, or bringing them progress or closer to civilization. On the contrary, it ruined them, and forced them into idle exile. They recall instead days of plenitude and abundance, days lived amongst loved ones and friendly neighbours, days of purposeful work, days when their lives were complete, days when their existence was coherent. They recall spring flowers, birds and insects. Palestine is the lost paradise and they are frozen in time. They collected honey. Besides farming, they kept goats and cows and sheep and made ghee, yogurt and cheese. Palestine was a place of good pasture. Food (its cultivation, preparation, consumption, food as celebration) was one of the recurring themes evocatively brought up by these teary-eyed, regretful old people. They recited poems and sang songs about it:

How beautiful is the farmer's life, void of unpleasant thoughts ...
At night we meet in the square for entertainment, for songs and for stories ...
The stories of Aantar and Salim al Mighwar ...
And the stories of Banu Hillel or the best of stories ...

In the winter we sit around the fire, gather on the mattresses and wait for
the dawn prayers ...
We gathered to pray, each one calling out to God: 'Oh Lord, send me rain
for my fields ... '
We planted courgettes, wheat and cucumber, yeast, corn and sesame ...

How great is the yoghurt of my goats ...
My harvest fills barrels.
Oh mother I wish I could go back to my hometown,
To see what has become of Dammoun ...
To see the hills on my left and the sea on my right ...
I would call out for our home, and it would call out for me ...
You know I haven't left you willingly,
I ask for your forgiveness.
Even if I, my friends and all my sons become rich in exile,
Nothing is worth the figs from your fig trees.
Oh watermelon of Dammoun, how red you used to be!
Like blood running through my veins!
Even if I prosper in exile,
My heart remains in Dammoun.
My faith is in God Almighty.
Oh people of Dammoun, take care of me and bury me under its amber
trees.

Oh God I remember the hot bread coming from the oven,
Fried birds in olive oil,
A *muhammar* dish with chicken,
And a big meal of rice and meat spread out on a large plate.[39]

How might the British initiative to 'settle' title, to draw maps based on new
boundaries, to overhaul Ottoman land law, to remove the evil *Musha'* system
from agricultural practice, have been experienced by the Palestinian *fellah*?
The reports of land experts, commissioners, surveyors and other officials
charged with 'improving' the countryside, their pronouncements on the *fellah* and
his wretchedness might as well be read as narrative fiction.[40] They become capti-
vating if read as such, for the rich and colourful insights into the personalities and
biases and pathologies of their authors.

There is an alternative way of presenting the story of land law and property
rights in Palestine, which is authentic and relies entirely on the colonial archive.
This alternative rejects the rationale of the Mandatory and disputes its claims to
development and progress. Instead, it questions its motives and focuses on its
absurdity. The following piece of creative non-fiction synthesizes the developments
I have enumerated in this chapter. It is a first person narration by an unidentified
land expert, and it is based on the reports and private papers of various government
advisors, Land Commissioners and Surveyors during the Mandate period.

To cure the country of its agricultural atrophy, and give the starveling peasant an incentive to improve his land, we must first clear away a thick layer of debris they call Custom. The apathy and maladministration of the Turk has brought Palestine to the brink of economic ruin. Begin with an authoritative investigation of Title based on full cadastral survey, including comprehensive data of agricultural land.

When The Turks retreated they destroyed or removed all court and Land Registry Records. An extensive attack on the entire system of land tenure is inevitable if we are to remedy this miserable state of affairs.

This would involve, in the very initial stages, the calculation of the azimuths of the northern and southern base lines (I believe the Arabs call this *Al Sumut*) and the assessment of the geographical position of their terminals. A Cambridge Mathematician will check on the work of the Survey. A Drawing Office, run by a British Chief Draughtsman, will be responsible for final tracings and for the production of large-scale maps which clearly determine the position, shape and area of all landowners' property. Only then may we begin to investigate and take stock of real rights throughout the country, village by village and in situ. I would recommend that we train a body of surveyors and draughtsmen from native elements for this purpose, who are fully acquainted with facts on the ground.

Unfortunately, we have found the military Triangulation made during the war unreliable. I will arrange for a reconnaissance party to investigate all the points of the old Triangulation. Since horses are unlikely to be available, the party should be ready to set to work with camels. We will prioritize the coastal plain, and should complete reconnaissance within 6 months.

Next, we will review village boundaries in each District. These should be demarcated since the current boundaries are completely inaccurate: enclaves of land may be geographically held within one village yet administered by another. The aim is to sub-divide them, and create self-contained village units which will operate as registration blocks. Property descriptions will be noted on paper and permanent marks fixed on the ground.

Thus, the many quarrels between various clans, so common in this primitive administrative environment, may be averted.

His Excellency might consider protecting these Marks, with an Ordinance which metes out exemplary punishment in case of interference with them – primarily to individuals but, where information as to guilt is not forthcoming, to communities – Collective punishment has been used with satisfactory results in Cyprus.

Progress has been slow with regard to Parcellation: completed transfer of allotments to individuals in Samakh, Kafr Misr, Kaukab, Fatur and Bira. However, as anticipated, considerable delays were caused by owners who refused to attend or point out boundaries. The list of defaulters runs to dozens of cases for non-attendance, some of whom have been charged.

To expedite the process, I suggest that Cadastral partitioning of communally owned land should be undertaken as part of the work of the Demarcation Commission, to put an end, once and for all, to that curse of the Palestinian agricultural system, the *Musha'*.

His Excellency will appreciate that it is in the Public Interest to discover and define Public Domain as a matter of urgency, so that the Administration may proceed with its resumption. Palestine is hardly a pot of gold, and vesting as much legal estate in the Government as possible will maximise its value to us.

Although the correct state of land ownership is likely to remain unclear, several Ottoman categories lend themselves to redefinition as State Lands. Land which escheats to the Administration in this way may then also be made available to immigrants on long leases. Since the native system of access to land relies more often on tribal lore rather than on registration or deeds, I suggest we enact legislation making it an offence to cultivate these areas without permission.

I have identified several Ottoman categories which lend themselves to redefinition as State Lands. These are: 'Mahlul', roughly meaning unproductive; 'Matrouka', which refers to land left for the use of the public in a particular area; and 'Mawat'.

This last is waste land, described in the literature as land which is so far from the nearest inhabited spot that a loud human voice cannot be heard calling there.

Notes

1 Le Ray Hugh Granville Papers (LRHG), box 1, 'Annual Reports of the Director of Surveys 1920–39'.
2 Although things are beginning to shift: recently Martin Bunton (historian), and Alexandre Kedar (legal geographer) have started to relate developments of land law in Mandate Palestine to their political context. Bunton's writings introduce Palestine into the debate about the 'invention' of tradition under colonial rule in general, whilst Kedar writes about spatial relations in Palestine in relation to wider discourses of power. Legal geography is a new field of studies that identifies the relationship between law and geography. Within this field, a critical stream examines how legal structures order and legitimize spatial hierarchies, and how law produces, constructs, legitimates and organizes social space. See Forman and Kedar (2003: 493) and Kedar (2002: 406–7).
3 For an overview of the literature on law and colonialism, see Comaroff (2001: 305).
4 The Tswana speaking people in nineteenth-century South Africa referred to law as the English mode of warfare. (ibid.: 306)
5 Peasant/farmer.
6 See Tomlins (2003) for an account of a recent body of work investigating the relationship between law and violence.
7 Tomlins (ibid.: 454), writing about the discourse of English colonizing in America, specifies law as: 'a technology of description and definition instrumental to the

process of realizing colonization as a practice', which contained 'those texts and
ideologies that fuelled and realised the coloniser's violent ideology of differentiation
and exclusion from the outset'.

8 I largely rely in this section, on Chapters 1 and 10 of Edney (1997). Edney (33)
places his study alongside the work of the South Asianists who question the reliability
of the official /colonial archive as resource.

9 Mark Neocleous (2003: 409 at 418) gives a succinct illustration of this: even though
it is supposed that maps are simply representations of pre-existing borders and
boundary lines, they are not, and they often create this so called reality.

10 See Inden (1992:36): 'Integral to the ideal of "imperial formation" is a notion of
"imperial knowledge".' Inden argues that this knowledge acquires hegemonic force
for it is not imposed by force on a passive population but is accepted and perpetuated.

11 Triangulation or 'trigonometrical survey' involves the drawing of a series of straight
lines connecting the tops of hills/mountains/tall buildings. These are selected so that
lines form either linked or interlocking triangles across the landscape. The surveyor
then measures the interior angles of the triangles and their size by means of
trigonometry. The result is that each point is defined in relation to another by
means of a mathematical. See Edney (op. cit.: 19). A Topographic map is one that
depicts the characteristics of land in terms of elevation, slope and orientation.

12 The Hague Convention 1907, prohibited substantial interference with the laws of
occupied territory.

13 For nineteenth-century land tenure in Greater Syria, which comprised Palestine, see
Sluglett and Farouk-Sluglett (1984).

14 Palestine (Amendment) Order in Council 1933, Article 16 A (in Goadby and Doukhan
1935: 40). *The Land Law of Palestine*, (Palestine 1935), 40.

15 Even though the claim was repeatedly made that the registry was closed in 1918 as a
result of the Turkish army fleeing with all the registers, '[o]ne must dismiss outright
any implication that these very records were not available to, and did not prove to
be extremely important to succeeding British Administrations.' (Bunton 1997: 140–
41) Bunton (fn. 8) says that in 1948, some 800 Turkish registers were photographed
with the permission of the High Commissioner, in order that they may be returned
to England. The missing link is possibly provided by Norman Bentwich, Attorney
General. Bentwich wrote in his private papers that when the Turks left, they carried
with them everything: court records, judges and records of the Land Registers.
However, he also states that 'the Registers were recovered after the fall of Damascus and have been brought back to the Districts to which they belong; but the pro-
hibition has been maintained to the present time for *various reasons*' (my emphasis).
(Bentwich papers: 'The legal administration of Palestine under the British military
occupation')

16 *Fellaheen*: plural for *fellah*.

17 Bunton (2000) explains that this approach, although a complete departure from
Ottoman practice, is similar to colonial protectionism elsewhere, such as in the
Punjab and in Egypt.

18 This included official and unofficial members. The unofficial members were unelected and
consisted of four Muslims, three Christians and three Jews. They were prominent
members of society: mayors, landowners and the Sheikh of a powerful tribe from
Beersheba.

19 S.3 LLAO 1933: 'All rights in or in relation to any public lands shall vest in and
may be exercised by the High Commissioner for the time being in trust for the
Government of Palestine'.

20 For instance, boundaries may have been named after one's neighbour, or by the
number of seeds it took to sow it. (Tyler op. cit.: 29)

21 Martin Bunton is the first historian to point out the importance of Dowson's influence on the British Mandatory administration, and on the formulation of land policy in Palestine (see Bunton 1999).

22 Muhammad Ali was influenced by Europe and carried out extensive legal, administrative and cultural reforms based on Napoleonic methods and European technology. See Mitchell (1991) and Maghraoui (2006).

23 For instance: Dowson thought that the long-term use of Public land led to a creation of *Mulk* title, whereas in reality, it could only ever lead to a prescriptive *Miri* claim. Dowson also had a staggeringly flawed understanding of local culture: whilst determining which language should be employed on maps and in records, Dowson wrote in his 'Notes on Land Tax, Cadastral Survey and Land Settlement in Palestine' (LRHG, box 1, file, 2: Dowson to Clayton, 'Notes on Land Tax, Cadastral Survey, and Land Settlement in Palestine', 7 Dec. 1923) that '[t]he language at present used is English as this at least avoids preference for either the language of Jew or Palestinian Moslem'. It is a mystery why he chose to separate the population in this way: had he momentarily forgotten that he was speaking about the land that had brought him Christianity, or did he think Palestinian Christians spoke Aramaic?

24 This is perhaps self-evident, but see anyway CO (10 Dec.) in which the government promises *Mudawara* lands around the Dead Sea to the Zionist Organisation, after it had ascertained the areas it required for its own mineral exploitation.

25 NB The first sentence of this quotation does not make sense, and it is unclear what Dowson is referring to when he assumes the existence of 'racial rivalry'.

26 Public Lands, State Lands, and State Domain were used interchangeably.

27 For instance, HC Samuel expressed reluctance to depart from government policy that State land should not be sold. (CO , HC to SSC, 23 July 1921)

28 This refers to the close settlement of Jews on the land per Article 6 of the Mandate and should not be confused with the effort to settle title begun in 1928.

29 1 *Dunam* = 1000 metres sq. (approx.).

30 Figures from CO 733/185/2 (Letter from the Director of Surveys to the Commissioner of Lands, 10 April 1930).

31 K.W. Stein (1985) examines how this happened at length – although it is not clear what the point of his study is: there is no controversy around the issue of whether Arabs sold land to Jews or not, as we know that this was a fact. However, it is a question of emphasis and proportion. Is Stein implying that the Palestine Arabs deserved what happened to them in 1948 or that the mass expulsion in 1948 was a natural extension of those land sales? See Khalidi's letter in Khalidi and K.W. Stein (1988).

32 Sales made by the absentee Sursok family took place over some six decades, beginning in 1881. See Stein's letter to Khalidi. (ibid.)

33 For instance K.W. Stein (1985: 61) writes that in the 1920s, the Land Question was unobtrusive. See also Bunton (2000). Bunton contrasts the decision of the Land Court in the case of the villages of Sajad and Qazaza with the government's approach to the Beisan lands, in order to demonstrate the emerging political sensitivity of allowing peasants disposable rights in land: In Sajad and Qazaza, the Settlement Officer had declared that the villagers had equitable rights according to Article 10 (3) LSO, and that, following the Beisan decision, their rights were hereditary and assignable. The Attorney General appealed the Settlement Officer's decision and the Land Court declared that the cultivators of Sajad and Qazaza had neither legal nor equitable claims against the government. Bunton interprets this as government reluctance to individualize tenure because of the rising fear of tenant dispossession, which was reaching an acute stage.

34 The Shaw Commission remained in the dark over the number of dispossessed farmers which resulted from land sales, because evidence offered at the proceedings

conflicted widely. For instance, with regard to the Jezreel Valley sales made by the Sursok family, Jewish witnesses estimated 800 displaced tenants, whilst Arabs estimated 8,000 displaced tenants.

35 See Adam Ashforth (1990) for what he calls 'the question of questions'. Commissions of inquiry are 'schemes of legitimation' (8).

36 The Survey Ordinance 1920 provided for the demarcation of boundaries in preparation for a full-scale Cadastre.

37 For instance, we know that for the sake of accuracy, it was a strict hierarchical requirement that Survey must be preceded by Triangulation. Things were a little more haphazard in reality, where sequential requirements and the precision they promised gave in to other more pressing exigencies. When he came to visit in the winter of 1923, Dowson insisted that survey, settlement and 'assessment' of Palestine should be 'attacked' based on a system of Triangulation. Dowson also despaired over the prosecution of cadastral survey prior to the investigation of real rights (i.e. settlement), which he called 'a most considerable misdirection of effort, misapplication of funds and misuse of them'. Dowson compromised. He advised:

> there is no choice now but to proceed with sporadic registration in advance subject to effecting without delay such amendments as are practicable. Of these the most obvious, as well as the most urgent, is to define the areas which registered transactions purport to concern, so that they can be located by the Government itself with certainty and in due course fall without serious error into their places in the cadastral map of the village in which they occur. At present, isolated and uncontrolled plans are made of such areas by surveyors who ... work without technical control or direction.

For Dowson, the cadastral survey was implicated in the investigation of rights and the settlement of title. The work of the Survey and that of the Land Registry complemented each other. Ideally, Land Book and Cadastre should operate simultaneously. However entry in the Land Book was conducted in the final stages of the operation. Although not ideal, it was an acceptable compromise.

38 These were held in camera.

39 Poem by Seoud Assaadi, a poet from Be'ni village in Accre, recited by Hussain Lubbani, originally from Dammoun village, currently living in Tripoli, Lebanon.

40 What is the difference between writing history and writing fiction? Both are 'premised on the recording, ordering, observing powers of the central authorizing subject, or ego ... The capacity to represent, portray, characterize, and depict is not easily available to just any member of just any society'. (Said 1994: 79–80)

Chapter 3

'Between the bazaar and the bungalow':[1]

A rebellion without rebels

Prelude

What is history? Who writes it? Who reads it? What are its assumptions? Who invented its rules? Can they be challenged? Can we read between the lines of historical studies? What is the difference between a historical study and historical fiction? What would happen to the discipline of history if historical studies were received as though they were works of art: as the emotive, evocative, subjective creations of their author?

Sometimes, often or too often, depending on what one likes to read, historical studies exclude the 'subaltern'. Gramsci defines the subaltern as part of a non-élite social group, an aspirant who could eventually move beyond a pure defence of his economic position in a capitalist society to participate in social and political leadership. Even though he was not originally part of the dominant class, there is potential for him to manifest in the domain of political representation (see Hoare and Smith 1991: 52–55). Spivak takes the concept further, and speaks about the subaltern in a colonial situation: 'You have the foreign élite and the indigenous élite. Below that you will have the vectors of upward, downward, sideward, backward mobility. But then there is a space which is for all intents and purposes outside those lines'. (Spivak 1996: 289) The question of silence, of the viability of any project of recovery of the non-élite colonized subject's history, is central to debates within and about the Subaltern Studies Group. The fate of the subaltern has been cleanly hijacked by Spivak's rhetorical question in her powerful essay 'Can the Subaltern Speak?' (1988). For Spivak, the state of subalternity is conclusive, undisturbed even by the attempts to rise above subaltern status and move into political ground, which constitute insurgency. She concludes that the subaltern cannot 'speak' – not because he or she is incapable of utterance, but rather because speech is a reciprocal interaction which involves talking and being heard, talking and being legitimated by the listener. According to Spivak, the most we can hope to achieve through our rereading of the historical archive and of colonial texts is the revelation of the West's misrepresentation of the subaltern, so that no matter how radical, projects of historical recuperation of subaltern consciousness are doomed to failure. Bhabha also asserts that the colonized subject is irretrievable, though glimpses of him may be perceived in the gaps, silences, ambivalences and chinks of colonial history.

The danger in a pre-emptive line of attack on élitist histories is that we, whose intentions are pure, who champion the subaltern, who want to hear his story and engage with his experience, instead end up colluding in gagging him. But there is a positive side to keeping an uncompromising stance regarding the subaltern's eternal silence: if he cannot speak, if he remains elusive, then neither can he be normalized, nor his experiences or recuperated narratives straitjacketed to comply with the crushing rules, debasing limitations and establishment buttressing values of Western historical studies. So the Palestinian rebel which emerges out of Mandate histories, the mysterious mutineer whose movements are subterranean, laws irregular, fighting methods spontaneous and identity amorphous, represented more than a material challenge to colonial power. His endlessly mutable ways signalled a severance between knowledge of the native population, and power over them. His emergence from the wings to the centre stage of the colonial theatre, with an Arabic script all his own, disturbed the official description and characterization of the native.

But the rebel also represents a conceptual challenge to the contemporary historian. Shall he be condemned to eternal darkness? To hear/tell the story of the Palestinian rebel, we have to altogether sidestep the study of British colonialism according to the institutional structures it devised for itself (Guha 1987: xx) (even if these structures are ostensibly native ones). Although I hesitate before a project of positivist retelling, hesitate to pin down and trap the subaltern or compete for knowledge in the quest for power, neither can I with a clear conscience, declare the Palestinian rebel subaltern completely irrecoverable. For Spivak's subaltern is a nineteenth-century Bengali queen who committed ritual suicide on her husband's funeral pyre, leaving nothing behind. Spivak's subaltern differs from mine in that hers only appears when conjured by the texts of the foreign élite. (Spivak 1988: 213–17)

Did the Palestinian subaltern rebel speak during the Mandate, and if so, why is he so absent from Mandate histories, so quiet? Secondly, if he spoke, then what did he say, and how did he say it? Several old men and women, who had either participated directly in the 1936–39 rebellion in Palestine or had relatives who did, spoke to me, and I listened.[2] I did not listen critically, I had no specific questions, or an empirical theoretical framework. I did not listen out for reliable or verifiable information which could be used to counteract Western histories of Mandate Palestine. Nor was I particularly attached to the idea of a clear, recuperated past. I was perhaps a little too late for that. Some of those I did find were either infirm or a little forgetful (sometimes confusing the events of the 1936–39 rebellion with the 1947–48 war). Nonetheless, my desire to hear them was matched by their desire to speak. Existing historical accounts had jarred against both my cold intellect and my visceral intuition. And it frankly does not take too much of either to realise that there was another story dying, literally dying, to be told.

When the rebels or sons and daughters of rebels spoke, the cathartic effect was considerable and there were tears, laughter, tirades against oppression, the wisdom of the old. Some were fasting, some were ill and in visible pain, some interrupted the day's work, everyone skipped prayer times, in order to speak. They happily spoke for hours. One man, (Lubbani, in Tripoli, who recited poem after poem) suffering clearly from severe back pain, positioned a stool to face me as I sat on the sofa and spoke for seven hours, pausing only to take his prescription pain killers. In that chronological order, the British ('the English'), the 'Jews' (Jewish migrants in Palestine) and now Lebanon, had not been kind to them. They cursed everybody but mostly, it has to be said, 'the English'. Free of the need to establish knowledge, truth or facts, I had the luxury to simply follow and let the lyrical, dreamlike rhythm of their stories wash over me instead.[3] The subaltern speaks in subaltern language. To listen, to intercept his dreams, we must accept and become accustomed to that language. In this vein, it is also clear that the Palestinian subaltern rebel equally spoke during the rebellion, and spoke loudly and threateningly enough to exasperate the British administration with his rebel propaganda for instance. The decrees which were posted on buildings and mosques made the Mandatory exquisitely uneasy (see, for instance, CO 733/372/4, 'Rebel Propaganda', discussed in more detail below). Even though the Palestinian subaltern rebel was not granted an audience to speak, and even though those instances when he did constituted an outrage in the culture of the dependency with its clearly defined avenues of expression and amounted to an ideological trespass, nonetheless the Mandatory was forced to listen. Here is the rebel: he does not know the alphabet, but somehow he is talking. Not only is he talking, he is kicking up a huge fuss. The Mandatory heard the subaltern rebel and reacted with some bemusement, some dismay and considerable worry. The rebel spoke without being spoken to, daring to disobey the configuration of Palestinian society according to meticulously prepared colonial grids (see Cooper 1994: 1526).

In a chapter entitled 'Of Mimicry and Man', Bhabha describes the result brought about by colonial ambivalence towards local leadership. This local leadership, whose power is circumscribed by the foreign visitor, is forced into a theatrical role play, where the parody of self-governance is splayed out across a treacherous screen. The screen is treacherous because the images projected on it are a little bit magical in the sense of trickery and conjuring – 'trompe l'oeil, irony, mimicry and repetition'. So far so good. However this model becomes really interesting, according to Bhabha, once it collapses under its own weight, so that the full potential of mimicry is revealed in its 'slippage', 'excess' and 'difference'. Here, it is the rebels who represent the ambivalent model's slippage and excess. It is they who highlight both the effort to civilize (psychologically colonize) natives as well as its spectacular futility. There was no such window of opportunity with the rebels, who serve as a powerful marker of the sensationally abortive efforts to normalize the native. The effrontery of their attempts to create alternative legal and other state structures, their literal appropriation of the symbols of state control, all blur the lines between 'mimicry' and 'mockery'. (Bhabha 2004) We can imagine the sense of alarm and confusion that the following must have instilled in the Mandatory authorities at the height of the rebellion, on 30 November 1938:

> In Galilee the rebels concentrated towards the end of the month, on widespread destruction of roads, particularly these which had been opened up during the summer. There had been a number of armed gangs active in the Acre-Safad area at this time, and 16th Infantry Brigade, in the course of several actions, succeeded in capturing a Headquarters group, complete with banner and documents, and a Court of Justice, with wig, warders and witnesses. (CO 733/379/3)

Whereas the élite were granted sufficient pardon as to ape the colonizer and don wigs and gowns, the same gesture, when carried out by the rebels, becomes a menacing, pointed travesty and parody. The rebels, according to Bhabha's model, emerge as a reminder of the 'excess' and 'slippage' which is bound to occur wherever mimicry has been successful.

A quick chronology

Let us look now at the series of inauspicious events which gave rise to all this mimicry, excess, and slippage.

Background

Sir John Hope-Simpson, a senior civil servant appointed to expand on the Shaw Commission's inquiries and assess the agricultural and industrial absorptive capacity of Palestine, concluded in his October 1930 report that Jewish immigration was unsustainable in Palestine and that it was causing unemployment. His findings were later backed by Lewis French, the British Director of Development for Palestine, who stated in his Reports on Agricultural Development and Land Settlement of December 1931 and April 1932 that Palestine's natural resources could not withstand a further Zionist influx. SSC Passfield's White Paper (Cmnd. 3692), published at the same time, reflected the same findings. Passfield upheld Hope-Simpson's report and emphasized the dual obligation of the Mandate, negating the precedence of the Jewish National Home over the Mandatory's other obligations. The White Paper linked Jewish immigration directly to the number of unemployed in Palestine, ignoring previous guidelines regarding the country's capacity for absorbing new immigrants. Passfield proposed a Legislative Council based on Churchill's White Paper of 1922 (Cmnd. 1700), which provided for ten official and twelve unofficial members, with the real power resting with the High Commissioner. Most significantly, the White Paper provided that State Lands were to be reserved for landless Arabs, in an initiative defined as a public purpose, thereby giving it priority over Jewish settlement on those lands, which had been assured with Article 6 of the Mandate. The White Paper called for a cessation or at least reduction of Jewish immigration and was welcomed by the Palestinian population.

Almost immediately, for political reasons, for reasons outside our scope, the government recanted and Prime Minister MacDonald delivered what became known amongst Arabs as his Black Letter. (Hansard, vol. 248, cols. 755–57)[4] In it, he denounced the policy outlined in the White Paper as incompatible with the Mandate and reiterated that Britain's commitment to the Jewish National Home was foremost.

Land acquisitions, immigration

A sombre mood crept over Palestine. Continuing Jewish land acquisitions and increased immigration contributed to a feeling of helplessness. By the 1930s eviction proceedings and disputes between Zionist settlers and peasants were being regularly reported in the press (ibid., cols. 155–56), and Arab sales to Jews with the help of brokers and intermediaries increased: in 1932, 18,895 *dunams* of land, in 1933, 36,991 *dunams* and in 1934, 62,114 *dunams* were sold to Jewish immigrants. (Lachman 1982: 53)

By 1936 Jewish immigration also increased by an unprecedented 250 per cent. There were now some 400,000 Jewish immigrants in Palestine, accounting for 31 per cent of the population. (ibid.: 67) The new arrivals fiercely coveted cultivable land in competition with Palestinian peasants. In 1930, British reports had calculated that a family needed 130 *dunams* of average land to support themselves. Yet by 1935, a Jewish Agency and Jewish National Fund report estimated that in the hill districts, each family was making do with 45–46 *dunams*. (K.W. Stein 1991: 155)[5]

The land settlement initiative, vaunted as a means of empowering the countryside, concentrated on the valleys and the plains and thereby attracted accusations that it was a process aimed at facilitating Jewish acquisition of the most fertile lands. PCO 1929 and its following amendments were not equipped to ensure that evicted tenants were compensated with land instead of cash, as provided. The Landless Arabs Inquiry, which aimed to identify and resettle landless Arabs was a disastrous failure, and applied narrow definitions of 'landless': by 1932, 3,737 claims had been submitted. Even though 899 of these families were found to be 'landless' a trifling 74 of these were resettled by the Development Department set up for the purpose.[6]

The administration remained reluctant to spend money. Even though both Hope-Simpson and French had suggested that the government invest more in the development of the agricultural sector and the protection of the Palestinian peasant, and even though the administration enjoyed a large budgetary surplus in the 1930s,[7] this was not done. Palestine boomed, and a disgruntled underclass was being created. In a despatch to the War Office, Peirse, writing from the Headquarters of the British Forces in Palestine and Transjordan, distinguished the current troubles from previous unrest:

> In April 1936 … the general situation was different. The feeling was more intense. The Arabs were unanimous in the belief that something had to be done to check the increasing flood of Jewish immigrants. They believed their national and economic future to be at stake. They were encouraged by the recent concessions made to Arab nationalism in Syria and by the changed situation in Egypt. (WO 32/4177, 15 Oct. 1936)

Strike, rebellion, civil war

The start of the Arab rebellion has been officially recorded as 1936, when a nationwide strike was imposed. Some writers mark 1935 as the launch of significant Arab grass-roots resistance against British imperialism and Jewish settlement. There were two main phases: the April–October 1936 strike and then, after the resumption of economic activity, the descent into violence between September 1937 and 1939. I will refer to the entire period, from 1935, as the rebellion.

Bands causing trouble in the hills started to appear as early as 1929 with the Green Hand Gang, a small collection of agitators who went from village to village raising funds and stirring up villagers' frustrations. Though the Green Hand Gang's activities were crushed swiftly and their leader Ahmed Tahfish fled, they had set a trend. A few years later, Izz Al Din Al Qassam emerged in the Galilee preaching an austere, puritanical, redemptive Islam. Qassam was born in the mountains of Northern Syria, to a conservative community where agitation against central government was part of the political landscape, and had flourished throughout the ages. (Johnson 1982: 38) He was a rebel fighter on the run from the French in Syria where he had been sentenced to death *in absentia* for his resistance activities. He received his higher education at Al Azhar University in Cairo, a world-class Islamic institution. He arrived in Palestine in 1921, already aged over 50, and settled in Haifa where he became a teacher, preacher and marriage registrar. This last job enabled him to wander around the Galilee, some say preaching *jihad* whilst recording marriages. Qassam was also a social reformer, and he set up a school for illiterate adults with the aim of rehabilitating (through religious education) men who had fallen foul of the law and other marginals. His followers consisted mostly of the desperate, silenced, urban poor, whom he stirred up with his fiery sermons. In the early 1930s Qassam formed the Black Hand Gang, a secret association through which he trained cells in paramilitary combat, organized the acquisition and distribution of arms, proselytized and forged political contacts. Initiates of the Black Hand Gang grew long, unkempt beards and their religious practices have been compared to those of ascetic Sufism.

Qassam combined religious austerity with anti-élitism. He denounced political affiliations based on familial or clan lines. He criticized the materialism of the urban political leaders. He told the members of the Supreme Muslim Council (SMC), an institution established by the Mandatory and which consisted mainly of heads of the urban notable families: 'The jewel and the decorative implements in the mosques should be transformed into weapons. If you lost your land, how are the decorations going to help you, when they are on the wall?' (quoted in Nimr 1990: 54). Qassam was not completely excluded from mainstream Palestinian leadership, and he was connected with the secularist Istiqlal (Independence) Party.[8] The Grand Mufti, President of the SMC, refused to openly associate with Qassam even though he may have secretly financed some of the Sheikh's ventures.[9]

The trigger to the first phase of the rebellion came in October 1935, when an apparently Jewish arms consignment was discovered at the harbour in Jaffa, the old Arab town adjoining modern Tel Aviv. There, it is said that a barrel of cement fell from a crane as it came off a lighter and broke. Qassam took the opportunity of this latest provocative action to declare open war against the British administration. He left the town of Haifa for the hills with some of his disciples in tow, only to be killed by British police in a famous battle at Ya'bad in the hills surrounding Jenin in November 1935, after he and his men refused to surrender the refuge of a cave. This was not his first military operation, but it was his first confrontation with the British authorities. The cult of Qassam burgeoned. He was the only member of native political leadership to have embraced martyrdom. Six months later, in April 1936, two Jews bore the brunt of native anger and were killed on the Nablus-Tulkarem road. Jews reprised almost immediately with the murder of two native workers in Petah Tikva near Tel Aviv. Rioting broke out in Jaffa and quickly spread to Nablus and Tulkarem. National Committees (NCs) were formed in all the major towns and villages, with the aim of resisting the Mandatory and Zionist colonizers. These NCs declared a unified, general strike. The Arab Higher Committee (AHC) was established on 25 April 1936, ostensibly as the strike's national coordinating body although the NCs were autonomous and financially independent.[10] On 26 April, the AHC, which consisted of the representatives of all the political parties of Palestine, issued its first communiqué and articulated their demands: the cessation of Jewish immigration, an end to land sales, and total representative government. They refused to continue to cooperate with the British administration unless their ultimatum was taken seriously.

In the hills, a word-weary rural population prepared to communicate their own demands with fewer syllables. Bands of armed peasants began to spring from villages, mainly in the central massif and in Galilee, and accompanied the strike with guerrilla attacks on both British and Jewish targets. One Kawakji was in command, a man with a wide span of military experience. A Lebanese/ Syrian by birth, he had fought against the French in Syria in 1920 and had been in exile ever since. He was also a former Ottoman officer, an advisor to King Ibn Saud of Saudi Arabia, and was lecturing at the Military Academy in Iraq when he was granted command of the rebellion in Palestine by the Palestine Defence League in Iraq. On 22 August 1936, he crossed the Jordan River with a couple of hundred volunteers. He issued his first communiqué a few days later, which he signed Commander of the General Arab Revolt in Southern Syria. A few days after that, six leaders of the largest bands bowed before him and accepted his authority.

The AHC called for a cessation of the strike. None of their demands had been met. Yet on 10 October 1936 the AHC, following an intervention by two Arab Kings and a Prince (King Ibn Saud of Saudi Arabia, King Ghazi of Iraq and the Emir Abdullah of Transjordan), capitulated. They ditched their ulti-matum and agreed to appeal for an end to the strike and violence. The High Commissioner wrote to the Colonial Secretary in November:

> The AHC now seems as anxious as is Government to ensure that armed bands should be dispersed and order restored in the countryside. Indeed they made an unconditional offer through one of their members to take any action the Government wished in order to ensure that Fawzi Kawakji and his band left Palestine forthwith. (CO 733/317/1, Memo by Hall, 13 Nov. 1936)

The effect of economic inactivity had taken its toll on the rest of the population. The bands dispersed, Kawakji was driven out of the country. The strike, one of the longest in history, had come to an end. The Peel Commission was appointed to investigate the causes of Arab unrest and arrived in Palestine on 11 November 1936. The Commissioners rendered their report in July 1937 and recommended the division of Palestine into two states, with Galilee to be included in the Jewish state despite its predominantly Arab population. It was also mentioned in passing, that the Mandatory would be in charge of guarding the sanctity of Jerusalem, Bethlehem and Nazareth, since 'that, in the fullest sense of the mandatory phrase, is a "sacred trust of civilization"' and would therefore be in keeping 'with Christian sentiment in the world at large'. With breathtaking short sight, the report declared that 'Partition offers a chance of ultimate peace. No other plan does.' (Summary of the Report of the Palestine Royal Commission, Series of League of Nations Publications, VI. A. Mandates) This would mean displacement, uprooting. A Miss Newton wrote to the Government:

> Everyone is simply pole axed. ... The core of the Arab treaty is the necessity for the transfer of the Arab population. ... It is difficult to see how

adequate compensation is to be made for the orange groves in the north and round Ramleh etc. These trees cannot be transported to the barren lands of Transjordan as easily as can their owners. ... One thing to be thankful for is that the proposal to terminate the Mandate is a vindication of the stand of the Arabs have made it against it. ... I fear that the oil and the water will remain suspended for the ingredient necessary to form an emulsion. i.e. frank recognition that this land is in Arab possession, is still lacking. (Chancellor Papers, box 15, file 7, Letter from Miss Newton, 12 July 1937: 58–60)

The rebels could not speak English or argue their case and if they could, they might have gone blue in the face. Instead, with unhesitating animal quickness, they ambushed Lewis Andrews, the Acting District Commissioner for Galilee, in a narrow alleyway as he was walking to Evensong at the Anglican Church in Nazareth on 26 September and assassinated him. The assassination is said to have been the work of Qassamites.[11] This launched the officially recognized second phase of the rebellion. Even though the AHC issued a statement deploring the crime, and Andrews' funeral was attended by one of its members, the murder provided an unmissable opportunity to rein in the Palestinian élite leadership. Andrews' murder is regularly cited in literature on the rebellion as the reason for the severity with which the Palestinian politicians were treated. It was not. Haj Amin Husseini, Grand Mufti, member of the AHC and President of the SMC, had long been a thorn in the side of the administration and the Secretary of State for the Colonies had written to the Prime Minister some six months prior to Andrews' assassination, of General Dill's suggestion to bar Husseini from re-entering the country after his pilgrimage to Mecca:

> [I]f we were to try and get rid of the Mufti in such a tricky way, he would be free to roam the near and Middle East and even India exposing our methods and stirring up Moslem feeling everywhere. If there ever was a time when such a step should *not* be taken, it is the present, when the Mufti is at Mecca on a religious pilgrimage! If we ever can or do get rid of the Mufti, for whom I have no love, I want him deported fairly and squarely from Palestine to the Seychelles and kept there. As to whether we can do that depends on whether he gives us a decent excuse for such action after the Peel Report and our decisions are out. I cannot agree to Dill's proposal which to my mind would not be 'cricket'. (Cmnd. 5634, SSC to PM, 2 March 1937, 'Policy in Palestine, January 1938')

Hall, the Officer Administering the Government during HC Wauchope's leave, wrote to the Secretary of State for the Colonies shortly after the murder that 'the murder of Andrews cannot be traced directly to the Mufti whose interests definitely lie in maintaining peace at present'. With regard to the AHC and the

NCs, he explained: 'If therefore we do not attach great importance to future negotiations the Executive Council advise and I concur that these bodies should be declared illegal forthwith.' (Cmnd. 5634: Telegram from Hall to SSC, 27 Sept. 1937, Policy in Palestine, January 1938') Andrews' murder was a perfect pretext to sever all ties with the local urban leaders. The rebellion was eased into its second phase. The Palestine Defence Order in Council of 18 March 1937 (PDOiC, superseding PDOiC 1931 and 1936), empowered the High Commissioner to make Defence Regulations for the purpose of securing public safety and order and suppressing mutiny and riot. Haj Amin Husseini, Grand Mufti, was removed from his post as President of the SMC. He went into hiding in the compound of the Golden Dome Mosque in the Old City of Jerusalem (the Haram Al Sharif). Two weeks later he grabbed an opportune moment to flee the country, frustrating Ormsby-Gore's fantasies of him languishing in an Indian Ocean archipelago. His nephew Jamal Bey Husseini also fled. Other members were deported. Hussein F. Khalidi and Fuad Saba were arrested in their homes in Jerusalem early one morning. Hilmi Pasha was apprehended in Gaza. Yacoub Ghossein surrendered at Ramleh. All four boarded the Destroyer HMS Active and sailed to Mahé, in the Seychelles. (CO 935/21, HC to SSC 'Narrative Despatches', Sept. 1937–Dec. 1938) Rashid Al Haj Ibrahim, a bank manager, was also deported with them, even though he was not a member of the AHC. There was a rumour that his arrest and deportation were compensation for the authorities failing to catch Awni Bey, secretary of the AHC and a much naughtier native (see Chapter 5, 'The last word: the unusual suspects').

Further regulations were issued throughout the year under the banner of Public Security. On 30 March, District Commissioners were empowered to billet additional police if the locals were a little reticent to assist the authorities. As a further punitive measure, the local inhabitants would bear the cost of this extra expense. On 14 October the High Commissioner took the power to prohibit anyone who was out of Palestine at the time, from returning. On 11 November 1937, the Emergency Regulations establishing military courts were published. These courts could sentence to life imprisonment anyone *in possession* of firearms, ammunitions or bombs, and to death anyone *carrying* any of the above named weapons (see Report of the Mandatory to the League of Nations, 31 Dec., 1937, Colonial No. 146: para. 26). The military courts were summary courts, with no possibility of appeal, although the General Officer Commanding was to confirm conviction and sentence. The military could now act independently of the administration. In 1938 local officials could restrict individuals from moving within Palestine, impose collective fines, order house demolitions and intern detainees in concentration camps, the unfortunate term used for British detention centres and gaols.[12]

The rebels were gasping for oxygen, but they redoubled their exertions. The headquarters of the rebellion moved to Damascus, where the Central Committee of the National Jihad in Palestine, a coordinating body for the rebellion, was established. By mid-1938, the rebels controlled almost all of Palestine, including the Old City in Jerusalem. Palestine had come under the people's control through the actions of the primitive and primitively armed peasantry. The cry of challenge to authority could no longer be ignored. The rebellion's command structure was targeted with the formation of the deceptively named Arab Peace Bands composed of collaborators to act against the rebels. British troops flooded the country, a curfew was imposed and the rebellion was crushed. The rebellion had transmuted from a strike in 1936 to a fully fledged violent uprising in 1937. It reached its peak in 1938 and from then on, suffering from infighting and under attack by the military machine of the world's greatest empire, is regularly said to have degenerated into an internecine struggle which has been compared to a civil war.

Now, what is the story behind this story?

We strain to see

Histories of the rebellion we read and reproduce, read and accept, read and internalize, are histories of the Mandatory state. The devil is in the detail: how many ordinances were passed? How many were hanged/tried/interned? How many 'Jews', how many 'Arabs'? How many troops were deployed? How much money spent? Why was martial law not applied? What is the difference between martial law and Emergency Regulations? How was this rebellion, this rioting, different from previous unrest, in terms of causes, names, numbers, scale?

Since there was a rebellion in Palestine, then blatantly there must have been rebels. Strangely though (or not so strangely), these rebels are all but absent from the historical literature. So absent — from literature which otherwise details every breath, every whim, every after-dinner conversation between members of the ruling élite (in the main, British), with meticulous care. Histories of the rebellion are actually its hollow bones, stories with half the actors missing. The more histories we read the more elusive are the rebels. We know they must have existed, but *how* did they exist, *what* did they exist for, *why* did they exist, what was the *texture* of their anger, what did they *value*, how did *they* view the Mandatory, what did *they* say about the Mandatory? Will we ever know? Do we need to know? What would we do with that knowledge? Where does it belong? How would it affect Western histories of the rebellion? Can it be integrated in them, or can the two only ever exist in parallel? Edward Said (1988) writes that élite and subaltern histories are interdependent on each other and that the subaltern enterprise ought not to be a separatist one, or it would run the risk of mirroring 'the writing whose tyranny it disputes' (Edward Said, 'Foreword', in R. Guha and G. Spivak (eds), viii). Perhaps not — not as long as the playing field is tilted, the official narrative is asymmetrical, the discourse is Eurocentric, the amorality of the Mandatory project is obscured, the historiography is élitist, and progress/modernity constitute an unproblematic baseline.

First: how have Western historians portrayed the rebels, and how far does this reflect the rebels portrayed in the colonial archive?

What historians see

Look at the chalky outline on the floor. That is the Palestinian rebel.

Or, that is all the Palestinian rebel we get from historical texts. Texts rich in political nuance, bolstered by reliance on indifferent facts, driven to and by (more or less the same) conclusions, relying on major events to trace political developments, relying on the lives of major figures as reassuring reference points, acquiescing (even if reluctantly) to the fundamental and intrinsic validity of the Mandatory's position, dominated by dubious, inaccurate and weighted linguistic choices. Western historical accounts of the rebellion are achingly repetitive and blissfully free from doubt. Terms which have come to be acceptable as value-free are in reality laden with values. Analyses which are careful to grant that Palestinian Arabs had legitimate grievances are in reality laden with prejudice and innuendo. In other words, the only acceptable way of writing about the rebellion, seems to be by chronicling reactions to it. It is not the rebellion itself which is chronicled, but the chain of diplomatic and political events it set in motion.[13]

What do historical studies teach us, beyond the fact that Qassam inspired the whole thing, that the murder of two Jews followed by the murder of two Arabs led to the formation of NCs and a national strike, that the AHC was established to coordinate the NCs, that rebel bands began to form and that they were led by Kawakji, that the AHC eventually called for a cessation of the strike, that the Peel Commission recommended partition in 1937 and that this drove the Arabs mad and that Andrews was assassinated as a result, that AHC leaders were arrested and expelled after that, that violence escalated during this second phase of the rebellion, and that an overwhelming military government crackdown as well as internecine violence weakened and put an end to the rebellion? With minor adjustments of tone, pitch and colour, this is the story which is reproduced again and again across the range of historical studies.

For instance, Qassam is routinely described as a bandit/criminal, and one writer dismisses the entire rebellion as 'an extension of traditional brigandage'. (Bowden 1975: 151) The more balanced accounts of the rebellion will concede that the struggle was multifaceted and multidimensional, that it was part class war, part *jihad*, part anti-imperialist and part feudal, and that this together with its skeletal and unstable political structures, left it open to the exploits of a bunch of opportunistic, parochial and self-centred commanders.

The rebellion's lack of effective leadership, its much stated incoherent/immature political ideology, the rise of intercommunal or internecine violence and the turning inwards of suspicion and anger, are regularly blamed for its demise. It is true that dozens of bands were left to operate each of their own accord and that the absence of central leadership from Palestine left the chiefs to squabble amongst each other. Even if the urban political leaders were powerless to influence the direction of the uprising, nonetheless their expulsion dealt the rebellion a substantial symbolic blow. The common conclusion is that the underdeveloped political consciousness of the rebels finally damaged their efforts at national liberation: the Arabs fought each other, never mind the British or the Jews. (ibid.: 147)[14] Bowden writes that the military campaign was conducted by 'what were little more than feudatory retinues of bandit marauders only marginally inspired and motivated by loosely held, inchoate notions of liberation and *Jihad*'. (ibid.) He elaborates on the 'deep Arab fighting traditions' that eventually took over the rebellion and lost it. Arnon-Ohanna (1981) also blames its lethal flaws on the '*Hamula*' system of Palestinian society, referring to its lineage based tribal structure.[15] He explains that old tribal jealousies could simply never be transcended.

Yet here is the rub: at the peak of the rebellion in 1938, the whole of Palestine, including the Old City of Jerusalem, was under siege. In August of that year, a British doctor stationed in Hebron wrote in his diary: 'The Law Courts are closed, forests, PWD [Public Works Department] and Lands have all been withdrawn, and the police reduced to a cipher.' (Dr Eliot Forster Diaries, entry for Aug. 1938) The feral farmer, the barely armed, myopic rebels were presumably operating with some sort of cohesion, *savoir faire* and discipline to achieve this. Yet it is the familial and clan lines of rebel (dis) organization, their localized and microcosmic understanding of politics, which is focused on. Peasant political fervour is based on emotional and therefore presumably irrational attachment to the soil, which in turn is infused with feudal undercurrents. Evolved political consciousness and the particularity of each peasant's attachment to his own access to a cultivable area, are ideological worlds apart. So when the peasant picks up a gun, it is to fend off an immediate threat to his intra-communal boundaries, and usually when he has been whipped up into a racial/religious/class frenzy by some urban leader or other. The flammable *fellah*, instinctually identifying with a patch of earth, who is genetically, educationally and culturally incapable of formulating a political ideology, or of rising above each impending individual battle.

Time and again the rebellion is said to have failed. It is said to have failed because it did not achieve its main objective, which was to bring and end to British imperialism and Zionist settlement. It failed because the peasants were innately incapable of real revolution, incapable of organizing themselves into effective alliances. They engaged in undisciplined and self-defeating Arab-on-Arab violence, as government employees and others perceived as traitors were made to pay for their affiliations. The rebellion became plagued by factional rivalries, and pre-existing blood feuds were settled under the guise of political competition. End of story.

What the Mandatory saw

It is true that the rebellion suffered from the lack of a central command, and that rivalries between band leaders existed. It is true that the predilection of certain rebel commanders for the assassination of perceived traitors was legendary. One Abu Dorrah for instance, was known as the slayer of *Mukhtars*[16] – the final figure of how many he did kill varies between 20 and 80. (Swedenburg 1995: 118)[17] Things are not completely as they seem in the literature though, and the Mandatory government itself may have experienced the rebels quite differently. As an example, even though the execution of collaborators is a recurring theme in historical studies of the rebellion, we know that the British authorities were frustrated at the poor quality of Palestinian intelligence.[18] Similarly, it has been suggested that Fawzi Kawakji, first Commander of the rebellion, attempted to set up a discipline and structure consistent with his training but that his efforts were wasted on the essentially undisciplined rebels.[19] Yet Ted Horne, a Mandate policeman, gives us a tantalizing taste of the true rebel style:

> Fawzi's [i.e. Fawzi Kawakji] troops were from rural peasant recruits for the most part, with limited weapons, no armour, few cavalry and no aeroplanes. Training was also very sparse and there was always a shortage of ammunition, food and ready cash. In spite of this, the rebels managed to burn down 40 police stations and posts, damage the railways and postal system severely, establish whole 'no go' areas in rural Palestine. They held their own courts and even used their own stamps ... the real point to be made is that nobody thought the Arabs capable of launching such a campaign in which British prestige was sorely tested and lessons were learnt of military value. ... The rebels had fought the good fight and lost but they had frightened Whitehall. (Palestine Police Old Comrades Association Collection (PPOCAC), Horne Photographic Album 'Arab Rebellion': iv)

The rebellion was ultimately crushed by the overwhelmingly superior military, political and financial power of the Mandatory. Never mind the historical literature, the Mandatory itself certainly did not underestimate the threat posed by the rebels, nor their own options to deal with it. The authorities were aware of the rebels' potential for disruption and prepared for it. A memo prepared by the Headquarters of the British Forces in Palestine and Transjordan as early as 1936 stated:

> [I]n the hill country of Palestine where movements off roads by ground forces is restricted, the destruction of armed bands is best achieved by the action of the air striking force in close cooperation with a ground striking force in support of ground forces, aircraft or the civil organisation on which attacks develop ...

> The outstanding military problem at the moment in Palestine is the vigorous action of armed rebel bands ... armed bands vary in size from 5–70 rifles ... their fire directed against aircraft is effective and aircraft have been hit on many occasions ...
>
> Under prescribed conditions, air action by machinegun fire can take place over the whole of Palestine. (CO 733/317/1)

As the rebellion showed no signs of abating, and violence escalated despite the arrest/deportation of the urban political leaders, the military vied for complete control of Palestine and for the application of martial law.[20] Martial law was not applied, lest the British government lose face in the Middle East,[21] and Emergency measures were introduced instead. According to these, the General Officer Commanding (GOC) could appoint Military Commanders to replace District Commissioners. The police was placed under the operational control of the General Officer Commanding, a night curfew was imposed on the whole of rural Palestine, and all males were prohibited from car and rail travel if they did not have a pass from a Military Commander. (Report of the Mandatory to the League of Nations, 31 Dec. 1938, Colonial No. 166) Other informal mechanisms, more sneaky, were also deployed. The government gave the rebel bands their nemesis: the so-called Peace Bands, which co-opted the collaborative elements of Palestinian society and which operated in the countryside against the insurgency. GOC Haining thought this was a good thing:

> There are moreover signs that as the grip of the rebels on the countryside is weakened by *military action*, the situation will be further complicated by the emergence of Arab anti-rebel gangs formed by those moderate elements who wish to take revenge on those who have supported the rebel terror. (WO 32/4562, GOC Haining, 'Hostile Propaganda in Palestine, its Origins and Progress in 1938. My emphasis.)

Orde Wingate's Special Night Squads were deployed to the countryside in May 1938. Orde Wingate was an intelligence officer with a Christian Zionist upbringing. His Night Squads were led by British officers and consisted of British and Jewish personnel, the latter mostly members of the Haganah, a Jewish armed group, to conduct offensives in the countryside. The Mandatory's methods had drawn complaints, but the authorities' conscience was clear. Acting HC MacMichael wrote in connection with the disarmament of the village of Halhoul:

> [I]t is true that in this village 8 male Arabs died from heat exhaustion. This was due to a combination of *unfortunate circumstances* which included abnormally hot weather and the extremely low powers of resistance to these conditions of the older men, to which category those who died belonged. (WO 32/4652, MacMichael to McDonald, 'Palestine 1938, Allegations Against British Troops', 22 Sept. 1939. My emphasis.)

Well that is ok then.

By December 1938, Palestine had been reclaimed by the British. The rebellion did not unavoidably self-implode, it was crushed. The Mandatory explained to the League of Nations:

> The main difference between the course of events in 1938 and that in 1937 lay in the gradual development during 1938 of Arab gang warfare on organized and to a certain extent coordinated lines. By the end of the year, *as the result of the arrival in the autumn of large military reinforcements,* this gang organization was first dislocated and finally reduced to comparative impotence in the field. But in the towns terrorism persisted and the roads were still largely unsafe for normal traffic. In fact, the events of 1938 succeeded in seriously affecting the economic and social life of the country to an extent far greater than was the case in 1937. (Report of the Mandatory to the League of Nations, 31 Dec. 1938 op. cit. My emphasis.)

The Emergency Regulations provided for an impressive form of collective punishment – blowing up houses in guilty villages – and a ludicrous and disingenuous justification was given for this:

> Criticism is often directed at the system of collective punishment but it is probable that the critics fail to realize that the principle of collective responsibility of a community for a crime or disorder committed within its boundaries is fully recognized and understood by Palestinian Arabs. (WO 32/4652, GOC Haining, 'Hostile Propaganda in Palestine' op. cit.)

That may be so, but what about the crime or disorder for which the punishment was administered? Was that as fully recognized or understood by Palestinian Arabs?

The rebellion failed in the sense that it did not achieve its stated objective of liberating Palestine. But if we were to take it on its own terms, if we were to suggest that its stated aim of liberating Palestine was chiefly rhetorical and a non-starter, that the rebels acted in the only way a population under the same conditions could be expected to react – imagine a boot stamping on a human face, and imagine that face to be your own – that their rebellion was a reclamation of the self and of their dignity, that they cleansed themselves and were truest to themselves when they armed themselves, that the courage they displayed in the face of the greatest world power was humbling and inspiring – then there is no failure and the rebellion's achievements can be appreciated as truly colossal. Moreover, the Mandatory never underestimated the damage the rebels could do or were doing. Mandatory reports, despatches, investigations and minutes provide a glimpse of rebel life. This is the type of thing they said in the 'bungalow':

> [T]he damage and dislocation caused to government property and communications forbids their dismissal as trivial. They are, in fact, symptomatic

of what is now a very deep seated rebellious spirit throughout the whole Arab population, spurred on by the call of a Holy War. The rebel gangs have now acquired, by terrorist methods, such a hold over the mass of the population that it is not untrue to say that every Arab in the county is a potential enemy of the Government. (CO 733/379/3, GOC Haining, 'Disturbances: Appreciations by GOC, Military Forces', Report on Events in Palestine during the period 1 Aug.1938–30 Oct. 1938. Report dated 30 Nov. 1938.)

As Fanon said, the colonialist begins to panic when good natives become scarce. Since we are starved of information, we have to be grateful for those indicators from colonial sources that serve as evidence of rebel consciousness. So for instance, when the Mandatory during the rebellion refers to the '*notoriously bad* villages of Beit Rima and Halhoul' (WO , 'Palestine 1938, Allegations Against British Troops', my emphasis), this does not only point to a mindset which criminalizes resistance, but also reveals those villages as centres of resistance (cf. Guha 1983: 17). The hostility is rising daily and the Mandatory is, momentarily, helpless to do anything but observe and note it down. This in itself is a triumph for the rebel resistance movement. It is a challenge to authority. A CID Intelligence Report prepared in September 1938 reveals the administration's preoccupations in some detail. The report gives a detailed analysis of the leadership and composition of the rebel gangs. The report cites Sheikh Khalil Mohammed Issa as the executive head of the rebellion, on orders from the Grand Mufti, the Haj Amin Husseini, who was believed to be directing operations from his base in (exile in) Damascus. Abdul Rahim Al Haj Mohammed is described as the nominal Commander-in-Chief of the rebel forces, and together with Abu Dorrah and Aref Abdul Razak, formed a Committee or Council which was to 'decide unanimously upon all questions of the distribution of contributions and sentences on traitors, and that disputes must be referred to Damascus'. (PPOCAC, Intelligence Report, Sept. 1938: 2) The report identifies Abdul Razzak as the organizer of the rebel courts, and as the one who banned the Turkish *tarbush* (fez) from the streets in favour of the peasant's *hatta* (or *keffiye*, the traditional chequered scarf). He issued ultimatums off his own back and requested all Arab officials to resign from their posts with the British administration within forty-eight hours. Abu Dorrah is said to be 'ruthless' in enforcing his verdicts. Abu Khaled is 'the chief executioner of the rebel court', the one who apparently issued a proclamation calling for the formation of a dispute-settlement/trial of collaborators committee in every village. The report portrays the rebels as organized and disciplined:

[T]he machinery for cooperation between the gangs is more efficient than it was and gives the rebel movement certain claims to the dignity and power of a national cause. One of its most characteristic and potent institutions is the system of rebel courts, which is increasing daily in popularity. The majority of villagers no longer complain to the police. Instead a court is convened, composed of the leaders of the detachments operating in the area concerned, and the cases heard and dealt with as expeditiously as possible, generally to the satisfaction of both parties. An order has now been issued by the Committee in Damascus that the Mukhtars of every village in the country together with 4 elders are to sign a declaration that no criminal cases are to be reported to Government. Cases of minor importance will be dealt with by a village court but those of a serious nature by the rebel courts. Cases in which a village court is unable to come to a decision will be forwarded to the rebel court. (ibid.: 10)

The report goes on to comment on the rebel bands' most prominent recent developments, and notes:

They have also noticeably tightened up their own internal discipline and shown increased severity with armed robbers who oppress the villagers without authority from the leaders.
It is reported that recruitment is being carried on in Syria and Transjordan; that machine-gun and anti-aircraft guns are expected from across the border and will be operated by experienced Turkish ex-Army Officers; that large quantities of first-aid equipment have been bought and distributed throughout the country.
These are but a few examples of the initiative and attention to detail shown by Rebel Headquarters. (ibid.)

Ted Horne wrote of the rebellion as 'having all the characteristics of a classic peasant revolt', and that it was 'the last chance the Arabs had of keeping their country'. (PPOCAC, Horne 'Palestine Diary': 2) The colonial archive itself then, yields a little more marrow for those hollow bones, is a little more nuanced than Western historical studies typically let on, even if rebel activity still only *exists* where the Mandatory has reacted to it. Even if rebel activity only *exists* in the Mandatory's reports, despatches, investigations and minutes. Even if it is only noticed once it has posed a security problem. It is not the rebels which are conjured in the colonial archive but their silhouettes as they step in and out of the shadows, in and out of their cave-dwellings, in and out of towns and cities, in and out of fields, in and out of their disguises, in and out of the collective consciousness of the Palestinian population, in and out of the real and the metaphoric night. The rebels come into focus when they gravitate towards the centre, when they come within a stone's throw away of the 'bungalow', when they start trespassing into privileged ground and desecrating sacred territory. H.M. Wilson, a British schoolteacher living in the town of Bir Zeit in 1938, experienced the rebels thus:

When I had passed this way on Saturday morning, on my way into Jerusalem, there had been a stone wall built across the Bir Zeit tracks, just above Jifna. This was to prevent lorry-loads of British troops from surprising the rebels, who had spent the whole of Friday in Bir Zeit, feasting on the sheep they had demanded from the villagers, and holding judicial courts ... Today I found that the stone wall had been tidied back on to the hills. This meant that the rebels had moved on. (PPOCAC, Wilson, 'School Year in Palestine 1938–39': 3)

One of the sacred territories desecrated by the rebels was that of law. The rebels made a go of establishing a revolutionary juridical system to replace the functions of the boycotted British courts.[22] They dispensed justice on the hoof. Their trials were mostly held under the cover of darkness. Caves, fields and empty wells were used as prisons. There was clearly more to this than the trial and punishment/execution of collaborators and traitors. Dr. Eliot Forster, a physician working in Hebron, wrote in his diary:

The Rebel Courts sit not only for Courts Martial but also to settle all the land, feud and financial cases that in normal times are heard by the government. Their justice and common sense does not appear to me inferior, and their expedition is demonstrably many degrees superior to that of HMG. (Dr Eliot Forster op. cit.)

Eight months later, Dr. Forster wrote in his diary that he had gone up to Jerusalem for a District Court case. He continued:

The President of the Court, one Plunket, was the man whose decision was upheld by an oozle[23] court last year. As one of his colleagues acidly remarked, 'About the first time that Plunket has ever been upheld on appeal!' (ibid.: 17 April 1939)

H.M. Wilson also provides a first-hand account of the these rebel courts. Wilson recounts that two neighbours in the village of Bir Zeit clashed over the building of a wall. Some rebels who happened to be passing through the village unsuccessfully attempted to arbitrate between them. Two nights later,

miss (sic) Naser told us that a rebel judge, Abouji, had come into the village to try the case that night, upstairs in the school's sitting room ... Abouji was already installed there, together with the Mukhtar ... and several other villagers. The masters from the boys' school presently came across, all arrayed with their white head cloths. It is amusing how these, worn with European suits, have the effect of turning the mildest looking Arab into a complete desperado ...

> After about an hour of general talk he proceeded to the affair of Abu Suleiman and Nahum. ... A lot of noisy conversation followed, in the course of which Vera whispered in my ear that he was now discussing the case of a policeman in Ramallah who wanted to divorce his wife and that she was sleepy and was going to bed! (PPOCAC, Wilson op. cit.: 11–13)

The phenomena of the rebel courts and the boycott of the British courts were symptomatic of the extent to which the rebels wished to dissociate and disengage from British imperialism. These 'oozle' courts and their affiliated Legislative Committees, were more than functional, folkloric systems of dispute resolution. They had another, more historically cogent and surprisingly (?) lucid aspiration: to counter the psychological ravages of a beautiful word: 'Englishism'.[24] The rebellion's working class, peasant, unadulterated Arab character was its defining feature. Rebels drank rainwater, slept huddled in the wild, roamed the hills by foot, ate every few days and depended on the charity of strangers. In 1938, they issued a notice declaring a moratorium on debts, the discontinuation of all court actions in respect of debts, and promised to summarily execute ('merely at the complaint of the debtor'), any creditor who contravenes the order more than once. (CO 733/372/4, 'Rebel Propaganda', 16 November 1938) The rebels prohibited the entire population from wearing the *tarbush*, the red fez which was a sign of notability under Ottoman rule,[25] and instead ordered men to wear the chequered scarf, the *keffiye* or *hatta* of the peasant. This completed their symbolic rejection of the conciliatory attitudes of the urban notables towards their foreign masters, and it worked. The Mandatory noted that whole country was in the grips of rebel fever:

> Practically all Arabs, Christians and Moslems, have assumed at the behest of the rebel 'High Command' the head-dress of *Kaffiyeh* and *agal* ... women are wearing the veil more and more; edicts have been issued by the rebels calling on all Arabs to come to their courts to settle their complaints rather than go to the King's courts; other decrees forbid strong language and loose morals and invite the wives of faithless husbands to seek redress in the rebel courts. The rebels conduct a continuous and largely successful propaganda to show that their courts are more just, and above all more speedy, than the King's courts. Incidentally, it is no doubt for this quasi-administrative business that the gangs require typewriters: a considerable number of these machines have been stolen chiefly from Government offices. (CO /733/935/21: HC to SSC, 'Narrative Despatches', 29 Oct.1938)[26]

The rebels were not merely keen to settle disputes/scores, expedite justice, or to fill the gap left by the suspension of the British courts. To drive the point home, they thought they might do this by appropriating the paraphernalia of

British justice and parading it as their own. Were these attempts to negate their own perceived inferiority, an indication of the colonization of consciousness of the native and of his low self-esteem? Or were they genuine triumphal gestures, the brandishing of spoils of war? Alternatively, the gestures can be seen as pure burlesque. The rebel may very likely have been simply revelling, sensually and spontaneously, in the topsy-turvy carnival, for no other reason than to make his master squirm.

'We were farmers'

There is another language in which the rebellion is remembered and told, remembered and circulated between generations. It is a language in which the individual's direct experience claims centre stage, and which is made up of many different voices. This is the language of oral history, with its mixture of memory, emotion, fantasy, collective identity and activism.[27] The activism is implicit in the act of both giving and hearing oral testimony, since the interviewer and interviewee are engaged in an act that will inevitably confront and question tidy historical grand narratives. Memory reconstructs, deconstructs, evolves, flows, recedes and is transferred. The men and women who spoke to me seamlessly weaved the past, the present and the future. The memories being handed down to subsequent generations (three? four?) interlace emotion with detail, reflection, repartee.

The flexible structures of their narratives, their declaratory style, might unhinge you if you are a historian. Where then, does the value of these stories, part truth and part legend, lie? In this case, their primary value is not in the counter-facts they reveal. Quite simply, I wanted to hear the refugees' accounts of a story I had read which had left me unconvinced. It was an unconvincing story because half the protagonists were missing. Most seriously though, it was a story without heart, without character or feeling, without colour or temperature, without redemption or substance. Vexingly, tantalizingly, this absence seemed wilful and deliberate, since the protagonists, and their experiences and their words, had been there all along. More than *what* they would tell, I wanted to know *how* those protagonists would tell and the language they would use to tell it. Histories of the rebellion have been written, as a rule, by historians too conservative, within a discipline itself too conservative, too susceptible and too loyal to the skewed colonial framework which has dictated historical discourse, to evoke rebel world-view.

How and where do the following testimonies fall in relation to Mandate Palestinian histories, those dominant, hegemonic accounts of the past which nonetheless pass for unqualified studies? Can we allow the rebels to speak, to preach, to declaim, and tell *us* about the rebellion? It is not only their accounts of the past which are disturbing, but the marginal place from which they utter them: for almost 60 years, the refugees have been living on dirt floors, amidst open sewers, some of them in camps actually surrounded by barbed wire,[28] without Lebanese citizenship or even refugee status to protect them. Despite the fact that their lives are in shreds and are defined by displacement, loss, insult, humiliation, slight and idleness, inside them they harbour gold. As we listen to the subaltern rebel tell his own story, according to his own values and logic and in his own tongue, according to his own transcendental dialectic, we should keep in mind Fanon, who writes that violence on the part of the colonized in a colonial situation is a reclamation of the self, that it is only when 'his rage boils over that he rediscovers his lost innocence and he comes to know himself in that he himself creates his self'. (Fanon 1963: 21) Not only that, but his resort to weapons is life-affirming, and 'proof of his humanity' (ibid.: 22), and the act of killing in that context is doubly liberating, because the rebel has killed both the oppressor and the oppressed man who lived inside him, his own oppressed heart, so that what remains is a dead man and a free man. (ibid.)

Similarly, Memmi (1966: 164) writes that rebellion was the only viable solution to a colonial situation, (*'la seule issue ... qui ne soit pas un trompe l'oeil'*) for such a situation is humanly unmanageable. It is a choker/restraint which must be ruptured. It is only when the native rejects the colony and his master that he may begin to regain himself. If we understand this, then we can listen to the rebellion as a story of untold heroism and bravery (not mindless and apolitical violence), of personal awakening for the Palestinians who participated in it (not degeneration or banditry), of social transformation and cohesion (not factional infighting), of significant, symbolic, disruptive challenge to authority and of redemptive potential (not doomed to failure).

When the rebel speaks, we are struck with the extent to which he has refused to adopt the colonist's mode of thinking, in contrast to members of the élite, who use the same vocabulary as the colonist. The rebel's speech is unselfconscious because it does not seek to persuade. It is not strategic or tactical speech: 'the fellah, the unemployed man, the starving native do not lay claim to the truth; they do not *say* that they represent the truth, for they *are* the truth'. (Fanon op. cit.: 49) We might shirk at hearing such profuse talk of violence and of killing, but our shirking would be insincere. Violence should not surprise us: 'the argument the native chooses has been furnished by the settler, and by an ironic turning of the tables it is the native who now affirms that the colonialist understands nothing but force'. (ibid.: 84) The fact that their truth consists of simple, single syllable words such as land, life, bread or blood does not make him narrow-minded or dull-witted, but amounts to the most authentic, natural and healthy way of thinking and being. (ibid.: 50)

The rebel though, is not completely free. For even though his rebellion and acts of violence hold redeeming potential, he has taken on the methods and lessons of his master and of the settler. He generalizes and does not differentiate between 'the English'. He sounds racist and xenophobic. His racism and xenophobia however, are justifiable and are not based on a belief in the inferiority of the hated group but in the conviction that the hated group is aggressive and harmful. It is a defensive, rather than offensive racism (see Memmi op. cit.: 166–67). Perhaps the aboriginal, authentic native is irrecuperable after all, and really only exists as an invention of his master, and continues to find it impossible to *be* himself. (ibid.: 175)

How, though, do the dormant frustrations of the rebel turn to active violence? Fanon writes that one of the triggers for action within a colonized community at boiling point sometimes comes in the form of a battle in which someone considered a reprobate by the authorities is confronted by them and dies a valiant death. This event is enough to provide a blueprint for action and renders the rebel a hero. (Fanon op. cit.: 69) Qassam clearly was one such trigger. One who emerged like a phoenix from the refugees' narratives, is the figure of Al Asbah, who was mentioned by almost every single interviewee. The following transcripts are excerpts from a selection of interviews conducted in the Baddawi, Nahr Al Bared, Rashidiyye and Shabriha Palestinian refugee camps in Lebanon, over a six-month period, between January and June 2004. I italicize the names of their home towns and villages because they do not exist anymore. More than half the interviewees I met have died since. The following narratives provide a fleeting glimpse of the rebels' 'reverse-discourse' (Parry 1996: 172) but a vivid one nevertheless. The subaltern is speaking fast and furiously, his memory is fading and his health is ailing, but the opportunity to tell his tale brings a glint of joy and mischief to his old filmy eyes.

Here it is. The last of the candle for the cave:

Anonymous

The English were governing Palestinian land while the Palestinians wanted independence so this is how the rebellion started. Some people went up to the hills. I was very young, I was born in 1926 so I was 10–12 years old. During that time, the English would come and circle the town and look for rebels. I walked with the rebels but the English never said anything to me ...

It was a rebellion. The English knew it was a rebellion and the whole world knew it was a rebellion. No one thought it was anything else. The rebels were attacking military and government posts, so the English knew it was a rebellion. They knew very well that we were not criminals. Listen, I don't remember very much. I remember one thing from the rebellion. It was 1936, I was still young. There was one man fighting with the rebels and the leadership was harassing him for some reason. He was under a lot of pressure. The leadership stopped paying him or giving him clothes or anything. His name was Rabah. Then he changed sides and became a policeman with the English. One day the English came to the town and called on loudspeakers for everyone to gather in the squares. Men, women, children. They gathered us like cattle. They put one Arab policeman on either side of the street, each with a whip in his hand. They gathered 40 young men. Rabah was one of the policemen. They stripped the young men naked and said 'come on you dogs, come on'.[29] Each man had to come forward to get whipped. One got two lashes, another three, another five. Then the fourth man stood in front of Rabah and said, 'You can whip me to pieces Rabah, I will not move. Shame on you, for bringing our women here for the English to look at.' Rabah pushed him away and started crying. He regretted what he was doing. I will never forget that.

Listen to me. We couldn't digest the English. They are worse than the Jews. The English were fairer with the Jews than with the Arabs. They armed the Jews and gave them ammunition but they didn't give anything to the Arabs. The reason for our *Nakba* [catastrophe] is the English. Go and tell them. They are the ones who ruined our houses and made us refugees. They slaughtered us. We don't like them. I'm sorry, what am I saying? Are you English?

Hussein Fayyad Al Toqi, b. 1921. From Balad Al Sheikh, Haifa, currently living in Baddawi refugee camp

The colonial government was unfair to us so we organized a rebellion. I was young and active. I was 16 but I was in good shape. Now I am 82 years old and have only one leg but I am in good health. Praises to God, even though I only have one leg, I've just come back from the mosque. At least I can still go to the mosque. I go about my life. Some of my relatives were rebels. I'm not giving you names! Whatever happened happened and those who died died. Ok I'll give you my cousin's name: Ali Zeidan. Our leader was Sheikh Rashid. He was from *Tiret Haifa*. My cousin told him that I wanted to join, but he said I was too young and my father might be upset and object. But I joined anyway and they trained me ...

We attacked whoever: English and Jew. Of course we were armed, what do you think! Everybody carried arms, the Arab countries gave them to us. We were not told where the arms came from as the leaders feared that collaborators would tell the occupiers the source. When we needed arms, there were special places where we could go and get them. Grenades and cartridges, etc. were all in the same place. There were different kinds of arms: the Ottoman, the German, the British. We only used Ottoman and German rifles with five rounds. We didn't use the English ones even though they had eleven rounds because they were the enemy's.

Of course they imprisoned me. After I was shot. I was shot during the rebellion in the battle next to the river *Moqatta'*, next to *Tell Al Nahel*. The river springs from Nablus and goes straight into the Mediterranean. We ambushed the Jews at night because we knew they would come out to check on their fields. We started shooting at them. The land was flat and there was nowhere to hide. It was damp. The battle started. My friends disappeared. In the end I was shot in the leg. The English commander came and the tanks came. They found me bleeding. They took me to hospital and they operated on me twice. They amputated my leg. When they took me away I was unconscious. They fell on me and grabbed my gun and they anaesthetized me.

They took me to a hospital with a very famous doctor, Dr. Hamzeh. They treated me in the hospital until I was better and then they took me to court and sentenced me to death. Then my parents spoke with the one who was responsible and asked him to reduce my sentence and my sentence was reduced to a life sentence. I don't know how many Jews died in that battle. None of us were killed, none of the rebels. I went to prison in September 1939. I came out of prison on 15 May 1945. That date is engraved on my chest right here. For the last two years, I don't remember as well as I used to. I am getting tired. I am even forgetting the Quran ...

Haj Khalil Mohamad Soueidan, b. 1926. From Houleh in Safad, currently living in Baddawi refugee camp

I remember when the rebellion started. There was someone called Abu Dorrah who was a porter in Haifa. When he saw how the Jews and the English oppressed Palestinians, he collected arms from the rich for 12 rebels ...

God bless our prophet Mohammad, let me get this right: there was one rebel leader called Al Asbah. The rebel does not stay in one place. He moves from one place to another. Al Asbah was from *Wadi Arous, Nabi Yushaa'*, which the English occupied. He attacked English soldiers and Jews. God bless our prophet, let me count them. There was Abu Jeldi and Al Asbah ... I can't remember the others. Then more and more people joined. Musa Zrayef was from our town and he had a vineyard next to our house. The English were observing him. One day when he was coming home, some elders were sitting outside after afternoon prayers and they shouted to him: 'Musa run!', and he ran. He was a tall man, *mashallah*![30] The English soldiers searched the house but they didn't find anything. They started vandalizing his food. They mixed all his grains together:[31] the bulgur and the rice and the wheat. Then they set fire to his vineyard before they left. The villagers replaced his food and rebuilt his vineyard ...

After that the rebellion was crushed because there were disputes between the rebels. The English caused these disputes. God bless our beloved Prophet Mohammad, let me see if I can remember: Ahmad Shukeiri had three brothers, one lawyer, one doctor, and one whose profession I don't know. The English got a fake identity card for this third brother in the name of Husseini, and told him to assassinate one of his own brothers. When he was caught, the Husseini family was very angry. This caused disputes between the Husseinis and the Shukeiris. And there was another family from Jerusalem ... God bless the Prophet, what was their name? The Nashashibi family. The English caused arguments between them and the Husseini family as well. They interfered in everything, those people.

What destroyed the rebellion was the internal conflict caused by the English. This is typical of them, this was not the first time they do it! We will never forget what they have done to us. It is the English who gave away our country to the Jews. It was our country! What's his name? May God have mercy on my soul … Balfour! When they left, they had accomplished their mission. They gave the Jews their tanks and their planes. You know what they gave us? All they gave the Arabs were rifles that didn't work … do you want to know about 1948? No? As you like my dear. Maybe next time. I remember more from 1948.

The rebels were young men who fought without being paid or even fed. When they wanted to eat, one or two rebels would go down to the villages. And they would gather food from the villagers: a few lentils, a little cooked food, bread. They just took whatever they were offered. They would spread their *abaya* [mantle/coat] on the floor and people would just leave food on it. They didn't take anything by force. They just said to the villagers: 'your brothers are hungry'. And they would take a few figs, olives, dates. Some bread. The rebels drank rainwater. Where rainwater collected in pools in the mountains, this is what they drank. When they got sleepy they wrapped their *abaya* around themselves and slept between rocks or in grottos when it rained. They didn't even have donkeys or horses or mules. All they had were their legs. Yes ma'am. They just focused on their mission. On the settlements and the checkpoints. Rebels didn't care about anything, they just wanted to get the enemy. That was their duty. Back then, when the rebels used to ambush Jews, they would distribute grain and bread to the people of Galilee afterwards … Not like our leadership today, who only ride in the finest cars and who only function with a salary!

Do you know what? I don't want to talk too much. I've been imprisoned by the Lebanese government 12 times already. I don't want this to be the thirteenth!

Anyway, in the days of the Black Hand Gang, if someone was a traitor, he got a warning. They sent him a written warning. That's how it was with the Black Hand Gang: you betray Palestine, you die. They would go to the spy's house and tell him: you repent or you die. They shot people down in public, like at the coffee house in Haifa. One of these traitors I really want to tell you about is Nayef Sobh. He was very unfair. During the time of the Ottomans he married two sisters at once. He was such a persecutor. In the north, he took our land. He said our land was his and he registered it in his name and the English gave it to him in court. And who did he sell it to but the Jews. Nayef Sobh got two written warnings but he didn't take any notice. So they killed him.

My cousin and my uncle were also rebels. My uncle is dead now but his friend is still alive. He's over 100 now. He was really something in the rebellion. But he's ruined now, he's a wreck, you should see him. What do you want to talk to him for? He doesn't know anything, he's a shell of a man. Wait, that's his voice. That's him outside. Would you like to say hello to him? He was a hero in those days. A true hero. Abu Musa! Come in Abu Musa, come and say hello to our guests! …

We never went to the English if anything went wrong. We knew what the English were doing. We knew they were traitors. You don't go for justice to a traitor, do you? Listen, we were living in the century of our lord Jesus Christ, whom we praise and pray for. We were farmers. And the farmer is never as happy as when he is harvesting. The English ruined us by forcing us to sell the land or lose everything. In the summer, they waited for the watermelon season and they would bring two shiploads of watermelon from outside and dump it on the Palestinian market and the peasant was ruined. Same with the wheat. In the wheat season, they brought one or two shiploads of wheat from outside and sold it so cheaply, the peasant couldn't sell anything. Our village was famous for its sesame, and its green beans, and its wheat and its corn. They brought a shipload of sesame in and we were ruined. These traders don't know the fear of God. So the traders got together and they fixed a single price for the sesame and they monopolized the market that way. No one dared go above that price. You sell or you keep your stuff with you! The English offered five piastres for a cow. Ok let's say ten piastres. Five piastres for a goat, five piastres for a sheep. Ten for a man. And you want me to like the English? They took my land away from me, they stripped it from me and they gave it to the Jews. May God bring them down. May God Bring America down. Say *inshallah*! [God willing].

What else do I remember from those days? Do you want to hear about Al Asbah? During the rebellion, there was Al Asbah, who had 15 men with him. He set up checkpoints. They ambushed Jews and English at night and then went back to hide in their grotto. Yes ma'am. This grotto was on a mountain. Then someone told the authorities about the grotto. They were surrounded for 15 days. Their water and food ran out. They were given an ultimatum to either surrender or die. One man after another came out shooting, and was shot dead. Rebels don't surrender. The last one to be martyred was Al Asbah, God have mercy on him. He was shot from above. This was in 1936. This is a battle amongst battles. Everyone knows about this. They didn't surrender. They died fighting. What's his name, Abu Dorrah, God have mercy on him, also carried out some amazing feats, killing settlers. Around Haifa and Jaffa. The rebel never had anything. They had to beg for each cartridge. You know, the guns we were carrying were completely useless. We might as well have been carrying sticks. We had to beg for ammunition. And these rifles we carried, the French and the English and the Ottoman, good for ten minutes' use ... ok, good for fifteen minutes. I know because I carried those arms. Those were the days. Not like the *Tanzimat*.[32] Those men are useless. Sorry my dear, you like the *Tanzimat* don't you? I can tell.

Ask me more. Ask. Ask. I've seen everything. I'm seventy-eight.

Fatmeh Haj Awad Salem, b. 1934. From Jaouni in Safad, currently living in Baddawi refugee camp

Jaouni was a big village. It was almost like a town, but it was considered a village.

My uncle was Al Asbah. That is not his real name, his real name was Salem. But they called him Al Asbah ... He was one of the leaders of the rebellion. He had a small army of followers, of soldiers. He trained them and taught them how to use firearms and together they fought the English. They also fought the Jews. They were against the Jews as well as the English. But they never attacked the Jews who were our neighbours because they might retaliate. So he never harmed them. He fought a battle in *Wadi Halawi*. A few were martyred in that battle, one of them being my brother-in-law, or rather my husband's cousin, so he was sort of like my brother-in-law. I mean I can now call him my brother-in-law in retrospect, because I wasn't married at the time he was killed, I was still a small girl. So in that battle they continued killing English soldiers until they drove them into the lake of Tiberias. The English soldiers who survived the battle threw themselves into the lake. The others were dead. Whenever he fought a battle he would immediately take refuge up on the mountain. He would leave his horse, which was a thoroughbred, safely in the village and then climb up the mountain to take cover from the soldiers. That is to say from the English. He also fought a battle at Morning Star. That was a Jewish settlement. At the end, after 4 or 5 years of driving the English crazy, at the end they got him in *Sa'sa'*. There they surrounded him and set fire to the fields all around him. He was trapped. He was shot down from a plane. The plane shot at him and blew off the side of his head. He was martyred. He was martyred and left exposed on the face of the earth unburied for 40 days. The people of *Sa'sa'* were too afraid to come anywhere near him or touch him in case their houses were blown up. Finally they let his relatives know that Abu Al Abed Al Asbah, may God's mercy touch his soul, had been martyred. My father and uncles went up to *Sa'sa'*. This was after 40 days. They found the martyr on the floor, blood still pouring from his head. They removed the *hatta* from around his shoulders and stuffed it in his head to stop the bleeding and they carried him and dug a grave for him and buried him in *Sa'sa'*. They didn't want to bury him in our village because they wanted to keep the whole thing quiet. May God have mercy on his soul and on the souls of all dead Muslims. The people of *Sa'sa* know about this. People stand witness to Al Asbah. They know him from *Deir* to *Sohmata* to *Shaeb* to *Safad* and in the entire region. They made up songs for him. Because he was incorruptible and a guerrilla until the end. ... During weddings and *Debkes*[33] they would sing for my uncle. I forget. I forget, I forget. I swear I'm forgetting everything.

...

My father is Haj Awad Hamad Salem. During the day he was an Imam and a teacher. At night he was a fighter. I remember my father as a fighter. I remember that at night he used to dig holes in the roads and place landmines in them. This was for the Jews. So when one of their cars or buses drove past they would blow up and they would die 5 or 10 at a time. People would wonder: 'What!? How!?' At night he trained people how to use firearms. We had a field in a nearby village and that's where he trained them, how to lay booby traps, how to kill, etc ... He used to get arms and dynamite from Syria which he hid in our field. He told his men where to place the grenades and landmines during the night. Come morning, whatever Jews or English were driving past would be blown up and torn into little pieces. Then the *Mukhtar* took issue with all this activity and with what my father was doing. And one day an English General came to the village to visit the *Mukhtar* and said to him: 'We are on the same side. The village must surrender its arms. Go and tell the young men to surrender their arms.' But my father had told the young men to never admit they had arms. He said: 'Never ever admit there are arms here, because we are going to need them one day soon. There's a war coming.' But the *Mukhtar*, I'm sure you know, had been co-opted by the foreigners. He was a traitor. You know how it was. My father stuck to his story. The English General insisted, he said: 'Tell the men to surrender the arms and we will slaughter a sheep and eat together'. My father refused. The English General put a gun to his head. My father said: 'We still don't have arms.' The English told my father: 'As you like. You leave us with no option but to take you away from your people. We will take you to Nazareth. We will pull out your fingernails and gouge out your eyes and in the end hang you.' Still my father kept quiet. I remember my father had two rifles: one English and one German. One was kept in the field and one was hidden in the wheel of a car that he kept in my uncle's house. The house was demolished by the English, because they knew he was a rebel leader and son of Salem and so they demolished his house. My father said: 'Next time they come for me or near my house, I am dying a martyr.' They told him they would take him in the Jeep, to torture and hang him. My father said 'Let's go, I'm ready.' They took him in the Jeep all the way to Tiberias. There he met a Christian called Albert. May God shower him with blessings if he is alive. Albert carried letters for people. When he saw my father he said to him: 'Peace be upon you, Sheikh! What are you doing here?' and my father told him he was on his way to be hung. The General told Albert that my father was a troublemaker and an agitator. Albert spoke with the General in English. Albert told the General (I am telling you this in Arabic but Albert spoke to the General in English): 'This man is like a priest. He is an upright person. Hang me in his place. This is a holy man.' The General let my father go because of what Albert had said to him. When my father came back everyone ran to our house to congratulate my mother, and they ululated from one end of the village to the other. My father was unremorseful. He carried on digging holes and planting landmines until we finally had to leave in 1948 ...

My father owed his reputation to that of my uncle, Al Asbah. We are known as rebels and revolutionaries. From Palestine. My father couldn't stand the Jews or the English and he tried to die a martyr but never succeeded. He understood the value of arms and of fighting. He told the *Mukhtar* that he was corrupt, and that he was cheap and that he was easy to bribe and that he sold his people for a kilo of tea, or coffee or sugar, and that he was a traitor. My father was a revolutionary and my family is a family of revolutionaries.

Don't switch off that tape recorder, girl, I have more to tell. More about us. My father's been dead 23 years. He wanted so much to die a martyr but he died the death of cowards in his bed. God have mercy on his soul. May you live. Everything I've told you is the truth. I grew up hearing these stories. I grew up with people talking about my father's and my uncle's accomplishments. Their names were always mentioned. I heard the songs women sang about Abdallah Al Asbah and Abu Al Abed. Wherever you went you heard their names and about what they did and the battles they fought. This is how I know. Even now people continue to talk about these events. What's left to do but talk and remember? May God unify us.

Said Hassan Me'ary, b. 1920. From Shaab, Acre, currently living in Nahr Al Bared refugee camp

Shaab is 15 km from Acre. Ask me anything you want. Anything. I'm ready to talk.

I was 16 when the strike began. I didn't go to school. We were peasants and we owned camels. I was with the camels and on the farm. That's what we did, farming. I did not officially participate in the activities of the rebels. But I did go to *Layyath* valley to ambush the English night patrols. There was someone called Farhat who ambushed a British patrol once with a hand grenade. He placed the grenade near a well and a patrol with a reinforced car drove past. The grenade blew up the reinforced car. He killed four English soldiers with one officer amongst them and injured three more. Farhat came to *Shaab*. Why he didn't stop at *Dammoun* I don't know. He kept going until he reached *Shaab*. He stopped at the first house in *Shaab*. The people of the house had no idea what he had done. He drank coffee there and left. The next day, I was checking on our fig trees up on the hill. It was the beginning of the fig season. I was checking for children near the trees or whatever. It was just before dusk. The trees were about 3 km from the village. From the hill I looked over to the town and there was a lot of dust. Between *Shaab* and Acre is a valley. Slowly I realized that there were tanks and soldiers approaching the village. It was prayer time. I came back to the village and told the people that the army was here. I was in mid-sentence when they started firing. There were at least 60 soldiers on horseback and six tanks. They started forcing people into the street, everybody, both men and women. It was about an hour and a quarter before sunset. There were about 200 men. They paired the men up two by two and filed them up in a line with one tank in front, one tank in the back and one in the middle, and soldiers on horseback surrounding them. The women returned home with the children. They walked the men to a valley called *Al Aayadiah* near Acre. I was there but one of the men told me I was too young to be there. It was sunset and the men were thirsty. They threw themselves on the well. There were two men standing on the hill. One of them shouted: 'I am so and so!' and he started shooting. The English soldiers didn't know what to do, they got confused. The men ran into the valley and disappeared. But someone called Hassan Haj Khatib was killed. Someone told me not to worry, that my father and uncle were safe. The following day Britain came back and surrounded the village. 1936. They demolished 190 houses in the village, one of the biggest villages in the Galilee. One man whose house they demolished started shooting at them. They were retreating anyway. A lot of the British soldiers died. Hundreds. Yes, hundreds. Why are you looking at me like that? After that a collaborator was shot in Acre. People in the cities used to wear the *tarbush* and those who used to assassinate collaborators were peasants, so they stood out. So the *tarbush* was banned in the cities so that the rebels could not be recognised. ... They put a *tarbush* on a donkey and said: 'only the donkey wears a *tarbush*, buy a *hatta*!'

The 1936 rebellion was harsh. It was a threat. Britain lost a lot in it. The leaders were very strong. ... From the north to the west bank, it was strong. ...

Said Hassan Said, b. 1920. From Fer' em in Safad, currently living in Nahr Al Bared refugee camp

I was a rebel and my father was a rebel. I was imprisoned in 1937. We had a farm called *Kherbet Al Muntar* where we used to farm in the winter and during the summer we returned to the village. One day I tried to go to *Ashabi*. I arrived at the gate and showed the officer the permit that I had taken from a 70-year-old man. I was 15. When the Englishman saw the permit, he took me to the police station straight away. When my parents heard what had happened they tried to visit me but the soldiers refused to let them see me. The English then took me to *Safad* and then they took me to Acre. The Jewish guard told the soldiers that the firearm was mine. I had a German firearm. They put me in a tank and threw me in Acre. They imprisoned me in Acre and put me in cell number 17 and we were around seven or eight young men. We were kids. One was called Farid, from Haifa. They said to me, 'what are you doing so far from *Safad*?' They asked us who was from Safad and everyone kept quiet because I wasn't from *Safad*. I'm from *Fere'em*. They took the young men who were from *Safad* ...

I went to see the English officer in the interview room. He was Grant, the one who was shot in the knee and his leg was stiff as a stick. He told me that when I am questioned, just to answer 'yes, sir' to the officer so I just said 'yes, sir' to everything. They asked me if I could read and write and I said 'yes, sir'. They told me to stay in the watch room on the lower ground with writers and employees and that at night I could sleep in the prison. I spent six months there before I went to trial and they sentenced me to one year. It was a military court. They sent my papers to Jerusalem and realized I was only 13 years old and that they couldn't sentence me because I was a minor so they set me free ...

Mahmoud Abou Deeb, b. 1924. From Saffourieh in Nazareth, currently living in Nahr Al Bared refugee camp

When the rebellion started, young men used to go to the hills and ambush the Jews and the English. The rebellion was in the hills. See these mountains in front of you? Yes, hills like those. That's where the rebels used to be. Day and night, in the hills. The English and Jews who came to the hills paid for it. The rebels beat the hell out of them. They eliminated a lot of people. The rebels sometimes kept one person alive so he could go and tell his people to come and collect the bodies. So his people would send in tanks, or do whatever they needed to do. We did what we had to do and they did what they had to do. The English had an interest in all this you know. The rebellion continued despite their harshness. They stepped all over us until we couldn't take any more. This went on until the rebellion was smashed. How do you think it was smashed? Well, the English warned the villages that they would destroy every village and every town that shot at an English soldier. For instance in our village, two officers came and spoke with Saleh Salim, one of our leaders. They said: 'Listen Mr Saleh, Britain is about to go to war with Germany. We don't want you annoying us as well. If one single shot is fired from this village, the whole village goes down.' Every young man in Palestine was told this. Every young man was warned not to carry a gun. Not to fire a single shot. The English were so strong. There was no one as strong as the English. We thought they were just like any other country but we were wrong! The English also warned the Bureau[34] in Damascus not to send any more arms into Palestine. The Bureau closed and the rebellion fell apart. Now, after they smashed the rebellion we became useless. We had to use aubergines instead of guns. Yes we pulled aubergines on people to scare them at night. It didn't work.

Miss, please have some coffee. No? some tea? No? What's the matter with you? Hot water?! No I can't offer you hot water. Please don't behave like a guest. This is your home. Well I can't drink coffee if you're not drinking. You've been drinking coffee all day but you refuse to drink it here?

Now then, where were we?

Listen to me now girl, let me continue with the story. Let me end the story for you.

There was this guy called Abu Dorrah and he was 90 cm tall. Plus 10 cm from me. Yes I'm saying I can spare 10 cm. So let's say he was 1 m tall. And his chest was 25 cm. He was from *Qebleh*. He became popular when he started to enforce justice on the street. He was against lynching and robberies. He was just. But people said he was tyrannical because the English considered him so. The English turned justice into injustice and injustice into justice. Listen to me, they turned us into terrorists. According to them, aren't we terrorists? You know this as well as I do. Abu Dorrah used to deal with people who broke the law. He would arrest the criminal and ask him: 'Who is your *Mukhtar*?' and punish them instantly. This is what the short guy did. Then his men would bring the *Mukhtar* to the short guy to be punished, dragging him before the short guy like a woman. Because it is the responsibility of the *Mukhtar* to prevent crime and to preserve order in the towns. Within a month, Abu Dorrah dealt with all the *Mukhtars*. More than 15 in one month. Maybe more. How should I know? This is what I heard at the time.

Oh those days were full of fear. We sat in fear, walked in fear, ate in fear, slept in fear. We were scared even as we laughed. Can you imagine laughing and feeling scared at the same time? ...

Listen, do you want to hear some poems for my country? What do you mean who wrote them? Of course I wrote them. What's left for me to do but sit and write poems? My heart is scorched. My heart is on fire for Palestine, don't you know? I want to recite you my poems but I don't want you to think I'm a senile old man. I still have my dignity!

Ok now listen to my poems, listen to my voice ...

Fatmeh Farida Al Ali, b. 1930. From Acre, currently living in Baddawi refugee camp

(Fatmeh was too young to remember the Rebellion. I include her testimony anyway.)

We are the *Ghawarneh*[35] of Acre. We had lands and we used to plant beans and wheat and lentils and blackberries and figs and peas and grapes and everything. We didn't want for anything, we were farmers. My father had lands. We had so much wheat. Yes. But you know how the story goes, what happened happened. We had to leave after the massacres of Haifa. We came to Acre. We couldn't stay. The whole village left and came down to Acre. Now we're living in a refugee camp. You know the story ...

My father was a farmer. We worked our fields. We were farmers. My father was a farmer, he just planted and harvested, planted and harvested. I didn't think about life when I was younger, all I knew was that we were farmers. When I played with other girls we would get some onions and some dandelion and we would pretend to fry them and we ate them with bread. We were farmers. Look, we planted beans and stored them, we planted peas and stored them, we ploughed and planted, ploughed and planted, ploughed and planted. I went to the fields when I was eight or nine. I would collect apples, and beans, and okra and aubergines, and I worked in the fields until I was 15. When I was old enough I went to Haifa to sell what we harvested. God forgive you and may He forgive your parents! You're asking me about things that happened more than 60 or 70 years ago. Look, all I remember is that we planted and harvested, planted and harvested, and stored our food. We stored berries, and grapes and aubergines, and tomatoes, and *mulukhieh*,[36] and okra. This is what we were about ...

Some young women worked as seamstresses but you know, we were mainly farmers. We didn't do anything else. The young men in the village were also farmers. I come from a big village, sort of a small town. We were all farmers. People kept cows and sheep and goats and chickens. But when the English army installed a camp in our village, the men started to work for them. It was nasty work. But what could they do? They worked anyway. We took the car and went to the markets there to sell our stuff. When we were in Haifa or in

Acre, we would buy sugar and olives and rice and oil and so on. There were about 20 or 30 shops there! …

I lived next to a Jewish village. Our Jewish neighbours had nothing to do with the war. The English left them all their ammunition and materials. But our neighbours were peaceful, the aggressors were outsiders. They were just like us. Those Jews spoke Arabic just like us. We worked the fields side by side with them. They came to us to buy chickens, eggs, everything. We used to go to them too and buy things from them. There was no fear then. No politics. No nothing. Who knows why things happened the way they did?

God is great …

Of course I tell my grandchildren everything that happened to us. I tell them everything we used to plant on our land: figs, apples, melons, potatoes. We planted everything! Some people tell me that our land is a big field now and that our houses have been destroyed.

Omar Ziad Shehadi, b. 1922. From Safad, currently living in the village of Barr Elias in Lebanon

The *Mukhtar* and the *Imam* of the town were my uncles. We were farmers. We used to plant wheat and olives. I used to feed the cows. That was my job. When I was old enough I helped out in the fields. My father was a farmer.

When I turned 13, the rebellion started. So I carried a rifle and went to the rebellion. I thought it would be better than farming. I told my father I was ready to die. I was with Al Asbah, Abu Sultan, and Abu Atwi Al Moghrabi. We were together for six years and we forbade the Jews from the land. Don't you know about that? We didn't let the Jews near the land. We stopped them from working the land. My father didn't want me to join the rebellion. So I ran away and he came to look for me. We had courts you know. These courts tried the criminal and the collaborator. There were many rebels from *Zeitoun* and from *Sofasaf*. There were many rebels. I witnessed many battles. I was the youngest and the older rebels looked after me and kept me by their side. We used to sleep outdoors. We weren't allowed to go home. We wore rebel outfits in the hills and when we went into town we wore civilian clothes. We had to wait to reach a village before we could bathe and wash our clothes. Our khakis.[37] This was about once a week. We left our rifles and guns behind olive trees until we picked them up again on our way back into the hills. We didn't tell people in the towns that we were rebels because we were wanted by the government. That's how it was.

I was at the battle at *Mallaha* in *Wadi Arouss* and we ambushed an English troop killing four soldiers and one commander. We took off the soldiers' decorations and stitched them to our outfits. We sent them to Abdallah Al Shaer from *Safad* who was one of the rebels.

We lost one of the rebels in that battle. His name was Sheikh Ahmad. We took him to his hometown, we carried him home. But of course his family didn't tell anyone how he was killed. They just said he had been killed by mistake by his own people. They didn't tell anyone he fell in battle. That would have caused trouble.

So we sent the English soldiers' decorations to Abdallah Al Shaer from *Safad*. We sent them to him because he was a big *qabaday*.[38] He was tall and powerful. The girls embroidered the decorations on his outfit and he wore the decorations on his shoulders. After that, we fled to the hills and slept in the wild and in caves like in *Sa'sa'*. You know, this battle at *Mallahah* drove the English mad. They just couldn't figure out how we did it, and where we disappeared to. We were everywhere and nowhere. We always found a source of water, and somewhere to sleep. When we wanted to come to a village, we would send news to the *Mukhtar* that we were coming. The *Mukhtar* would prepare us dinner. That's how it was.

And Abdallah Al Shaer walked around with his English decorations. Of course, what do you think? Right on his shoulders. Whenever he conducted a trial, he wore the English decorations. If two people quarrelled, they would complain to one of the leaders of the rebellion, like Abu Atef, or Mahmoud Osman Abu Sultan from *Ber'em* in *Safad*. Then there would be a trial. There were no English courts at that time. The rebels didn't intervene in people's business, people went to them themselves. If someone was accused he would be taken to the hills and beaten until he confessed. If you didn't confess, you would get killed. It was justice you know. Not like English persecution. It was proper, immediate justice. There was no waiting around and postponing. If someone was a traitor, he was shot or thrown into a well. Bye Bye. Done. What's worse than being a traitor? What's worse than betrayal? The rebellion was just. The rebels brought justice. It brought us dignity. We made the Jews afraid. They couldn't work their land, or even switch their lights on at night or go about at night. This rebellion drove the English mad. This was a dark period for them. That's the rebellion for you. It was really something. I wish it had gone on.

Ali Said Louhayek, d.o.b. unknown. From Ma'athar in Tiberias, currently living in the village of Barr Elias in Lebanon

You want to hear about the strike. Very well. I'm ready. The strike started in 1936, and it went on. Not for one month or two, but for six months. It started in the cities and we were in the villages. It didn't affect us in the villages too much because things were banned from the cities. But you know, we were farmers ... we had everything we needed, we didn't depend on shops for our things. And the rebellion happened. Leaders started to get rebels together to attack the settlements and ambush the English. They joined forces. So each region had its leadership. There were leaders in Tiberias, Nazareth, *Safad*, Nablus. The rebellion continued and then it ended. There you go.

In *Ma'athar* we had a leadership. In the region called *Shafa*, which included four or five villages, we made our own leadership. One of our boys was called Mohammad Ibn Issa. He was a leader and he had with him some people from *Kufr Subt* and from *Ma'athar* and from *Olam*. A mixture. Plus a few Arabs.[39] He was responsible for that region and those villages. At the beginning we had another leader. He was a famous leader. His name was Sheikh Nayef. Sheikh Nayef was from *Ndour*, from around *Ndour*. From *Zaabiyyeh* and the villages around *Zaabiyyeh*. He was an important leader and he had many followers. And he went from village to village until he came to ours. He came to our village and he stayed overnight because it was late, so we hosted him in the village. Eventually we separated and we formed our own leadership. And so it was ...

At the beginning of the strike, even though we weren't really affected, we refused to go to the cities. We didn't come, we didn't go, we just stayed put. We supported the strike that way. Also, there were settlements all around us. So if we heard gunfire at night we knew rebels had gone to the settlements. So whichever one of our young men had a firearm would pick it up and go and join in and take part in the operation. Then each one returned to his own house. That's it. That's how we supported the rebellion ...

Every leadership had its own court. So in the south there was this Sheikh Nayef. He was the rebel leader in that region, and he formed tribunals and tried criminals. In the north we had Hayat Abu Atef and Al Asbah, leaders from *Safad*. Big leaders. They would arrest someone if he'd killed or whatever, and bring him before a tribunal and try him. Then there was someone who never came to our region but who I heard about. He was a solitary judge who worked on his own. They called him Sheikh Yehya and they put him in *Lubya*, around there, in the region of *Lubya*. This one would put people on trial and then send them to the rebellion leadership. Witnesses would swear: 'We saw so and so talking with the Jews. We saw so and so going to the Jews.' This was in our region. They didn't condemn anyone without witnesses. Not like Abu Dorrah up around Mount Nablus. This Abu Dorrah judged people according to his own mood. He was known as the *Mukhtar* killer. He specialized in *Mukhtars* because he considered them spies for the English. He killed lots of them. Anyway they kept their cave-prisons secret. They had to keep moving from one place to another in case the English discovered where they were imprisoning people. Otherwise they will come with their planes. Immediately. This one I was telling you about, Ibn Issa, the leader from our region, news got out that tonight he was sleeping in *Olam*. There were spies. They told the English. Two planes arrived the next dawn. The army came at night and surrounded the village and the two planes circling the village. There were fields just below the village and Ibn Issa, poor thing, and his men fled into those fields. The planes lit up the fields and they started to attack the men with machine guns. They killed him. They got Ibn Issa and one of his companions and they wounded a third. The army brought him. Whenever the English put a village under siege, they would call out all the people into the squares and gather them. Not together. They separated the men from the women. They brought him before everybody and they told the villagers 'Take a good look at your leader, we've killed him.' And they left. God have mercy on his soul. Then the one who told on him, he was discovered. Discovered. In Tiberias, in the town of Tiberias, we had the Black Hand Gang. The Black Hand Gang of Palestine, followers of Sheikh Izz Al Din Al Qassam. There were some of them in Haifa and in Tiberias. They discovered him and as he walked in the street they killed him. Yes they did …

Now then, if they were going to try someone, the rebels would just come and take him. They would take him to the leadership. Wherever the leadership was, they would take him. The leadership moved around in secret. No one knew where they were, because they moved from one village to another, from one mountain to another, from a field to a cave to another field. It was secret. The English were on their heels, and everywhere and in every village looking for rebels. My village was under siege twice. They loved to pull us out of our houses and drag us out onto the squares. One day the English army came to our village because they heard the rebels were on their way there. The army went into the olive groves at sunset and waited. Now in our village, there were these two: one young man who was a little vain, and another one who was a notable who had a *madhafa*.[40] He told him: 'I need to clean my rifles.' So he replied 'Go and get them.' He brought his gun and the house owner's gun and accidentally fired a shot. Now the army was sitting waiting in the groves. When they heard the shot, they thought the rebels were there. They threw themselves at the village and surrounded it. The doors of the *madhafas* are always open. So they went from one *madhafa* to the other shouting at people: '*yalla, yalla, yalla!*[41] come on, come on, come on!'[42] until they reached the *madhafa* with the rifles in it. There the doors were closed. It was a little rainy and cold. They had brought food and they were eating. And the rifles, the two guns, were against the wall and they were sitting down having their dinner. The English looked and saw the rifles and surrounded the *madhafa* properly. One of them pushed the door. Inside they noticed that the door had moved and the young man tugged at the door. When it didn't open, he tugged harder and the English man pulled a gun and said 'Nobody moves.' They seized the rifles and gathered the people there. One of them was my grandfather, who was at his *madhafa* and had guests with him. I was at my neighbours' *madhafa* and when I heard the English were there I ran home. But thank God I found my father there. I told him 'They're here.' He hadn't left the house and poor thing he had crashed out. My father was a *Mukhtar* in those days. The English came and arrested my grandfather. They told him '*Yalla* come on.' He followed them to the *madhafa* with the guns in it. The English heard screaming inside. They said to my grandfather 'Wait here' and left him and they went into the *madhafa*. My grandfather stood and stared at the groves and fields and at the valley and he thought to himself 'Where do these English think they're taking me? By God I'm not going, let me escape ...' and he ran past the groves and fields and dived into the valley. And he walked through the night until he reached *Tireh*. This was a village near us. It's the same distance as between here and just before Sidon. He reached his friend's house and knocked on the door. His friend was a rebel leader and he was startled and he thought to himself 'Who is knocking on my door at this time of night?' and he shouted 'Who's there!' and my grandfather said '*Haj*[43] Sharif,' and his friend thought 'No it can't be! How can it be *Haj* Sharif? How can the *Haj* come at this time, and on foot? He can't come on foot, he has horses and children.' And my grandfather swore he was who he said he was and his friend opened the door and shouted '*Ya Sultan Ya Haj*!'[44] and my grandfather said this is what happened, this is my story. Meantime, that night the English took the men they arrested – '*yalla* come on come on' – to the settlement of *Nazha* at *Kfar Tabur* close by. And on the way they came across one young man, the poor thing, from our region, who used to work at the convent and he had joined the rebellion and he had bought a gun. He wanted to walk with the rebels. He heard the English were around and he came out of his house – instead of staying put in his house, which was hidden from the road and where he would have been safe, he came out to the main road. He saw the English and threw the gun down and threw his jacket over it to hide it. The English commander saw him and pulled a gun on him and arrested him. There was another *Mukhtar* in our village. He was very mean. The Englishman asked him who the man was and the *Mukhtar* said 'I don't know him', instead of telling him the truth. The English commander took this young man to the settlement and he took him behind a tree and shot him dead and left him. Yes. The next day, the people went to look for their relatives. My uncles went to try and find my grandfather. They couldn't find him. They went to a prison called (inaudible). It was a military prison. He wasn't there. He wasn't home. By sunset they heard he was in *Tireh*. But he became very afraid. After that, every time he heard the word 'English', he would take his horse and jump on it and split.

And Nazareth was a revolutionary town. And the Fahoum family were a big part of the rebellion.[45] And the rebellion was Christian and Muslim.

Notes

1 Guha (1983: 259).
2 Oral interviews conducted in Baddawi, Nahr Al Bared, Rashidiyye and Shabriha Palestinian refugee camps in Lebanon, over a six-month period, between January and June 2004.
3 I felt free to do this thanks to Vincent Crapanzano's *Tuhami: portrait of a Moroccan* (1985).
4 The reasons for this are excluded from the scope of this analysis.
5 Stein links the economic plight of peasants from the central range (between Jenin, Tulkarem and Nablus, the so-called 'Triangle of Terror' although arguably from

the point of view of the inhabitants of that triangle, it was they who were terrorized), to the fact that they participated most intensively in the rebellion.

6 For an overview of the failures of the Landless Arabs Inquiry, see K.W. Stein (1985: 150–63).

7 According to W.P.N. Tyler (2001: 105), 1934–35 yielded a surplus of over 2.2 million, the administration's 'largest ever budgetary surplus'. K.W. Stein (1985: 146) provides the figure of 4 .7 million in 1935.

8 See Porath (1977: 137–39) for an account of Qassam's involvement with Palestinian urban notable politics.

9 Qassam apparently approached the Grand Mufti and suggested that they launch a coordinated revolt against the British administration, with Qassam leading the north and the Mufti leading the south. The Mufti refused (see Nimr 1990: 73–74).

10 The AHC was brought together when the High Commissioner decided to consult prominent leaders regarding the creation of a Legislative Council in the summer of 1935. After the strike began, the Committee diverted its attention from the Legislative Council to the strike. (CO 733/317/1, HC to SSC, 28 Nov. 1936)

11 For an account of the role of Qassam's followers in the rebellion, and for a breakdown of the positions they occupied within the rebel bands, see Lachman (1982: 78–86).

12 For instance:

> Proved offenders punishable under Emergency Regulations are then transferred as soon as possible to permanent concentration camps, while those against whom no charge is proven are normally released. In some cases they may be held temporarily for further periods for work on roads, etc. for security reasons. (WO 32/4652, G OC Haining, 'Hostile Propaganda in Palestine, its Origins and Progress in 1938')

13 The rare accounts of the rebellion based on oral sources break the mould. See Swedenburg (1995) and Nimr (op. cit.) for example.

14 By the end of the Rebellion, almost as many Arabs were killed by Arabs (494) as were killed by Jews (547).

15 According to Ylana Miller, Palestinian villages at the time of the Mandate were divided into one or two *Hamulas*, which were each led by one elder. Individuals were protected according to this clan structure, in return for complete loyalty to one's extended family. The *Hamula* system of control emphasized collective responsibility and also granted considerable autonomy to individual communities (see Miller 1980: 128, 144).

16 The office of *Mukhtar* was established by the Ottoman Vilayets Law, 1864. The *Mukhtar* was a sort of lowly government official with administrative functions. For a discussion of this post, see Baer (1978).

17 Swedenburg (op. cit. 119) provides an oral account of the pressure placed on *Mukhtars* during the British Mandate to collaborate with the authorities. British search parties used *Mukhtars* to accompany them around villages and identify wanted men, deepening or creating divisions within communities.

18 'The collection of intelligence was unsatisfactory during the strike.' (Summary of the Report of Palestine Royal Commission, Series of League of Nations Publications, VI.A Mandates) Also, even though rewards totalling £26,000 were offered by police in 1937 in exchange for valuable information, the money remained unclaimed.

19 For a detailed account of Kawakji's attempts at organizing the rebellion, see Arnon-Ohanna (1981: 234–36).

20 For an account of the martial law debate, see Bowden (1975: 163–65).

21 An Inter-Departmental Conference in October 1937 decided that it was more important to 'restore the prestige of the Civil Government' in Palestine. (WO 32/ 9618: 'Palestine Disturbances 1936–38 Martial Law Policy')

22 The NCs called on the Palestinian population to boycott the British courts after the conference of NCs in May 1936. Disputes were to be adjudicated by the regional commander (see Nimr 1990: 167).

23 Short for 'oozlebaht', which is slang for bandit /rebel.

24 This word is taken from a notice, which read: 'Ask the remnants of IRTAH – the last village abolished; there you find the last witness against the Englishism. A poor innocent father with his two children were killed inside their peaceful house.' This notice was signed 'The Arab Revolutionary Council, Southern Syria', and was one of many similar posted on buildings across Palestine (see CO 733/372/4, 'Rebel Propaganda', 16 Nov. 1938).

25 The *tarbush* was also associated with the pro-British /collaborationist faction of Palestinian politics.

26 Two more references to the Rebel courts were found in the official records (see CO 733/398/2).

27 '[F]or Palestinians to have their own memory of life before 1948 ... and of life prevailing throughout the hardships of half a century in exile, for them to remember and preserve all this while living clumped in refugee camps or scattered across the world's metropoles is to hold a fantasy of no little activist value'. (Scheid 1998: 3)

28 'Ein Al Helwe' refugee camp in Lebanon is surrounded by barbed wire.

29 Anonymous said 'come on' in English.

30 'Praises to God', or 'God bless him'. Used when praising someone to protect them from envy/the evil eye.

31 Thus making the grains unusable.

32 Palestinian guerrilla organizations in the refugee camps of Lebanon.

33 Traditional Palestinian folk dance.

34 Rebel headquarters, established in Damascus by the exiled élite political leaders.

35 *Arab Al Ghawarneh* are a group of sedentarized, previously semi-nomadic families whose livelihood had consisted of raising buffalo, producing and selling dairy products, chopping and selling wood and weaving baskets and mats out of marsh reeds. See Forman and Kedar (2003) for more detail.

36 Stringy green vegetable: Jew's mallow.

37 Shehadi said 'khakis' in English.

38 Word of Turkish origin, meaning 'strong man'.

39 'Arabs' are Bedouins. This is how they are distinguished from farmers and townspeople, who are considered of mixed lineage.

40 A room for receiving guests – a guest house, or guest hall.

41 'Come on!' or 'let's go!'

42 Louhayek said 'come on' in English.

43 'Pilgrim' – someone who has completed his pilgrimage to Mecca. Sometimes older people acquire the title without having gone on pilgrimage, as a sign of respect.

44 Approximately{:} 'Oh respected *Haj*!'

45 I.e. Nazareth is a mainly Christian town and the Fahoum family is Christian.

so dressed in his Grand Mufti robes, presiding over the sonorously named SMC. The masses would not suspect a thing. Since then, historians have focused on the extent of the Mufti's involvement in the violence and on his culpability. Had he been speaking with a forked tongue, whipping up his congregation against the settlers and the colonialists, whilst making appeasing statements to his masters? Historians have been preoccupied with whether the Mufti turned a religious situation into a political one in order to further his own ambitions. Was he at least guilty of 'negativism' (Taggar op. cit.: 64) if not quite belligerence? Did the Mufti's Arab nationalism really integrate 'anti-Semitism'? (ibid.: 81) Who was the Mufti *really* loyal to? What political strategies did he deploy during this critical period? What *could* he have done? What *did* he do? What were the religious undertones to his political leadership – i.e. were there more signs of moderation or of zealotry? The question which pre-occupied the Mandatory, and which continues to preoccupy historians, is this: even if the Mufti and/or the rest of the urban politicians had not directly incited the masses to violence, why did they so spectacularly fail to control them?

How drastic would it be to suggest that this question is inappropriate? That this legendary folk hero, for whom Palestinians still sing songs, this figure hated by the Zionists for his perceived violence on Jews, this diplomat who charmed many a senior official in the administration, was basically a creature of the Mandatory's, something they put together in their laboratory? Is there anything to be gained from suggesting that even though Husseini was a man in flesh and blood, the Grand Mufti on the other hand, did not really exist at all, beyond the type-casting and mystique? That his power, as well as that of the whole of the élite class, was figurative and that his role and influence, as well as that of the whole élite class, was predetermined and had little to do with personality, talent or political strategizing? The Mufti's relationship with the Mandatory authorities and his strange political career reflect the Mandatory's attitude to the rest of the élite/aristocratic social class. Within the context of the British imperial story, that of the Grand Mufti is banal. It is a particularly familiar fixture in the archive of Orientalist knowledge. Here, again and again, we witness: 'the centrality assigned to religious orders, the charge of manip-ulation by élite groups of "leading native inhabitants"'. (Pandey 1989: 150). The Mandatory can barely help themselves: they are led by their own com-pulsive thoughts in this regard, by an obsessive pursuit of the ethnic and the religious, by an urge to reduce, essentialize, domesticate, twist, freeze and institutionalize aspects of native culture for their own specific purposes. The results are ready-made fantasies paraded as observation and description, lies deployed as moral high ground. These lies are more disconcerting for their gen-erality and un-specificity: which colonial official is speaking and which native is he describing when he evokes: '"Fanatical and clannish" entities, "disorderly sections of the population", communities "prone to dacoity and rioting", "fires of religious animosity", "indiscriminate affrays"'? (ibid.: 167–68) In this case, it is India, but how might we have guessed? Natives – any natives, anywhere – are prone to communal/religious strife. This is the picture that the colonialist – any colonialist, anywhere – focuses on in his frame of mind. When the colonialist is unlucky enough to witness the natives' convulsive collisions (with each other, or between them and the colonial authorities and/or settlers), he attributes this to their perceived pre-existing internal politics and blood feuds and resistance to progress and genetic programming. It is inconceivable (but why is it?) that the colonialist might attribute communal jitters and volatility to the new military order, the new power relationships, the new economic programme, the super-imposition of a new *language* on the very being of each native.

For these reasons, it is unrealistic, imprecise and even insincere, to talk about a Palestinian National Movement, Palestinian political organization, or even to discuss the merits of individual Palestinian politicians. Similarly, it is imprecise to conclude that this alleged National Movement failed in anyway: it was stillborn. There was no institutional cachet to being a Palestinian politician under the British Mandate. The Palestinian élite were captives. They were locked up, locked out, and locked down. They were the suave inmates of the dungeon, they had the ear of the screws and all we can sincerely do is observe how they behaved under those conditions of captivity. We can observe how each tried to adapt to his new environment. We note, somewhat disappointedly, that they never produced a united, exciting and integrated oppositional dis-course to that of the Mandatory. We note that whereas the peasant had screamed his attachment to the Motherland in Arabic, the élite nagged their masters in stilted English for a Government. We know that they know that the Mandatory's plastic smile dissimulated a wicked intention, even as they were showered with flattery and accorded some 'prestige'. We feel sorry for them.

First, who was the local élite as they lived and flourished in the early twentieth century and what did the government think of them?

All the king's horses

Who was the élite?

Élite politicians during the Mandate belonged to a particular socio-economic group, one which emerged seamlessly from the Ottoman period, when social and political offices were hereditary (see Nashif 1977). This most influential status group relied on wealth, property, landownership, reputation and mar-riage into powerful families – as well as on political association with the imperial centre, to maintain their position. At the tip of the socio-economic pyramid were the heads of large clans, members of the landowning aris-tocracy, wealthy traders and some professionals. (ibid.: 114)[6] They lived in the urban areas as absentee landlords, professionals or merchants. (ibid.: 114–15) Beneath them was an urban middle group made up of shopkeepers, teachers, government clerks, professionals and religious functionaries.

The urban élite began to replace the rural élite as holders of power with the Ottoman reforms known as *tanzimat*. These were centralizing reforms which gradually concentrated landholdings in the hands of the prominent urban families. The *tanzimat* instituted a more direct relationship between government and citizen, and curbed the notables' power as traditional mediators between the government and the rest of the population. Nonetheless the notable families were able to turn them to their advantage, huddling up to the imperial centre by sending their sons to professional Ottoman schools in preparation for military and civil service.[7] This development also stimulated competition amongst urban families, as they vied for positions on municipalities, provincial councils, and other administrative centres of power. The urban notables formed coalitions that spread from the towns and cities into the rural areas, and the rise to power of landowners and senior bureaucrats educated in the Ottoman government schools occurred at the expense of individual village leaders.

We know that a 'politics of notables'[8] operated in Palestine during the latter days of Ottoman rule. It was a practical matter. It assisted the Ottoman governors (strangers to their areas who may not have spoken Arabic, and whose military power was negligible) deployed to enforce the *tanzimat*. The notables had social functions: the local population needed them when new administrative measures relating to conscription and taxes were introduced and they acted as spokesmen for the rest of the population with access to central government. These factors guaranteed the power and influence of the intermediary notables, as long as they supported the status quo. (Mattar op. cit.: 3) The way of the notables was conspicuous in Jerusalem and other holy cities, where the prestige of the Ottoman Empire staked its hold as overlord of the Muslim world.

The old Muslim aristocracy were involved in running schools, municipalities and religious institutions. The Khalidi, Jarallah and Alami families of Jerusalem were influential in the eighteenth century. The Husseini family rose to prominence in the late nineteenth century. They were present in the Ottoman administration as delegates to the Parliament and as District Governors. They also occupied all the mayoral and Mufti positions. At this time, when the urban Muslim families held more sway than the rural clans, Christian merchants and professionals also began to yield more influence. The Muslim Jerusalemite Nashashibi family started to accumulate landholdings/influence at the turn of the twentieth century. The Dajani family was known for its intellectuals and scholars. In Nablus, there were the Toukans and the Abd Al Hadis. In Gaza, the Shawwas and the Husseinis (not related to the Jerusalem Husseinis) dominated the socio-political landscape. In Acre, it was the Shukayris. (Mosely Lesch 1979: 25–26; see also Muslih 1988: 25–31)

The arrival of the British did not immediately bode ill for these families. Their social status was not under threat. The British found them pleasantly pliant. They stayed cool: there was no need for undue anxiety simply because an Ottoman master was replaced by a British one. British colonialism was distinguished in the early days from Zionism. The élite reasoned: we will continue to run local affairs, and over there, far away, is the imperial centre.

How was the élite viewed?

It is often said that one of the main reasons Arab political leadership during the Mandate failed to achieve an operational level of ideological unity was due to the prominence of personal/clan interests within local politics (see Nashif op. cit.: 120).[9] 'Tension' between 'rival' clans was perceived and presented by the Mandatory as the most distinctive feature of Palestinian society. This 'tension', is safely allocated to a pre-Mandatory era, to a tradition outside of British rule. In fact, it is a feature of Palestinian society that is screaming out for British rule, for a rational rule, which is the opposite of base passions. This assumption was prevalent amongst colonial administrators themselves.[10] It is true that there was a cleavage within Palestinian politics, which became a fixed feature of political life during the Mandate, and it was most rudimentarily expressed in the divide between the Husseini and the Nashashibi families. The rivalry between the two families may well have pre-dated the British occupancy of Palestine. Nonetheless, it is generally said/accepted (but who really knows?) that the removal of Musa Kazem Pasha[11] Husseini from the Jerusalem mayoralty in 1920 for his role in the riots of that year, and his replacement with Ragheb Bey[12] Nashashibi rejuvenated the latent hostility between their two powerful clans. The perceived mysterious roots of ancient, primordial, local rivalries, far from falling outside British concerns and interests, were instead deemed worthy of high-level discussions even in the late 1930s, some twenty years into British rule. H.C. Wauchope's conversation with a Mrs. Alice Brooks, described as 'an Englishwoman who claims to be on intimate terms with all the Arab leaders – an Arab sympathiser', is fascinating:

> Apparently the Nashashibis sprang originally from the Husseini family – I think she said four generations back. But whereas the Husseinis are the senior branch, the Nashashibi family are the descendants of a slave woman. Their original name was El-Husni (meaning 'son of the slave'), and they adopted that of Nashashibi from an Egyptian notable who came to live in Palestine during the middle of the last century and died without issue. From these origins spring the perpetual inferiority complex of the Nashashibis and their desire to assert themselves at any cost, even at the expense of the Arab movement as a whole, against the hated Husseini. (CO 733/409/17)

What is the quality of this piece of information/gossip? Does it not reveal something about Brooks and Wauchope and their own state of mind? Where did Alice Brooks obtain her information? Is it amateur psychoanalysis? What use could such information/gossip/psychoanalysis be to Wauchope? How did it feed into stereotypes about the local population and culture? Wauchope, whose own inclination for gossip and intrigue was well known, nonetheless felt he could remark that '[a]ll Arabs, unless they are kept busy, will intrigue'. (CO 733/215/13, HC to SSC, 22 Dec. 1932) Yet it is said of Wauchope that he relied entirely on forging personal relationships with illustrious Arabs and Jews, preferring to consult 'privately with a few individuals' and then making up his own mind, rather than bringing them together for talks, which would be futile. (CO 733/215/2, Despatch, 13 Feb. 1932) Wauchope believed that the right combination of friendliness and pressure, a coercive bonhomie applied to a few influential gentlemen, could diffuse political tension and achieve nation-wide results.[13] So it was that as much as he may have berated the Arab tendency to 'intrigue', it either rubbed off on Wauchope or suited his personality. Harold Price, former head of the CID Palestine Police 1932–37, wrote in his memoirs: 'Arthur Wauchope played off one source of information on the others. I did not consider this at all funny, nor particularly clever, however "Oriental" he found it.' (Palestine Police Old Comrades Association Collection (PPOCAC) Price, Papers: 3)

In any event, it was convenient for the government (and subsequent historians) to divide Palestinian political allegiances according to the two dominant urban families. The Husseini vs Nashashibi rivalry in Palestine Mandate histories is convenient because it fits in with the paradigm of the resistance vs collaboration model that usually develops in a colonial situation. Nationalism became identified with the Husseini family and cooperation/collaboration with the Nashashibi family. Yet although certain families may have become associated with one camp or another, political alliances were far from determined by blood. So for instance, the Abd Al Hadi family included Awni, the Pan-Arabist leader of the Istiqlal party, as well as Ruhi, who was allied with the Opposition. Amongst the Dajanis, Sheikh Mahmud was a supporter of the Haj Amin Husseini, and was therefore at loggerheads with his brother Hassan, a member of the Opposition. (CO 733/248/22, 'Arab Who's Who') Within the Khalidi family, some were part of the Opposition, whilst others either chose to remain independent, or associated with the Mufti.[14] Also, the Mussa Kazem Husseini/ Ragheb Nashashibi alliance struck during secret discussions for a Legislative Council in 1929 does not fit in with the unhelpful Husseini/Nashashibi divide. Finally, whether true or not, it was noted down somewhere in 1930 that Husseini's style of leadership had made him unpopular amongst his own clan. (CO 733/193/9, Minute by Williams, 27 Aug. 1930) The crude clan-based dichotomy which most historians have resorted to to write Palestinian Mandate politics does not provide the most helpful paradigm for reading these politics since in reality, political alliances and allegiances formed and dissolved regardless of kinship and blood ties.

Both Mandatory officials and historians since have commented that it was difficult to extricate political platforms from private interests. It is often said that Haj Amin Husseini and Ragheb Bey Nashashibi sought to extend and consolidate leverage amongst their clients through their connections with the British administration, and that the private distaste they had for each other cut across their otherwise common interests – Ragheb Bey apparently famously asserted that he would oppose, on principle, whatever Haj Amin said or did. Whilst the Grand Muftiship/Presidency of the SMC was intended to mollify Haj Amin (the devil makes work for idle hands), meanwhile rewards were also in store for the accommodating Ragheb Bey. Following the removal of another quarrelsome Husseini from his post as Mayor of Jerusalem (Musa Kazem Pasha Husseini's participation in the 1920 riots cost him his job), Ragheb Bey was appointed in his place.

Far from balancing clan interests, the strategy deployed by Mandate officials on the contrary exacerbated friction and tension and institutionalized personal distrust. This interference with clan interests was also open to different inter-pretation by Palestinians themselves, who may not have agreed that the allo-cation of prominent positions according to a clan quota was helpful. Hussein Fakhri Khalidi (H.F.K.)[15] writes:

> The strategy of the British administration from the earliest days of the Mandate was to cause division amongst our ranks. So whilst they may have filled government departments with Arabs, they made sure to mix them up regionally. Arabs from the entire region were brought to work side by side with Palestinians, and they were encouraged to spy on one another. In other words, they made sure we would be unable to form a united front. Then, their strategy changed. When divisions between local families began to appear, they employed members of those families to work side by side. Finally, their last strategy was to create divisions between rural and urban clans, by bringing members of prominent rural families to work for the government. These are the ways the evil imperialist divided us and increased feelings of unease amongst us. (Memoirs: part 3)

H.F.K. specifically referred to Herbert Samuel's appointment of Haj Amin as Grand Mufti/President of the SMC, and to Ragheb Bey's appointment as mayor, as a divisive action which entrenched political biases into familial ones (ibid.). Competing local interests so realigned, they crystallized (during the Mandate period, and in subsequent history books) into two clear and distinct factions which became associated one with the Husseinis and the other with the Nashashibis.[16] The Mandatory after all had a template for this: 'horizontal solidarity' (Guha 1989b: 300) is inconceivable/unacceptable in a colonial con-text. Or rather, the colonialist cannot imagine that his subject might have the presence of mind, the gall, the intelligence and the spirit to conspire against him. What they can do is squabble amongst each other for his favour and vie for his attention. Under these conditions, it is impossible, as much as we want to, to have any respect for this élite. They are stripped of their dignity. They did not have a choice but still, they have compromised their essence. They are scrambling around on the floor for whatever might be tossed from the high table. It is unbecoming.

The Mandatory authorities also chose to deal with the Palestinian Arabs not as Arabs but as Muslims. The emphasis at the onset of the British adminis- tration was on conciliating and appeasing them *as* Muslims rather than as Arabs (see for instance CO , HC to SSC, Report for Dec. 1921). It was the effervescent Muslims who were prone to fits of zealotry, and who required priority handling. This may have also been because Britain was anxious to appease her Mohammedan subjects elsewhere (India). The first HC, Herbert Samuel, was so convinced of the strategic advantages which would result from pandering to perceived Muslim religious sentiment that he urged the home government to agree to this Supreme Muslim Council by expedited order rather than by ordinance, the 'special circumstances' justifying a departure from practice. This was a complete innovation of the Mandatory's and the ostentation of the title was a straightforward ruse to divert attention from the lack of genuine political apparatus for the Arabs. The urgency, Samuel claimed, was due to 'political necessities'. (CO , HC to SSC, 8 Oct. 1921) Again, his anxieties are related to Muslim rather than Arab opinion: even though the majority of Palestinians were Muslims, this was assumed to be/ assigned to be the factor which determined their political identity. It was a factor which could potentially replace their political identity. In reality, the 'Muslims' did not so much want a Supreme Muslim Council as much as they wanted a representative government. The anticipation of a scary type of Islam migrating from elsewhere was too much to bear, but it may well have been exaggerated. An ominously entitled file, 'Secret Despatch: spread of Wahabi tendencies', concludes as much. In it, the HC enclosed a letter from the Jaffa Governor:

> There has been much discussion going on lately amongst sincere Moslems as to the political advantages to be gained by preparing the minds of the people of Palestine to accept the Wahabite creed. It is acknowledged that the austere tenets of this creed will not willingly be followed by the people. The leaders, in order to avoid European domination and the imposition of the hated Balfour Declaration, are anxiously seeking a way out. (CO , HC to SSC)

British assumptions and preconceptions or even pretexts regarding the native characteristics bore directly on policy decisions regarding how they should be ruled and what institutions befitted them. These prejudices provided the foundation for negotiating with the élite Arab leaders. In summary, they were viewed as cliquey, vague on political ideology and touchy about religion (Islam. Christians: sidelined, even though Christians made up around 10 per cent of the Palestinian population). By pretending/hoping that the peasants would remain mellow as long as bread filled their stomachs, political unrest and protest were poised to be written off as despair.[17] Nonetheless, just to be safe, it was also essential to protect these peasants from the political meddling of their landlords, the (dangerously semi-civilised) urbanites. Peasants then, were considered unlikely to stir unless prompted by the urban leadership.[18]

How did these values and ideas shape the British administration's course of action when faced with the now grumbling, now conciliatory, élite local leadership? Assumptions that officials held about Islam, Near Eastern society and character, and the Ottoman Empire, were ideological ones which fed into their strategic considerations. The Mandatory needed these Muslims and clans, these clannish Muslims, these semi-Europeanised, semi-Turkified, hybrid Orientals and they went about forging relationships with them, setting them up against one another and encouraging their squabbles and grudges. Price, former head of the CID, admits that one of the 'best and most thrilling' pieces of information he ever received was passed to him by an Arab aristocrat. (PPOCAC, Price op. cit.: 3) Finally however, this relationship did not yield its entire promise: 'I don't think there was a sufficiently cohesive body of Arab leaders to organise a pukka Intelligence Service. It was mainly Bazaar gossip, possibly. Yet the leaders were in close touch with each other, and their life-blood was intrigue.' (ibid.)

Like all natives everywhere, the Palestinians were also childish: 'They are like children and very difficult to help', wrote HC Chancellor to his son, regarding a planned visit of an Arab Delegation to London. (Chancellor Papers, box 16, file 3: ff. 80; box 14, File 1: ff. 150–61) Other favourite classifications included 'agitator/extremist' and 'moderate'. The 'moderates' were also often described as 'clever'. In a report containing 'Biographical notes on the persons in the Arab Delegation to Europe', Musa Kazem Husseini is 'an agitator – not very clever'; Mouin Al Maadi on the other hand is 'a very clever person' who 'supports a Moslem/Jewish entente'; Refik Tmemi is 'an agitator'; Ruhi Abd Al Hadi is 'quite clever' and 'can be attracted towards the Jewish side'. By sheer coincidence, the three Christians in the Delegation, Fuad Saba, Ibrahim Shammas and Shibli Jamal are all 'anti-Semites'. (CO 733/13, Government Report on the 4th Congress, Despatch of 21 June 1921) Similarly an 'Arab Who's Who', prepared over a period of two years between 1931 and 1933 by Eastwood, the HC's private Secretary, and presented with the disclaimer that it may not be completely accurate because reliable information was hard to obtain, follows the same lines: Abderrahman Salim, a member of the Arab Executive (AE), is 'a notorious agitator of the most unpleasant type'; Awni Abdul Hadi, the General Secretary of the Pan-Arab Istiqlal, is said to care only about 'his own prestige, position and pocket'; Haj Shafi Abdul Hadi, who opposes the Grand Mufti, is 'the biggest liar in the country'; George Antonius, whilst 'the cleverest Arab in Palestine', 'like all Arabs has personal piques and jealousies and is quick to take offence' (especially when he can sense the enemy is aiming straight at the jugular, perhaps?); Izzat Darwazah, a member of the Istiqlal party, for his suggestion that Arabs 'embrace the spirit and faith of Ghandi', is branded an 'extremist'; Hassan Dajani, a member of the Opposition which associated itself closely with the authorities, 'has many of the qualities of a Jew: business capacity, self-assurance, bounce, a thick skin. But he also has the Arab gift for intrigue ... said to smuggle drugs'; Yacoub Bey Ghossein, who formed the Youth Congress, and became a member of the AHC is 'a fat unpleasant creature'; Fahmi Bey Husseini, the Mayor of Gaza, is 'fond of the ladies, even those of Tel Aviv', 'unscrupulous and immoral' and yet, startlingly, it was judged 'difficult to find in Gaza a better Mayor'; Jamal Husseini, the Grand Mufti's nephew and protégé, is 'rather slow witted, inclined to be pig-headed'; the bouncy Sheikh Muzaffar, on whom the authorities kept a watchful eye from the earliest days of the Mandate for his energetic activism, is 'a notorious agitator and firebrand', 'one of the most dangerous men in Palestine', 'a first class stump orator who in 5 minutes can make his audience do anything he wants' (surely that would not include anything his audience themselves were not predisposed to doing, or is the dark creature attributed with supernatural powers?); Suleiman Bey Toukan, a member of the Opposition, is 'given to the methods of intrigue'; Omar Bittar, a member of the AE and President of the Jaffa Muslim Christian Association, is a 'drunkard' whose involvement in politics 'does not improve their tone'; Haj Amin Husseini, President of the Supreme Muslim Council and Grand Mufti, who owed both positions to HMG, is 'affable, courteous, dignified and close. A dangerous enemy and not a very trusty friend'. ('Arab Who's Who' op. cit.) Reticently neutral, comparatively innocuous remarks were reserved for those personalities who may not have been soft targets. In those cases, their seemingly genuine and principled commitment to politics was noted with bemusement: Sheikh Sultan Atrash is 'one of the few Druzes whose interest in politics is more than parochial. Still in revolt, somewhere in the *Wadi Sirhan*. Has always been in revolt against one government or another'; Haj Tawfiq Effendi[19] Hammad, a member of one of the Arab Delegations to London, even though against the Mandate, is 'old-fashioned and honest' – Haj Tawfiq's greatest ambition is noted on file as wanting to cultivate the loveliest garden in the world until he visited England and was taken to Kew, 'which he felt he could never rival'; Ahmad Khalidi MBE, the Principal of the Arab Training College, 'has strong political feelings' and 'finds it at times a little difficult to reconcile his *prejudices and politics* with his official position'. (ibid., my emphasis)

This is a rough sketch, seen from the British point of view, of the gentlemen with whom HMG purported to form political associations. The Arabs *themselves* did not think of themselves as moderates/extremists etc. These are labels forced upon them by the Mandatory for the latter's own convenience and self-delusion. The Arab Women's Committee addressed a memorandum to the Officer Administering the Government in 1937, in which they protested the deportation and exile of political leaders, the detention without trial or even charge of hundreds of Arabs, including judges of the religious courts, notables, cultivators, labourers and merchants. The ladies ended their appeal by saying: 'There is not one Arab in Palestine ... who is an extremist or a moderate as all Arabs are alike in this respect.' (See ibid.)

Relations formed with the Arab leaders relied on reductive notions of Arabs, Islam, the Orient and even of the generic native. The Arab leaders were seen as either compromised and corrupt, honest and stupid, or stubborn and evil. The subsequent approaches and offers made to them must therefore be read in this dim light, where distrust, suspicion, apprehension, fear and paranoia determined the quality of every Anglo-Arab personal relationship mediated through Government House.

Councils: 'Advisory', 'Legislative'

The Palestine Order in Council 1922 gave the World Zionist Organization official consultative status in Palestine. There was no equivalent Palestinian body although several offers were made by the Mandatory, allegedly to redress the balance. The Arabs mostly held out for representative, autonomous self-government. In some circles, they held out for representative, semi-autonomous self-government subject to British supervision. The greatest obstacle was the JNHP and the incorporation of the Balfour Declaration in the Mandate. Holding out did not work.[20] Members of the élite more or less played along for the first twenty years of the Mandate, anxious not to antagonize their masters or miss out on potential power-sharing. They hummed along. They tried to learn the tune. In reality though, and in terms of real self-determination, the offers consisted of one non-runner after another. Self-government under these conditions did not relate to sovereignty, which would threaten the JNHP. Nonetheless, in an effort to harness local élite energy and deploy it into that colonial hybrid, the British JNHP, the Arabs were 'offered' an Arab Agency, one or two Advisory Councils and even one or two 'Legislative' Councils. The Arabs were said not to be ready for the business of real self-government.

HC Samuel (1920–25) introduced a purely consultative Advisory Council (AC) in October 1920. None of its 20 members (10 from the British administration, four Muslims, three Christians and three Jews) was elected. The composition of the AC was not representative of the population. The members seemed to have been carefully handpicked for their non-combative nature. The meetings consisted of harmonious and congenial elucidation of administrative matters. Compared to the status of the Jewish Agency, the role of the AC was severely limited. Churchill explained in a telegram: 'The special recognition accorded to Zionist bodies arises out of special conditions attached to Mandate, viz.: establishment of National home for Jews. There appear to be no grounds for giving similar non-official representation to other elements.' (CO 733/3, 2 June 1921) HC Samuel's ideas about imperial rule were different from Churchill's, who could not bring himself to identify Arabs other than by an oblique reference to 'other elements'. Samuel sought to reassure members of an Arab Delegation to London: 'I would wish to say from the first that it has always been the intention of the Government to proceed with the formation of self-governing institutions.' (CO 733/4, 23 June 1921) What could Samuel have meant by 'self-governing institutions', and how did this sit with Churchill? Churchill reminded him:

> The difficulty about the promise of a National Home for Jews in Palestine was that it conflicted with our own regular policy of consulting the wishes of the people of a mandated territory and giving them representative institutions as soon as the people were fitted for them. (ibid.)

The POIC of August 1922 provided for a Legislative Council. The envisaged body would consist of 12 elected members (eight Muslims, two Christians and two Jews) and 11 government officials. This translated into 43 per cent Arab representation, even though they formed 83 per cent of the population. The AE (see 'Who are you calling Muslim?' below), argued that if they agreed to this scheme they would be outnumbered by the Government officials and the Jewish members of the Council, who were likely to vote together on issues affecting the JNHP, such as immigration. The Mandate had not yet been ratified by the League of Nations. The AE called for a boycott of the elections to this Council in 1923. The government refrained either from pressuring electors to vote, or from taking any action against those who used undue pressure to discourage voting. Perhaps they felt the mood in the country. Perhaps they were indifferent. Or it may be that the incidence of intimidation was negligible. The boycott was a success and the vote was nullified. The Arabs had refused to lend constitutional legitimacy to the Balfour Declaration. Samuel responded by calling for a reconstituted AC. In May 1923, he issued invites to eight Muslim and two Christian Arab leaders to join a new AC. All accepted. The composition of this new AC was identical to that of the rejected Legislative Council. The new AC was a Legislative Council 'lite', which undermined the elections boycott and implied acceptance of the constitution. The invitees, after an intervention from the AE and extensive discussions, withdrew their acceptance.

Next, during the summer of 1923, the Cabinet Committee came up with the idea for an Arab Agency. This was ostensibly to match the Jewish Agency. They said:

> HMG are accordingly prepared to favour the establishment of an Arab Agency in Palestine which will occupy a position exactly analogous to that of the Jewish Agency under Article 4 – i.e. it will be recognised as a public body for the purpose of advising and cooperating with the administration in such economic, social and other matters as may affect the non-Jewish population and, subject to the control of the administration, of assisting and taking part in the development of the country. (From Cmnd. 1989, cited in John and Hadawi 1983: 194.)

Neither the status nor the brief of the proposed Arab Agency was 'exactly analogous to that of the Jewish Agency'. The Arab Agency's status would not be formalized within the constitution. Its members were to be appointed by the HC, whilst membership of the Jewish Agency was elected by Jews around the world. Its proposed functions were local, rather than international, and unlike the Jewish Agency, development activities would remain completely outside its ambit. The macabre insult was not lost on the Arabs. Musa Kazem Pasha commented: 'the name of the Arab Agency would make them (Arabs) feel they are strangers in their own country'. (Co 733/51, Musa Kazem Pasha's letter to HC, 23 Nov. 1923)

In the meantime however, Samuel, dedicated to the idea of local institutions, appointed a Commission to 'consider the present and former systems of local government in Palestine and to make recommendations with regard to the constitution and powers of local authorities'. Discussions about this revolved around a favourite British fetish, the 'Eastern mind':

> On the general question of local government in Palestine the pious hope expressed ... that the existing tradition should be maintained must, I think, be entirely disposed of. The Commission seem ... to have come near realising this. The truth is that no Eastern country has ever really had an efficient local government, partly because the idea of doing things for themselves is foreign to the Eastern mind, the daily round of routine duties is onerous to the Eastern, and partly because there is no public opinion of any sort to keep the local government up to scratch. *Any local government tradition, therefore, which exists is actually bad.* The fact that ideas of local self-government are foreign to the Eastern mind should not, however, I think, be used as an argument in favour of abandoning such a project. Nothing has greater educative value, and nothing in the long run, helps to the same extent in winning the sympathies of the inhabitants of the country for the central government, as having to struggle with the difficulties of their own local affairs. (CO 733/90, Minute by Blood, 5 March 1925, to Local Government Commission's 2nd Report. My emphasis.)

Field Marshal Lord Plumer (HC 1925–28) stuck to municipal elections. He wanted to train Arabs in the administrative business of government, and municipal elections were a necessary prelude. By focusing on local government, Plumer avoided the wider political questions, for which the Arabs, who had yet to mature into a discerning electorate,[21] were not considered ready.

With HC Chancellor (1928–31), there was talk of a Legislative Council. Chancellor understood the importance of allowing the Arab national movement a constitutional outlet, and spoke of Arab self-government in London. Once again though, this was not the same as representative democracy.[22] He told the AE that he supported 'local autonomy in Palestine'. (CO 733/167/6, HC Chancellor to SSC Amery, 15 Jan. 1929) The AE, which at this stage of the Mandate comprised a sizeable number of the 'moderate' Opposition, pressed for a Legislative Council supervised by the Mandatory, similar to the ones in other countries under Mandate.[23] The Legislative Council envisaged by

Chancellor was conceived as an ingenious and efficient way of undermining the 'extremists': The names forwarded by Chancellor to London included 'a generous representation of what may be termed the Constitutional Opposition', he wrote. Those designated should not be approached until the last minute, so that the extremists may be 'faced with a *fait accompli*'. (CO 733/167/6, Secret Despatch, 14 June 1929)[24] In any event, the outbreak of violence over the Wailing Wall in 1929, whilst Chancellor was in London discussing them, killed these proposals.

The next HC to tackle the issue of a Legislative Council was Arthur Wauchope (1931–37). In 1935, HMG announced plans to create a Legislative Council with five official members (all government employees), 11 nominated unofficial members (to be appointed by the High Commissioner), and 12 elected members. The plan was opposed by the Arabs because the basis of the Mandate had not been revoked, and because the High Commissioner maintained full legislative veto. It was also opposed by the Jews (now 20 per cent of the population) because it granted the Arabs majority. The proposal was shelved when it was debated in Parliament.

Peering now at the 'Secret', 'Confidential' and 'Private' official correspondence of the colonial archive spanning 1920–36, one does not have to read much between the lines to understand that these 'offers' of limited institutional representation which were made to the Arabs were conceived as safety valves, constitutional safeguards which would allow the Arabs to vent within clear allocated parameters, rather than as baby steps towards the full adult stride of self-governance. Even the establishment of the SMC with its vast powers, was such a safeguard. We can hear, for instance, HC Samuel fretting about the 'extreme impatience' of the Muslim 'community' and pressing upon the home government the necessity for expediting the establishment of a Supreme Muslim Council: 'For political reasons it is urgent that Moslem opinion be satisfied as soon as possible.' (CO 733/8, HC to SSC, 8 Oct. 1921) During HC Plumer's rule, a memo was submitted to the High Commissioner suggesting a bicameral Legislative Council, suited to the 'special circumstances of Palestine'. According to this, an Upper House would have the official majority, whilst a Lower House would

> [p]ossess little more than deliberative functions ... I believe that a con-
> stitutional reform on these lines, if proposed soon, might be made satis-
> factory to Arab *amour propre* and prove to be of educational value
> besides providing a safety valve for Nationalist sentiment. (CO 733/155/9,
> Symes, 'Question of Establishing a Legislative Council', May 1928)

This produced some apprehension:

> My own view is that, while we certainly shall not be able to resist indefinitely
> the demand for a Legislative Council we had better go on resisting it, at
> any rate, for the present. I doubt whether the risks of political trouble are

so great as Colonel Symes apprehends. His own plan ... does not seem to me a very practicable one. His 'Lower House' might be harmless enough so long as *all* power could be withheld from it. But how long would that be? Once such a body were in existence it would be difficult, if not impossible, to prevent it from acquiring powers similar to those enjoyed by Legislative Councils elsewhere in the Empire. I would hesitate to embark on so hazardous an experiment. (CO 733/155/9, Minute by Shuckburgh, 7 May 1928. My emphasis.)

Another official noted: 'I can't help feeling that the longer we can put off its being raised the better.' (CO 733/155/9, Minute on 'Question of Establishing a Legislative Council', 10 May 1928) Later on, outgoing HC Plumer himself told incoming HC Chancellor: 'Arabs will press for establishment of a Legislative Council and responsible government. Put off granting them as long as possible.' (Chancellor Papers, box 11, file 1, Notes on an Interview with Lord Plumer, 15 Aug 1928: ff. 14–20.) HC Wauchope's advice to the Colonial Secretary was also along those lines. He told the Colonial Secretary, who was reticent to receive an Arab deputation in London, since he was sure to disappoint them and cause them to return home more frustrated than before: 'I know of no way by which present feelings of the Arab resentment can be so mollified as by giving Arab deputation opportunity of stating their case in London.' (CO 733/307/10, Telegram HC to SSC, 31 March 1936) Clever resource to protocol diffuses political tension, and Wauchope repeated this for good measure: 'The mere fact of their reception in London would give great satisfaction to the Arabs.' (CO 733/307/10, Cabinet Meeting Extract, 1 April 1936) All the while however, the bottom line was that: 'the obligations devolving upon the Mandatory are incompatible with the establishment of a democratic form of government'. (CO 733/167/6, HC Chancellor to SSC Webb, 12 June 1929) This never wavered, gave, or shifted.

Who are you calling Muslim?

The Mandatory in Palestine then, was consumed by two major preoccupations: clans and Islam. Fraternal betrayals amongst the servants and alliances with the master were encouraged. Religious distinctions/sensibilities/identities were rigidified into English. Islam was a wild animal/psychiatric disorder. Their job was to capture, chain, medicate it. This is a universal impulse of the colonialist's: 'The status of "native" is a nervous condition introduced and maintained by the settler among colonized people'. (Sartre 1963: 20) Replace 'native' with 'Muslim'.

Making Muslims

Within Arab leadership, none is as confounding as the prominence and eminence enjoyed by Haj Amin Husseini between 1920 and 1936. The double game in which native agents of empire were involved is most exquisitely illustrated in the case of Haj Amin, whose status was exalted by the British administration although they periodically suspected him of spreading fanaticism and sedition. Aristocratic convict, devout Muslim, riot mascot and cautious diplomat all rolled into one, the prestige and pride of place accorded Haj Amin by the Mandatory surpassed that of every other élite politician who stood to compete with him for the spotlight. Some were more learned (such as Jarallah, the inspector of the religious courts, who lost the Grand Muftiship to him), some were more pragmatically inclined to check their nationalistic tendencies, (such as Musa Kazem Husseini, leader of the AE), and some were outright collaborators. And yet it was the diminutive Haj Amin, with his pale blue eyes and careful speech, who triumphed under British tutelage over each one of his potential rivals. Haj Amin was an ambiguous ally, and it is a matter of endless fascination and speculation as to why the British administration tolerated him so well. Sentenced *in absentia* by a British court to 10-years' imprisonment for his part in the 1920 riots, he was later pardoned and appointed Mufti of Jerusalem and Grand Mufti of Palestine. In 1922, he was elected President of the SMC, an institution conceived by the British to handle native affairs. The SMC dealt with all Muslim religious affairs, controlled large sums of money, and was responsible for the appointment and dismissal of religious officials. The SMC's activities, although restricted to those of a 'community' nature, were bound to straddle the political and legal divide. Whilst the SMC's breadth was carefully circumscribed by the Mandatory, the depth of its powers was fathomless. It functioned autonomously, perhaps even unaccountably. Still, the sphere of influence accorded the SMC excluded anything that touched on constitutional governance. The SMC was a politically inconsequential, vast and vague arena fabricated to relieve the British administration of cumbersome and complicated business (related to religious endowments and *Sharia* courts), whilst lulling their Mohammedan subjects into an opiate contentment.

Historians have focused on Haj Amin's efficacy as leader or representative of the people, on whether he helped or hindered the nationalist cause by his (in) actions. Haj Amin's strange career lends itself to studies which either vilify or glorify him. He is arch, inscrutable, and ambitious. He is a fearless and uncompromising leader. Or he is criticized for his shameless self-aggrandisement and self-interest. He is a diabolical chameleon. But the hero/villain equation of pro- and anti-Mufti accounts is unsatisfactory. Eastwood, HC Wauchope's private secretary, described the Haj's predicament in the 'Arab Who's Who':

> The Mufti is in the difficult situation of trying to ride three horses at once. He is a sincere Arab nationalist. He is an equally sincere Moslem and a leader in the Pan-Islamic movement. At the same time he derives his chief source of influence from his quasi official position as President of the SMC. It needs all his very considerable skill in diplomacy and intrigue to stay in all three saddles. (op. cit.)

But the Haj was riding for a fall. He did not stay in any saddle, let alone all three. Between 1921 and 1937, Haj Amin's position shifted from cautious Mandatory protégé with the highest religious appointment in the land, to political fugitive. By the end of the summer of 1936, SSC Ormsby-Gore was calling him the: '*fons et origo* of the murders in 1929' and a 'black hearted villain', finally concluding that: 'clearly too ... we ought to back any enemies of the Mufti we can'. (CO 733/341/20, SSC to Battershill (Acting HC), 8 Sept. 1936)

Whatever power and status Husseini possessed were part of the ornamental hierarchy instituted in the furtherance of Mandatory objectives. When he ceased to be useful, stopped fulfilling the role which had been allocated to him, stopped doing what he was supposed to do either because he was unwilling or unable, he was cajoled, castigated, threatened and finally driven out of Palestine. 'Reform of the SMC' became code for undermining the Mufti. In their minutes, officials mused upon various ways of curtailing his 'influence and prestige.'[25] The Memorandum of 1932 considering SMC reforms suggested that these might be a good idea if, by instituting them, his 'influence could be appreciably weakened'. (CO 733/222/7, HC to SSC, 4 June 1932) Husseini's predicament was unenviable as Plumer, Chancellor and Wauchope all made it clear who would be held responsible for outbreaks of violence in the country, and never hesitated to remind him that he was disposable.[26] By the mid-1930s, Wauchope was unwilling to give up on the relationships he had cultivated with so much pride, particularly with the Mufti, but cracks were beginning to show. Most writers forget to mention that his repeatedly quoted

I am confident that the Mufti likes me, respects me, and is anxious to help me. ... But he fears that criticism of his many opponents that he is too pro-British may weaken his influence in the country. The fact, however, that his influence is on the side of moderation is of definite value

had been preceded by the slightly paranoid proviso: 'It is hard to see clearly into the mind of any Arab but ... '. (CO 733/258/1, HC to SSC, 5 Jan. 1934)

Let us try, nevertheless, to look into the mind of this Arab.

Mohammad Amin, the man

Mohammad Amin Husseini was born during the last decade of the nineteenth century. The Husseinis were wealthy, influential, and accustomed to mediating between the local population and their foreign masters. They exerted authority through official posts as well as landholding, and their sway extended out of the city into the countryside. The Husseini family held the Jerusalem Mufti position since the seventeenth century, with the occasional anomaly. They were prominent in law, education and governance and were closely involved with the Ottoman ruling class, at times through intermarriage. They were conservative defenders of the status quo, and when General Allenby entered Jerusalem, it was a Husseini (Salim, Musa Kazem Pasha's brother and then Mayor) who dignified his military victory by handing him the Keys to the City.

The young Mohammad Amin was sent to Cairo for his continuing education. There he was enrolled at the school of Sheikh Rashid Rida to read Islamic philosophy. He may or may not have continued his education at the famous Al Azhar University, the world centre of Islamic learning. The 'Arab Who's Who' states that he was educated at Turkish schools in Palestine, followed by Egypt and Al Azhar. From Cairo he went to Mecca on Pilgrimage, and became *Haj*. He was in his early to mid twenties. During the war, he joined the Emir Faisal's army and fought with the British to drive the Turks out of Palestine. At the onset of the British military occupation, Husseini became a clerk in the office of Gabriel Haddad, the advisor to Storrs, the Military Governor. He was then transferred to the Department of Public Safety in Damascus, which functioned as the heart of the Arab nationalist movement.

Husseini was also President of the Arab Club. This club, like the Literary Club associated with the Nashashibi family, functioned as a lobbying, cultural, and political organization, through which the younger and more radical elements of the intelligentsia countered the Muslim Christian Associations' (MCAs) more conciliatory approach. (Kimmerling 2000: 79, fn. 60)[27] The three organizations differed in their overall objectives: the Literary Club was pro-French and wanted complete independence for Palestine. The Arab Club was Pan-Arabist. The MCAs wanted some form of autonomy under British rule. All three organizations were anti-Zionist.

It was in the wake of the April riots of 1920[28] that Husseini attained some notoriety when a festive religious procession became violent. The infamy he gained was incidental and did not necessarily reflect the true nature of his involvement, which may have been quite banal.[29] The disturbances erupted during the festival of *Nebi Musa* ('Prophet Moses'), and the rioting left five Jews and four Arabs dead. They had been cordial until then, but the incident took its toll on Husseini–British relations: Musa Kazem Husseini, Mayor of Jerusalem, was removed from his post and replaced with Ragheb Nashashibi. Kamel Husseini, the Grand Mufti, returned his British medal. (Mattar op. cit.: 17) Husseini, his friend Aref Al Aref (a young middle-class nationalist who also ended up a British civil servant, serving as District Officer for Beersheba), and Zeev Jabotinsky (founder of the Revisionist Zionist movement) were held responsible for the violence in the military trials that followed. Aref was said to have directed the mob, whilst Husseini was found guilty of incitement to violence. They were sentenced in their absence to some 10 or 15 years each,[30] (Jabotinsky received 15 years), and sought the protection of the Bedouins of Transjordan, who are honour bound to protect any fugitive in need without asking questions.

Shortly thereafter Herbert Samuel was appointed High Commissioner. Samuel was a Jew, a Zionist representing the King in Palestine and treading on eggshells. He may have been particularly anxious to allay Arab misgivings

about British intentions and immediately proceeded to amnesty political prisoners sentenced by the military court although he excluded Aref and Husseini.
The events which led to their eventual pardon occurred in a picturesque setting: during a visit to Transjordan in 1920 to meet with a delegation of tribal
Sheikhs, the Sheikhs publicly asked Samuel to pardon the two men. Aref
emerged triumphant on the shoulders of some youths, whilst Husseini refused
the pardon on the basis that he was not a criminal. It was only when Amin's
brother Kamel, the Grand Mufti, fell ill, that he swallowed his pride, accepted
the pardon and returned home to Jerusalem. There he was placed under police
surveillance, on a blacklist which described him as an agitator.

   In terms of his personality Husseini was by several accounts credited with
considerable personal dignity. The 'Arab Who's Who', despite its generally
virulent tone, reserved some kind words for him. Despite branding him as fundamentally untrustworthy, the report also describes him as 'affable, courteous,
dignified and close'. (op. cit.) Alice Brooks, the 'Englishwoman who claims to be
on intimate terms with all the Arab leaders' once again, provides a gentle portrait
of Haj Amin in the late 1930s, when he was under considerable pressure from
both 'extremists', 'moderates' and the Mandatory. She describes a

> sincere, patriotic, and simple gentleman, unfailingly courteous, kindly,
> considerate, and hospitable, with a pleasant sense of humour, son of an
> ancient and noble house, happy with a charming wife and family, a man
> reluctant to lose faith entirely in the good faith of the British people, and
> anxious to retain, even yet, their friendly advice and co-operation if pos-
> sible, a man of whom an official of the highest standing expressed the
> belief to me personally, at his own dinner table, that in all Palestine he
> was convinced that no man was more genuinely sincere and patriotic. (In
> CO 733/409/17, from the *Manchester Guardian*, 27 Oct. 1937)

Haj Amin was also apparently completely honest, even when he had large
sums from charitable endowments and officials' salaries at his disposal via the
SMC. Taggar (op. cit.: 72), a previous Israeli Secret service agent, describes
him as 'incorruptible'. A memorandum considering whether or how to curtail
the SMC's powers, determined allegations against the Council and its President with regard to the maladministration of *wakf* funds as 'unfounded',
'vague' and 'unsupported by evidence'. (CO 733/222/7, Memorandum: Palestine
SMC, enclosed in HC Despatch to SSC, 4 June 1932)

Grand Mufti

During the days of Ottoman rule, the Mufti of Jerusalem was subordinate to
Sheikh Al Islam in Istanbul. (ibid.) His status was unremarkable, and it was
equivalent to that of any other provincial Mufti. The administration of Muslim
affairs, *Sharia* courts and religious endowments, were also handled in Istanbul.

This changed when the link between Jerusalem and Istanbul was severed, and Jerusalem became a capital city. The British administration did not want these responsibilities for itself. Kamel, Amin's brother, was the Mufti of Jerusalem at the time. Kamel was apparently extremely moderate. He was friendly to the Jews and helped appease the situation after the Easter Riots of 1920. He was amply rewarded for his cooperative nature by successive promotions. Besides becoming known as Grand Mufti, he was appointed President to the Sharia Appeal Court, even though this was an innovative departure from the strict separation of the functions of Mufti (a jurist for consultative purposes) and *Qadi* (a judge with executive functions). Kamel also headed the Central *Wakf* Council, which put him in control of all religious foundations throughout Palestine.

The title of Grand Mufti then, was a fabrication. It had no precedence either in Islam or in Ottoman practice.[31] When Haj Amin became Mufti, he inherited the 'Grand' that had been Kamel's. In any event, the title was artificial, and it was to remain unofficial. Around this time, the British Empire was engaging in 'unprecedented honorific inventiveness'. (Cannadine 2001: 85) The Grand Muftiship may be seen as part of the many achievements of this creative surge.

After Kamel died in 1921 the administration appointed a Khalidi to replace him as President of the Sharia Appeal Court, but the question of the Muftiship and of religious endowments was left open. According to Turkish procedure, a college of electors – consisting of imams, preachers, mosque teachers, municipal council and administrative council members – selected a list of three candidates from which the government (through Sheikh Al Islam) appointed its favourite. In this case, the aftermath of war meant that the municipal council members were not elected, as required by law, but nominated by the military administration. A meeting of religious leaders and nominated municipal members was called instead. HC Samuel invited the religious notables to propose, after election, a list of suitable candidates from which he would select a Mufti. Husseini came fourth and failed to make the roster. One Jarallah, the candidate supported by the Nashashibi family, amassed the most votes. Jarallah was eventually forced to retract his candidacy, leaving the way open for the young Husseini to slither up the list to third place. There had been much lobbying on behalf of Husseini to the administration. He seemed to be popular with everybody: peasants and townsfolk, artisan and aristocrat, Muslim and Christian. There were suggestions of bribery and Zionist involvement in the selection of Jarallah, and the election was challenged on the basis that it was not carried out strictly according to Ottoman requirements.[32]

Although Husseini's pedigree was impeccable, there was the inconvenient detail of his conviction for incitement to violence, as well as a question mark over the extent of his religious education. Fortunately, HC Samuel did not let either of these facts get in the way of his appointment. He at least was clear about whom he wanted to see in the Jerusalem Mufti chair. On 11 April 1921, a day before the meeting of the electoral college, he held a meeting with

Husseini and the matter was settled informally between the two gentlemen.[33] Shortly thereafter, the Haj stepped into his brother's shoes and led the *Nebi Musa* procession which, in marked contrast to that of the previous year when he had vociferated and gesticulated on a balcony, was peaceful. Afterwards he reportedly invited Samuel for lunch.[34] The High Commissioner began to relax. It was all falling into place: the Haj would yield his considerable family influence to keep the masses in check.

Samuel either responded to an overwhelming popular appeal on behalf of Haj Amin for Jerusalem Mufti, or implemented a pre-existing *idée fixe*. Whatever his motivation, he had dismissed the official election results. Samuel had several motivations for appointing a Husseini: he compensated the family for their removal from the mayoral position and their replacement with a Nashashibi and he ensured that Haj Amin, who had acted up and received a 10- or 15-year sentence only 12 months previously, was safely within the fold of the administration. His new responsibilities would ensure that he was kept too busy for extra curricular antics.

The Supreme Muslim Council

Haj Amin became President of the SMC in January 1922 and remained in his post until 1937. Whilst the secular AE, representative of the broad section of Palestinian society, was shunned, the SMC was granted gigantic powers. The powers accorded to the SMC were so extensive that the Peel Commission commented disapprovingly in 1937 that Haj Amin had happily gone about building an 'imperium in imperio', running a sort of third parallel government (in addition to the British administration and the Jewish Agency). The Peel Commission also commented that 'the Mufti had contrived to accumulate in his person' multi-functions which extended his power and influence in the entire land.(Cmnd. 5479: 126) This is harsh – considering that Husseini's powers were clearly bestowed upon him by the administration, and that whatever his ambitions were, they were fanned by one administration after another. Moreover, some confusing drafting relating to Articles 2, 4 and 6, which dealt with the President's term in office, inadvertently granted Husseini a life appointment.[35] The scandalously and notoriously incompetent Attorney General Bentwich was responsible for this fiasco. Bentwich was disliked by the Arabs, not because of his incompetence, but because of his politics.[36] It was also generally agreed at home that he was a poor lawyer. His drafting, in particular, was inexact and even oblique. His December 1921 order constituting the SMC was 'lacking in precision, more particularly in respect of the procedure for the election of a new council'. (CO 733/112, HC to SSC, 19 Feb. 1926) They also said:

> His views are so extreme that I think he is unconsciously biased … Moreover, I am bound to add that he is not efficient as an A-G. His drafting is notoriously bad; his conduct of cases upon the rare occasion

when he appears in court borders on the ridiculous, and his knowledge and sympathy of English colonial law and institutions are lacking. (CO 733/175/3, Minutes, 4 Oct. 1929)

Every time an opportunity to reform the SMC and curtail the President's powers was bypassed, this was done deliberately and after extensive discussion between the Palestine and Home governments. In 1924, District Commissioners were asked to comment on the involvement of the SMC with the elections boycott of 1923. Even though it was unanimously agreed that the SMC had exceeded its powers, no action was taken. One official wrote in 1932: 'I feel we must be very careful how we proceed, as partly feeling between the Moslems is running high ... My personal feeling is that we should avoid as far as possible any tampering with the 1921 Order.' (Co 733/222/7, Letter Trusted to CO, 1 June 1932.) The Memorandum prepared to address the question of reform of the SMC in 1932 periodically stresses this one priority guiding principle: namely, that the Muslim 'community' should be afforded 'the widest possible autonomy in religious matters', both because this complied with British policy in other territories, and because it was the strategy most likely to guarantee peaceable rule. Any change of policy with regard to Muslims might entail 'serious consequences' and 'a religious outbreak' (Islam is a little bit like a continually mutating virus), even though this may not reflect the actual situation and even though no evidence has been received to this effect. Finally, we are left with the impression of an artificial, phantom threat, itself deduced from recourse to an outlandish and foreign rationale:

> The extent of this danger can only be gauged by those who are in close touch with the local situation ... But it is noted that the Mufti of Jerusalem is the head of the adherents of the Shafi rite, who represent 70% of the Sunni population of Palestine, and that nearly all the Moslems of Palestine are Sunnis. (Memorandum: Palestine SMC op. cit.)

Whilst admitting that the point may be pointless, nonetheless the pointless point is made.

Was there a more disturbing incentive for granting the SMC such deep powers? For there are also clear indications that by granting the SMC complete autonomy in the conduct of their affairs, even though the substance of those affairs is severely circumscribed to the religious, the urge of Muslims to participate in public affairs would abate a little, and hopefully sideline the more thorny question of a Legislative Council. In other words, a powerful SMC would keep the Muslims content and operate as a substitute for constitutional representation. During the summer of 1932, in the context of discussions relating to possible reform of the SMC constitution and elections to the Council, HC Wauchope told the Arab leaders that whilst the Government 'remains determined to establish a Legislative Council', nonetheless 'the reform which I think most urgent, and one very widely demanded among the Moslems of Palestine, is an election of new members for the SMC'. (Co 733/ 222/7, HC to SSC, 6 June 1932) In the same letter, Wauchope expounds against curtailing the SMC's powers. Whilst doubtful as to the Council's competence regarding the administration of *wakf* funds and *Sharia* courts, he counter-intuitively concludes that 'It may be wiser to leave Moslem affairs to be controlled by Moslem authority.' Wauchope was openly happy to sacrifice efficiency for political mileage, and he explicitly described the result he fore-saw. Again, he presented the SMC elections as a way to avoid discussions on a Legislative Council:

> The *extremists* will probably cry out for a Legislative Council, but I am hopeful, by taking no share in their party dealings, by consulting their leaders and by leaving as much as possible of Moslem affairs to be dealt with by Moslem bodies that these SMC elections will be successfully car-ried through before next winter. Once carried through the effect will be excellent throughout the country' (ibid. My emphasis.)

SSC Cunliffe-Lister also understood the value of swapping elections to a governmental body for elections to a religious one. He wrote to Wauchope that he agreed the need now was for 'early action with regard to the re-organisation of the SMC' and in the same breath, for 'going slow about setting up a Legislative Council'. (CO 733/222/7, SSC to HC, 5 July 1932)

HC Samuel had made a strategic decision to face the Palestine Arabs according to their several religious communities, rather than as a national group. The Muslim 'community' was the largest, and it was granted a Council which reflected this special position. Samuel recognized (overestimated?) the dual administrative/political usefulness of establishing a prestigious Islamic institution. But this was a not really a compliment: the description/identification of Muslims as a 'community' similar to the status of the Christian and Jewish minorities, was, in reality, degrading. The fact that an indigenous majority had been classified as a 'community' by a foreign colonizer set the tone for the way they would be dealt with. Nonetheless, by devolving the administration of religious schools, charitable endowments, orphanages, courts and mosques to an SMC, the Mandatory pandered to the majority of their subjects' attributed religious feelings. Here, the tried and tested rule of non-intervention with the internal affairs of a 'community' was applied, to the extent that Chief Secre-tary Luke commented in 1929 that the December 1921 Order amounted to 'almost an abdication by the Administration of Palestine of responsibilities normally incumbent upon a government'. (CO 733/222/7, Memorandum: Palestine SMC op. cit.) Luke then immediately goes on to describe how Haj Amin had opened orphanages, restored both mosques in the Haram complex, opened a library and museum within its walls. These social projects and cul-tural rejuvenation activities, especially his restoration of important Holy

Places, had endeared him to the population and apparently given Palestinians great satisfaction and 'a new sense of confidence and of pride and interest in their past'. (ibid.)

Once so intoxicated with their past, the people, one would hope, will eventually forget to worry about their future. They might as well have asked Palestinians to shut their eyes and count sheep.

Fear of the religious cry

The British government then, both in Palestine and at home, dreaded 'the raising of the religious cry'. Anxieties over a religious backlash to imperial rule in Palestine translated into virtually unqualified support for Haj Amin as a precautionary measure. It was a move which over-indulged the perceived Islamic susceptibility of the locals, considering that Islam had not traditionally provided a unifying national ideology in Palestine.[37] At the onset of the British occupation, Palestinian collective consciousness had emerged around a Pan-Syrian or Pan-Arab politics.[38] Apart from the Zionist funded National Muslim Association,[39] there was no religious sectarianism in Palestinian political activity. Yet the preferred imagined community in the Mandatory's mind was one made up of Muslims, flattered by appeals to and appeasements of their Mohammedan beliefs. So whilst the home and Palestine governments were reluctant to accept the AE as representative of the Palestinian population under the pretext that they were 'unelected', there was little parallel hesitation in appointing Husseini as uncontested Muslim representative.

Some Muslims were good, and could be of use to the government. Others were bad, and worked against the government. Husseini, besides being a Muslim, was also an aristocrat, and his masters could take solace in his social status. On the other hand, the authorities looked with trepidation upon the effusive, maverick, highly flammable and AE endorsed Sheikh Muzaffar, a wild and potentially lethal type who, they imagined, was capable of sweeping Palestinians into a blind, violent, mystical, anti-imperialist frenzy. In the early days of the Mandate, political reports regularly made note of the Sheikh's movements and of his speeches, and it seems that the wordy Sheikh was orating at every opportunity, particularly in the run-up to the failed Legislative Council elections of 1923. Muzaffar's popularity, together with the provocative and separatist contents of his message, confounded the administration's Muslim policy. The political report for January 1923 contains an appendix of his speeches. The political report for February notes that the Sheikh, in breach of directives forbidding political speeches to be made at the Haram mosque, spoke against the planned elections. (Co 733/43) A month later, another report read: 'The die-hards are touring the villages. The egregious Muzzaffar works and weeps in mosque after mosque.' (CO 733/44, Report of the Northern District Governor, in Political Report for March 1923) His hold over the common people was worrying: 'The effect of all this on the minds of the free and unenlightened electors is supremely perplexing and most of the villagers ... are withdrawing from a game the purposes and rules of which are incomprehensible to them.' (ibid.) The scope of his influence reached north and south: 'The visit and speeches of Sheikh Abdul Kadir Al Muzaffar undoubtedly turned the scale against any Arab participation in Jaffa'. (CO 733/44, Report of the Jaffa Governor, Jerusalem District in Political Report for March 1923) Meanwhile, the activities of Haj Amin Husseini during the same period were especially benign:

> The President of the Supreme Muslim Council, accompanied by the architect Kamal ed Din Bey, proceeded to Egypt with the object of investigating the procedure adopted in that country in respect of the preservation of monuments of Arab art, the formation of a Museum of Arab art, and of a library of Arab literature. (CO 733/43, Political Report for Feb. 1923)

The antithetical positions of the cooperative Mufti and the obstructionist Sheikh began to crystallize. Whilst Husseini talked and talked, hosted and argued, negotiated and compromised, Muzzaffar refused to make eye contact with the colonialist. Husseini may have felt piqued after Sheikh Muzaffar moved the congregation to tears during a speech at the Haram mosque in March, and he subsequently gave instructions to the mosque attendants that the Sheikh was no longer permitted to make political speeches. Muzaffar was consequently and rather humiliatingly removed from the pulpit when he did attempt to make a speech. (Political Report for March 2003 op. cit.) The Mufti, during these early days, seemed satisfied with the limitations of his brief. The national movement, with all the diplomacy, petitioning, protests and political appeals it entailed was left in the hands of the AE. The AE had a happy association with Sheikh Muzaffar, and the HC commented that Muzaffar and the Secretary of the AE 'spoke in similar terms' at a reception in Jerusalem. (ibid.) A few months later, on the sixth anniversary of the Balfour Declaration, the AE issued an open invitation to both Muslims and Christians to attend the Haram mosque, where they were to be addressed, once again, by Muzaffar. The government was uncomfortable with the united front Muslims and Christians presented via the AE. What happened next is peculiar – both for the interference of the Mandatory with the matter of Christian presence within the Haram, and for Husseini's collusion with it:

> The District Governor of Jerusalem on receiving notice of the proposed meeting reminded the Mufti Haj Amin Husseini of his promise to His Excellency the High Commissioner that the Mosque should never be used for political purposes. Haj Amin ... undertook to prevent the Christians from entering the Haram Esh Sherif area and promised to do his best to prevent Sheikh Abdul Kader [i.e. Muzzaffar] from speaking. (CO 733/52, Political Report for Nov. 1923)

Husseini could not prevent the tenacious Muzaffar from delivering his speech but he issued an order afterwards to the effect that only an imam, *mudariss* or *khatib* (teachers of religious scholarship) may speak at the Haram mosque, provided that they had previously obtained his written permission. Eager to please his masters, the Mufti was, in those early days, performing according to the demands of his post.

The Wall Riots in August 1929 then, played straight into British anxiety about international Islam, and officials indulged their passion: musing about frustration amongst the Arabs of Palestine, and its connection to worldwide Mohammedan intrigue. One official wrote to the Secretary of State:

> I would ask you confidentially to ask the FO whether they could obtain any information re. Zaki Pasha in Cairo, with whom the Grand Mufti has been conspiring for a considerable time and who was the focus of Mohammedan intrigue against Great Britain, not merely in Egypt and Palestine, but also in Irak and Arabia ...
>
> I'm afraid that this may merely prove to be a kind of preliminary attempt in regard to Mohammedan trouble which is always brewing all over the world against Western influences, and the Jews of Palestine or elsewhere are just once more the whipping boy of the circumstances ... having studied the whole eastern problem very carefully for many years, from Morocco to India, I've always felt that a moment would come at any time when the Mohammedan would challenge the supremacy of the West. (Co 733/173/3, Letter, Melchett to Passfield, in 'Activities of President of the SMC, 29 Aug. 1929)[40]

The Mandatory deliberately confused/blurred religious fervour with political resistance. They contorted their subjects into prototypes which reflected their own anxieties, not necessarily the truth. When Jamal Husseini (the Mufti's nephew) insolently spoke out of turn, when he discoursed back and challenged the Mandate's moral authority, they said he was courting 'Martyrdom' (see Co 733/258/1, 'Prosecution of Arab Leaders', 4 Jan. 1931). Jamal Husseini was definitely angry, but he did not sound like someone courting martyrdom. When he was bound over with surety for good behaviour on some criminal charge, he retorted:

> [I]f this means my personal conduct, I believe that such a conduct does not need my binding over with a surety, but if it meant my political behaviour, I assure the court, the Police and the Government beforehand that my behaviour will be during this year, according to their opinion, more wicked than any behaviour they have ever known. I will not spare one single minute to join in national activities and to embark upon the most rough behaviour, so long as I believe that will benefit the Arab cause in general. Because I believe that most of the Penal laws in Palestine have

been enacted to muzzle the mouths of the nation and to shackle its hands so as to deprive them of working in the sacred national movement, for the purpose of enforcing the government's colonizing ends ... On this basis, I will not be restrained by any surety of good behaviour, per their opinion, which, per my opinion, and to that of every loyal person to this country and nation, is a moral death. Hence, I wait imprisonment with quietude. (CO 733/258/1, Statement enclosed by HC to SSC.)

Palestinian political developments

So, whilst the Palestine Government preferred to relate to the native community as a 'Muslim' one, the Arabs themselves saw themselves, and organised themselves, quite differently.

The Muslim–Christian associations

Muslims and Christians did not need to unite against the Mandate, because they had never been disunited. Palestinian Christians actively contributed to political activities and were fully integrated in the national movement. They owned most of the newspapers, and took part in the negotiating delegations sent to London. They initiated the campaign against land sales to Jews in the north of the country.[41] The Palestine Government was bemused by this ideological unity. So much so that they commented on it in their political reports: 'From Haifa the Governor of Phoenicia reports that meetings have been held in the houses of a number of Moslem and Christian notables to discuss the means of expressing popular dislike of the Mandate in its present pro-Zionist form.' (CO 733/23, Secret Despatch from Acting HC Deedes to SSC Churchill, Political Report for June 1922) The reluctance/inability, to understand or acknowledge that resistance against the Mandate was one based on Arab rather than religious solidarity, persisted. When the AE wrote in a memorandum that, '[t]he fact that a Jew is a Jew has never prejudiced the Arab against him ... the question is not a religious one. For we see that Moslems and Christians alike, whose religions are not similar, unite in their hatred of Zionism' (CO 733/13, Report by 3rd Haifa Congress, presented to SSC Churchill on 28 March 1921), the reaction from Government House reflected the Mandatory's own preoccupations and prejudices: 'This passage is of interest as it indicates that the anti-Zionist movement is not part of any Pan-Islamic movement based upon zeal for the defence of the Mohammedan religion.' (ibid.)

In 1918, two MCAs were formed in Jaffa and Jerusalem. By 1921 there was one in each major urban centre: in Jerusalem, Nablus, Tulkarem, Hebron and Gaza. The movement excluded religion from its National Covenant and demonstrated public unity between Muslims and Christians (see Tshimoni

1978). H.F.K. wrote in his diaries that Palestinian political organization was completely secular, and that no one spared a thought for who was a Christian or a Muslim. If the MCAs were not representative of the nationwide Muslim/Christian ratio, it was because religion was not an issue. The MCAs comprised the religious and secular élites. Members' prestige was tied to lineage, wealth and prior association with the Ottoman central government. The local population accepted MCA members on that basis, and members needed no further confirmation of their representative status.

The Arab Executive committees

Until 1934, leadership of the nationalist movement was conducted by committees elected through secret ballot during seven national conferences between 1920 and 1928. It was this AE, under the leadership of Musa Kazem Pasha Husseini, which was in charge of the political affairs of the Palestinian community. The first AE was elected at the Third Congress at Haifa in December. Its remit was to coordinate national/political activities. The Haifa Congress drew up demands for a national government responsible to an elected parliament along the lines of governments in Iraq and Transjordan. In other words, autonomy under British hegemony, or some form of indirect rule.[42] The nine members of this AE were older men from leading families. The AE had tried to obtain acknowledgement of their representative status. HC Samuel did not like it:

> The information in the possession of the Government ... is to the effect that the members of the Congress were appointed by small groups, and are by no means representative of the population. Before taking into consideration, therefore, the resolutions which were passed, His Excellency would be obliged if he could be informed
> (1) by what societies the representatives were appointed,
> (2) what numbers of members of each society participated in the choice of representatives. (FO 371/6374, Political Report for Dec. 1921)

Later on the AE addressed a memorandum to Churchill:

> This Congress is a true representative of Palestine, her mouthpiece. In it all classes are legally represented. Town, village, factory and farm – in fact all the live aspects of the nation – acknowledged its leadership.
>
> But the enemy of Palestine, ever on the watch, has willed to distort the truth, and to paint Palestine to the Government other than she really is, by questioning the representative status of the members of the Congress. To such an extent were these intrigues carried that Sir Herbert Samuel became suspicious and would not recognize the Congress. It was then that the whole nation rose as one man and from Dan to Beersheba cried out

backing the Congress, and calling upon the government to recognize it as their true and legal representative. Unfortunately these peaceful demonstrations were powerless to convince the HC of the good faith of the people of Palestine, so he persisted in ignoring their Congresses ... whilst on the other hand he recognized the Zionist Congresses, congratulated them, encouraged them, and wished them good luck. (Report by 3rd Haifa Congress op. cit.)

This undignified begging reflected their powerlessness. It did not please Government House and the goalposts shifted:

Non-recognition of the Congress is not due to any question of its representative character, but the fact that it opposes the principles embodied in the Mandate. ... The committee of the Jewish Conference has been officially recognized as dealing with purely Jewish affairs on condition that it accepts the principles of the Mandate. ... This condition has been accepted. Should the Haifa Congress Committee take the same course as the Jewish Committee they will be similarly recognised. (ibid.)

In 1921, the AE appointed a delegation to London in an attempt to deflect Britain's Zionist policy. In the summer of 1922, a Fifth Congress in Nablus rejected the Palestine Order-in-Council, resolved to boycott the proposed elections for a Legislative Council, to form an arbitration committee to deal with differences between national groups as the need arises, and to institute MCAs in each District and Sub-District. (CO 733/22, Political Report for Aug. 1922) Until 1928 the AE represented the nationalist, anti-Zionist strand of Palestinian political leadership. Members of the Opposition (i.e. opponents of the Husseini clan and the SMC, commonly associated with the Nashashibi family) were sidelined from mainstream politics and lacked broad based support. Until then the AE was synonymous, in terms of ideology and membership, with the MCAs.

The government refused to acknowledge, on principle, either the MCAs or the AE as political partners. Their pretexts ranged from the 'unrepresentative' character of the organizations, to their rejection of the terms of the Balfour Declaration /Mandate. The MCAs replicated a traditional, élitist configuration and the Palestine Government used this to cast doubt on their authority. Whilst the MCAs' authority was traditional, and emanated from a power base of notables, dignitaries and Sheikhs, the selection of members, based on a system of secondary electors, did not differ in any significant sense from the electoral method to the Ottoman Parliament, which had been employed since 1876. (Porath 1974: 286) The AE seemed to enjoy popular support but the British administration expressed misgivings about what they considered to be an unrepresentative framework: there were no general elections and delegates were chosen by and from the MCA membership. Privately, the government agreed that the MCAs 'undoubtedly ... stand for a considerable body of opinion latent in the country'. (Samuel to Curzon, quoted in ibid. 126)

In 1931, the AE organised demonstrations against government policy. The government had refused the demonstrations permission. Disturbances resulted, during which the elderly Musa Kazem Husseini and others were beaten with clubs. The police used live fire and hand grenades against the demonstrators. The elderly Musa Kazem never recovered from the blows he received on the march, and he gradually retreated from political activity and from the world. (H.F.K. memoirs: part 3) During this time, the ineffectiveness of the AE was becoming apparent: 'Arab nationalist leaders in general seem to have given up their alleged unfruitful policies of protestation and appeal.' (FO 371/16926, CID Report for 16 Dec. 1932)

Musa Kazem Pasha's death in 1934 sealed the AE's demise.

The Arab Higher Committee

By the late 1920s, a new political vocabulary emerged with the pan-Arab Istiqlal (Independence) party. Awni Abdel Hadi, founder of the Istiqlal and Secretary of the AE, sought support among young professionals and government officials in and around the cities. They were anti-imperialist pan-Arabists. Between 1934 and 1935, four additional political parties were founded. The National Defence Party and the Palestine Arab Party were founded in 1934 and 1935 by a Nashashibi and a Husseini respectively. Both had access to the grass roots and were capable of mobilizing support in the countryside, although the Husseini branch were by far more influential. Meanwhile Haj Amin Husseini, Grand Mufti and British protégé, maintained a conciliatory position for as long as he could and was criticized for his perceived moderation by some sections of the nationalist movement.[43] The Catholic Alfred Rock was appointed Vice President of the Palestine Arab Party. H.F.K. founded the Reform Party. H.F.K. had defeated Ragheb Nashashibi in the bid for the Jerusalem mayoralty in 1934, but H.F.K. kept such a distance from factional rivalry that neither side seemed to know whom he supported. He said of the Husseini/Nashashibi divide:

> The Jerusalem families were all related to each other through inter-marriage, and we were linked in this way to the Husseinis. We remained neutral with regard to the Husseini/Nashashibi split, although some Khalidis did side with the Opposition. Some, on the side of the Council intervened in good faith and tried to bridge this potential gap. Musa Alami was instrumental in this regard. It was at his summer home that I met the Mufti. The Opposition were watching my every move. The Council agreed to back my candidature for the Jerusalem mayoralty. Ragheb was defeated by a very large margin. The Opposition lost out on

the other municipalities. Shortly thereafter, they held a meeting during which they expelled me from their ranks. Yet I was never one of them! I had been careful to stay out of politics. I was a Civil Servant. ... No one knew if I was with the Council or with the Opposition. Both Government and public opinion were split. The AE accused me of being the Mufti's man. But I was neutral, and had connections on both sides. (Memoirs: part 3)

Finally, Latif Abdel Salah founded the National Bloc. The AHC was formed in April 1936 as the national strike was declared. The AHC consisted of a coalition of all the major political parties.[44] According to H.F.K. (Memoirs: part 4), it was at Ragheb Bey's insistence that the Mufti joined the AHC, even though the SMC was not a political party. Ragheb Nashashibi also insisted that H.F. K. represent the Reform Party.[45] All factions were represented: Nationalists, Opposition, Muslims and Christians, the youth movement and the radical pan-Arabists. The formation of separate political parties was not a good sign. It was symptomatic of the divisions which had emerged over the twenty years of the Mandate: 'The wound had reached the bone, and there was no way of healing it', wrote H.F.K. (Memoirs: part 3) It is true that it was not a natural alliance, but one, as is often repeated, based on necessity.

Who is afraid of modernity?

Mandate histories chronicle one rejection after another by the Arabs, Arab élite dithering, ungratefulness, lack of foresight, impracticability and stubbornness. These were bewildering times for the Arab politicians. Palestinian élite political organization is often written about in terms of its weaknesses, defects and susceptibility to clan jealousies and competitiveness. It is true that élite leadership was ineffective: they never achieved their aims or anything. But there is an alternative way of reading and addressing and understanding élite failures (not failings) under the Mandate. To do this, we have to overcome 'the dialectic which liberal hypocrisy hides' (Sartre op. cit.: 14) and definitively place events within this dialectic. We have to step wide, remain committed to our starting point concerning the illegitimacy of the colonial state: and at once it becomes infinitely more sensible to ask, instead of whether the élite reacted appropriately to the Mandatory's offers, whether it is acceptable, today, to chronicle the Mandatory's approach to the élite without questioning their JNHP programme and their presence, in Palestine? Could there have been any other authentic Palestinian élite response, one in which neither their personal integrity nor the security of their future, are compromised?

The JNHP then, tested the usual policy of consent between local élite and colonialists. This did not prevent the Mandatory from marshalling the same useful techniques that had been honed elsewhere. They bolstered the social standing of the local élite, which was threatened by a severance from the imperial centre in Istanbul. This seemed the surest way of keeping the ripples of occupation as light as possible. The symbolic value to the British mandatory power of the existence of a native élite, who were apparently willing at least to a degree, to tolerate an abhorrent constitution, even where they did not amount to a wholesale collaborating group, was considerable. Did the Mandatory think that the success or failure of their plan for Palestine depended on the extent to which the more influential tiers of the educated class were engaged in a meaningful way? Did they hope that local suspicion could be deflected by leaving the local-level socio-political structures through which this class traditionally exercised their influence, intact? Did they hope to dissimulate the coercive and violent reality of cultural, political and military domination by seeking the acquiescence of a group of influential cooperators?

A range of motives inspired the empire – economic, military/strategic, and religious – but these alone do not explain the techniques of power and domination which were conceived on the ground or their implementation. In other words, historical contingencies are never just that. What was going on behind the scenes? How did British officials' view of themselves and their own society, become reflected in what they saw in the periphery, the field? How did this affect what we see read as history today? Cannadine (2001) argues that the Empire was as much about perpetuating sameness as it was about asserting difference. Perhaps it entailed a little bit of both alienating and drafting in, of pull and push, of mirroring and distinguishing. Perhaps it is too far reaching to conclude that they attempted to understand the world by analogy. But these gentlemen (some of whom may have been homesick), entrusted with overpowering, conciliating, ruling over and administering bewilderingly alien nations, set about replicating home. When it came to picking local leaders and anointing them they relied on identifying affinities between themselves and the locals, and these affinities were based on class and clan, the most constant and heartening system they knew. The techniques of rule and domination were largely dictated by how they saw themselves, let alone their subjects. Going further still, these techniques reveal more about the rulers and how they saw themselves than they do about their subjects. At the basis of these techniques lay the class system. (ibid.: 71)[46] So whilst race/culture accounted for and justified the British need to improve/dominate their subjects, nonetheless they resorted to notions of class and social hierarchy in devising ways of ruling over them. The mysterious people and their communities were decoded according to this variant. The policy was one of eliciting collaboration rather than enforcing marginalization. Never mind that in constructing neat hierarchical systems infused with British prejudices and colonial notions, local social structures were often misunderstood and eventually transformed. The unifying character of the empire was that it was 'first and foremost a class act', which eventually consolidated a 'pan-British, pan-imperial, elite' (ibid.: 23) through an elaborate system of titles, honours and rewards. A system of titles and honours was the basis for a sense of order, and eventually, homogeneity. It is this making visible of hierarchy that Cannadine calls 'Ornamentalism'.

The subordination of the chosen chiefs from the Palestinian élite class, the promising adolescents picked out for their potential and their interest in Western culture,[47] was not drawn on fear or the use/threat of force alone. So what if they were a little temperamental, a little stubborn? They would be gently reprimanded, they would eventually come to their senses. Their physical/political captivity under Mandate meant that they also were/became hostage to a mental construct. According to Chatterjee (1993), the subservience of the élite under colonial rule is illustrated in their restriction to a modern vocabulary. So once indigenous culture had been identified as 'the storehouse of unreason', élite leaders were bound in order to address their servitude and bondage, to do so by resorting to their masters' own cultural and political values. This symbolized their captivity in 'the prison house of reason' (ibid. 55). The currency of the inter-war years was 'self-determination', Legislative Councils based on a European model, though not exactly self-determining and subject to European supervision. This is what the Palestinian élite nagged their masters for. The skewed rules had been set, and the skewed games began. The Palestinian politicians did not ground their criticism of colonial rule in resentment towards foreign structures. On the contrary, by seeking the same legal-institutional forms of political expression as those of their masters, they had, arguably, already capitulated in a profound way. In their efforts to be heard, Arab leadership automatically adopted the terms of engagement of the Mandatory. Was this an imperceptible and conclusive confirmation of successful colonial hegemony, clearly distinguishable from the paradigms of nationalism which developed amongst the inhabitants of the countryside and the Rebels of the hills?

In order to integrate the élite into the political sphere and put them to work in a way which they, the Mandatory, found constructive, they demanded thorough, old-fashioned subjugation. The Mandatory was arguably indifferent to whether the élite were able to demonstrate true political maturity. This was not *really* what they wanted from them. They wanted their devotion and their servitude. What was required above all else was unconditional ideological surrender to an experimental project called the JNHP. This, the Palestinian élite resisted. They stuck to their argument about modernity. For that reason, the Palestinian élite can be distinguished from other colonial cases, where a 'blurring of boundaries' (Likhovski 2003)[48] between Western and native discourse may or may not be identified. Can we really speak of the 'blurring of boundaries' between élite nationalist interests and discourse, and those of colonial officials, i.e. between Western colonialism and native anti-colonial nationalism? The life and times of the élite leaders of Palestine during the Mandate is best understood in terms of what Chatterjee (op. cit.: 35) calls the élite's 'middleness'. They were the élite servants, but servants nonetheless. Can we really discuss the authenticity and merits or demerits of native élite nationalism under such circumstances, or was it carbonized at birth?

White master, brown servant: one scenario

About a year before the 1929 riots, SSC Amery, HC Chancellor, Col. Wedgewood, and a Mrs Dugdale had dinner together. Afterwards, they chatted. Apparently, Amery said something like this:

> [The] Scotch had differed from English in ideas of justice and toleration. But the Scotch had been the carriers of these English ideals into the empty places of the temperate globe ... the Scotch had served the mixture and become part of this thing called Empire. Now the gulf between the English or Scotch and the coloured races, or even the Mediterranean races, was too great. ... If this thing called Empire or British culture was to extend and graft itself onto Islam or Africa we needed a different, a new carrier of the English ideals. The Jews seemed there to take on the role of the Scots, to extend our conceptions of right and wrong and honesty into the East from Mediterranean to the Punjab. ... Palestine at present was neither East nor West. We could, if we chose, keep it East – ruling obedient servants, or we could make it West – the jumping-off ground for the new extension of the English Commonwealth and polity. Of course the first alternative was attractive to officials in Palestine, but no-one doubted that we had chosen the second alternative and were bound to it by the Balfour Declaration. (Chancellor Papers, box 11, file 1, Note by Col. Wedgewood of an after-dinner conversation on 26 July 1928: ff. 1–14)

British policy makers calculated at the Colonial Office Cairo Conference in 1921 that it would be a sound economic and ideological manoeuvre if 'local'[49] leaders could be installed to safeguard imperial interests in the Middle East, and so it was decided to introduce the politics of consent and indirect supervision there. The British were comfortable with chiefs, landowners, Sultans and Sheikhs. But things were not so simple in the Palestine section of the Middle East. In Palestine, the Mandatory took on a mission sympathetic to the Evangelical Christian world-view, decided that the natives were essentially Muslim, and racialized local relationships by inviting exclusively Jewish settlers.

The local élite, as in every other Dependency, had to contend with their ambiguous broker/victim role. They were initially comfortable in cooperating with the foreign power based on a mutual recognition of one another's social status. But as the Mandate advanced, other connections began to compete for their loyalties. Where class had been the determining factor in fomenting political alliances between British officials and their aristocratic local in-betweens, race and indigeneity acquired increasing significance. The JNHP project introduced new racial and religious affiliations, and transformed what it meant to be Jewish (this was quite different from what it had meant prior to the Mandate) and what it meant to be Muslim (ditto). It might be superfluous, but it is necessary to add that this was not a positive transformation. The 1929

Riots were significant in definitively resetting the way Arabs, Jews and British thought of one another, and an explosion of declamatory racial incantations erupted from all sides. Chancellor, who heard about the violence and murders which had taken place whilst sailing back to his job from a break in London, issued a Proclamation on 1 September 1929 that: 'savage murders had been perpetrated upon defenceless members of the Jewish population'. (ibid., box 12, file 2: ff. 95) Privately, he wrote to his son that: 'Every Arab thinks that there is no Jew like a dead Jew.' (ibid., box 16, file 3, letter dated 23 Oct. 1929: ff. 46) Chancellor's Proclamation shocked the Arabs and may even have reconciled those two supposedly intractable enemies, Amin Husseini and Ragheb Nashashibi: Chancellor wrote that the two had been spotted together, and that Ragheb Bey had his arm around the Grand Mufti as they strolled along a Jerusalem street. (ibid. box 12, File 2: ff. 94) Arab protests against Chancellor's Proclamation rhetorically asked whether the Arabs who had also died had been killed 'in an extraordinary Western civilised manner'. (ibid.: ff. 91–92) They judged the High Commissioner's Proclamation as 'untimely and insulting' (ibid.), and added that 'if His Excellency had waited until the results were seen, he would have realised that savageries were committed on the Arabs'. (ibid.: ff. 91–95) In terms of rhetoric, the Arabs were fighting a losing battle. They did not *own* the words of power. It was prescriptively and predeterminedly *they* who are violent, *they* who are bigoted. *They* are the ones susceptible to labels and to description. Foucault established our right to discourse against discourse when he asked:

> First question: who is speaking? Who, among the totality of speaking individuals, is accorded the right to use this sort of language? ... What is the status of the individuals who – alone – have the right, sanctioned by law or tradition, juridically defined or spontaneously accepted, to proffer such a discourse? (Foucault 1991: 50)

Cross reference India where the mob, and mob action, are of a piece: 'the marks of an inferior people and a people without history'. (Pandey op. cit.: 168)

The Mandatory's contribution to the racial tone of the violence was clear to the Arabs. Musa Kazem Husseini made the point to the High Commissioner: 'Had there been Jews in Jerusalem prior to the British Occupation? Had there been a Wailing Wall in those days? Had there occurred conflicts between Jew and Arab?' (Chancellor Papers, box 14, file 1: ff.16–23) The fallout was definitive. H.F.K. writes in his memoirs that the judges who presided over the trials held as a result of the riots became teary-eyed whenever Jewish women testified, but looked angry and full of hatred when it was the turn of Arab women. Jews stopped eating grapes from Hebron, saying they were grown on land soaked with Jewish blood. H.F.K. writes in his memoirs that the government armed British civilians, and stationed them as guards around the major cities. These trigger-happy, often drunk civilians, writes H.F.K., used Arabs as target practice. H.F.K., who treated their victims at the government hospital in Jerusalem, reports a conversation he overheard between two such civilians:

> 'What's your bag today?
> I've got 2 of them.
> Go on! I had a better chance, I bagged 4 of them!'
> (H.F.K. Memoirs: part 3)

The hollowness of local leadership

In the early days, Britain's sentimental and strategic reasons for wanting Palestine were compelling enough to ignore the discrepancies of the Balfour Declaration. Eventually, the impracticability and inequity of the venture would come to light. But the process took its own time, and it was a painful and ugly one to watch: 'Great Britain remained impaled on the horns of the dilemma, unable to abandon Palestine and yet unable to bridge the gap between the Zionist and Arab nationalist movements'. (Mosely Lesch op. cit.: 42) This would run and run as long as Britain's 'international obligations' took precedence over the locals' right to representative self-government.[50] As the Mandate advanced, this right, itself necessarily elusive under colonial rule, became progressively more ethereal. The élite, who assumed at the onset that the British would take sufficient heed of their status as aristocrats and in-betweens as not to thoroughly humiliate them, awoke to a state of gradual but irreversible despondency. They moaned politely: 'We feel that our existence as a nation is endangered, and that we only have to choose between economical and political ruin, and emigration.' (Chancellor Papers, box 12, file 2: ff. 95) Who cares? For whilst much was made of preserving local élite prestige, the reality was that in London, no one wanted to talk to the Arab politicians. The Home Government balked before the prospect of talking to the organized, secular Palestinian leadership under the pretext that they were not official representatives. Yet who was the British Mandate representing in Palestine, and why did the Arab politicians not refuse to talk to *them* on the basis that they had not been chosen by the local population? Fanon writes: '*Le monde blanc, seul honnête, me refusait toute participation. D'un homme on exigeait une conduite d'homme. De moi, une conduite de nègre.*' (Fanon 1952: 118)

Acceptance of the JNHP (by analogy to the above, '*une conduite de nègre*') was the only way forward, and conversations with them never transcended this circular argument.[51] Negotiations did not depend on the moderation or otherwise of the élite leaders. H.F.K., who was viewed as a 'moderate' by the British administration, who remained neutral and attempted to overcome the binary divide which developed within Palestinian politics, was neither as prominent a personality nor, ironically, as subservient as Haj Amin. He did not yield the same influence, nor was he held hostage to the impossible demands of his captors. Nonetheless he (with other political leaders), bore the brunt of the 1936 Rebellion with arrest and exile. H.F.K., then Jerusalem Mayor, recounts how he was asked to appeal to the residents of Jerusalem for calm or risk being removed from his post during the strike of 1936. He refused, replying that public security was not part of municipal affairs. H.F.K. was to be given one last chance before he was arrested and exiled to the Seychelles. He recounts an invitation by Chief of Staff General Dill to dinner in the latter's private rooms at the King David Hotel in Jerusalem. It was their very first meeting. During a very long discussion, H.F.K. explained that the Arab leadership was powerless to stem the flow of the strike if no government concessions, particularly regarding Jewish immigration, were forthcoming. The following exchange then took place:

Dill: What if we were to arrest members of the AHC?
H.F.K.:   I assure you the fall out would be very bad for the government.
Dill: That's a strange thing to say. It is not the opinion of everyone I have met. In fact one individual in a high and respected position has informed me that arresting the Mufti and the members of the AHC was certain to put an end to the rebellion immediately.
H.F K.:   If what that person says is true, and the solution were that simple, then why have there been so many casualties, and what are you waiting for?

This ended the conversation and H.F.K. left. (H.F.K. Memoirs: part 3)

Notes

1 See CO 733/297/3 (SSC Memo 4 July 1936).
2 Mystical winged horse on which the Prophet Muhammad is believed to have ascended to heaven on a night journey.
3 232 Arabs and 339 Jews were wounded. See Taggar (1986: 64).
4 'There is no evidence that the Mufti issued any requests to Moslems in Palestine to come up to Jerusalem on the 23rd August and no connection has been established between the Mufti and the work of those who either are known or are thought to be engaged in agitation and incitement'. (Cmnd. 3530, 1930, Shaw Commission Report: 159)
5 In particular, the Sheikhs Muzaffar in the early 1920s, Abu Suud in the late 1920s and Qassam in the mid-1930s. Qassam's influence is addressed in a CID Report on 4 December 1935: 'although Sheikh Izz el Din accomplished nothing, he expressed in practical form an idea, set an example to his countrymen, and opened a new avenue for political struggle'. (FO)
6 Nashif (1977) points out that of the 32 men who served on the AHC between 1936 and 1948, 28 belonged to this segment of society, with only four belonging to the bourgeoisie. Moreover, the concentration of power is reflected in the fact that about 18 members, i.e. 64.3 per cent, belonged to a clan with large landholdings (114–15). Muslih (1988: 45–47) describes the dominant social groups of Palestine as consisting of: urban notables/aristocrats; a commercial Bourgeoisie which emerged in the nineteenth century and which was made up of Palestinian and Lebanese Christians and Jewish and European traders; and foreign settlers and Lebanese landlords.

7 *'By joining the Ottoman "aristocracy of service", they saw an opportunity to pre-serve their power positions.'* (Mattar 1983: 4) Similarly Muslih (op. cit.: 47) speaks of this *'aristocracy of service'*, who by aligning with Istanbul, were able to gain property rights and thereby consolidate the power they wielded.

8 This term is attributed to the historian Albert Hourani. These politics are exercised under three conditions: the existence of relations of interdependence, the domination of urban landowners of the rural hinterland, and sizeable freedom of action for the notables – which, nonetheless, was ultimately circumscribed by monarchical control (see Mattar op. cit.: 2).

9 See Nashif (ibid.: 120). Robinson Divine (1983: 71) writes:

> That Palestinians did not unite politically during this crucial period in their history, nor cooperate economically, nor even band together militarily is considered corollaries of this organizational incapacity and reasons enough for their failure to achieve a national sovereignty of their own. ... *The intense scholarly concentration on what are perceived as Palestinian organizational failures has distorted our vision of Palestinian history.* (My emphasis.)

10 See HC Wauchope's comment on Haj Amin's allegedly waning popularity: 'The Press Campaign against the Haj Amin grows in noise, volume and violence. Its true cause is jealousy of his power and influence, family hatred, party feuds and personal antipathies.' (CO 733/278/13, HC to SSC, April 1935)

11 Pasha is an Ottoman title.

12 Bey is an Ottoman title.

13 See for instance, his beseeching of the AHC in the wake of the first signs of disturbance in 1936: 'I shall count on you, gentlemen, to use your influence to check all form of disorder, prevent all lawless acts and contradict any false rumours likely to disturb the peace'. (CO 733/307/10, 'Minutes of Interview with Arab Leaders', 21 April 1936)

14 See Dr Hussein Fakhri Khalidi (H.F.K.), (Memoirs: part 3), for his position concerning factional politics.

15 Civil servant (Medical Officer in the Department of Health), a public official (Jerusalem Mayor in the lead-up to the 1936 rebellion), founder of the Reform Party and member of the AHC.

16 Known as the Majlisiyeen, i.e. supporters of the SMC, with Husseini as its President and Mu'arideen, i.e. the Opposition, respectively.

17 Chief Secretary Deedes wrote regarding the impending publication of the Palestine Order-in-Council:

> The minority will no doubt vociferate. The attitude of the majority will, I believe, turn much on the harvest. Prospects so far are good. The thing to try and skilfully avoid is the agitating by the minority of the majority, the villagers. (FO 371/6374, Deedes to Tilby, 14 Jan. 1921)

18 See FO 371 /6374, Political Report for January 1921:

> The bulk of the population has been quiet. The rains promise to be sufficient. The people on the whole show as yet no inclination to devote their time or energy to giving any active backing to the political agitators of the Effendi or property owning class.

19 Effendi is an Ottoman title.

20 H.F.K. now definitively exiled and writing with the weight of expulsion upon him in Beirut in 1949, comments in his Memoirs that the Arab politicians were victims of

their own negativism, and that they were wrong to reject every offer presented to them. In the margin however, an unknown commentator had scribbled that 'there were some elements within the British administration, who claimed to be friends to the Arabs, who advised them to reject these offers' (H. F. K. Memoirs: part 3). Leila Husseini, H.F. K.'s daughter, thinks the handwriting is that of either Ahmed or Sameh Toukan.

21 '[W]ith the object of enabling the people of Palestine to obtain practical experience of administrative methods and the business of self-government and to learn discrimination in the selection of their representatives, Lord Plumer … introduced a wider measure of self-government than had previously obtained under the British regime.' (Cmnd. 3692)

22 HC Chancellor wrote to SSC Webb that even though there was no question of establishing democratic government in Palestine, still something needed to be done as the present situation was untenable. (CO 733/167/6, 12 June 1929)

23 A memo by the AE on the subject of self-government complained about the 'direct rule' under which the country 'groans'. (CO 733/167/6HC, Chancellor despatch to SSC Webb, 18 June 1929)

24 The men proposed are: Musa Kazem Pasha, Ragheb Bey, Aref Pasha, Assem Bey Said, Mahmoud Abou Khadra, Suleiman Bey Touqan, Shafi Abdul Hadi, Mahmoud Effendi Madi, Tawfiq Bey Fahoum, Freih Abou Meddein.

25 Mills, Acting Chief Secretary, who has just returned from Palestine, felt that the Mufti directly stood in the way of any rapprochement and compromise. (CO 733/193/9, Minute by Williams, 27 Aug. 1930)

26 Chancellor would ask him, rather dryly, if 'he liked a hot climate'. See Taggar (1986: 80, fn. 42) for threats made to Haj Amin by various HCs.

27 Also, Muslih (op. cit.) writes of Younger Politicians and Older Politicians, the latter being represented by the MCAs. Muslih attributes the MCAs' circumspection in relation to the British as attributable to 'the two poles of their power, namely, access to the ruler and their local positions' (160). The Younger Politicians on the other hand, who were not part of the imperial bureaucracy, had less to lose and so were less motivated to compromise or negotiate (164).

28 These are known as the Easter Riots, although Passover, Easter and the Muslim festival of *Nebi Musa* all fell at the same time that year.

29 For an account of events at the demonstration, see Mattar (op. cit.: 16–17). Taggar (op. cit.) points out that the Palin Commission, a military judicial commission of inquiry, found that the riots were spontaneous and that nobody could be blamed for them. Taggar also refers to the opinion of the Chief Political Officer of the OETA, Meinertzhagen, to the effect that the military administration, which was anti-Zionist, may have been encouraging the notables to kick up a fuss. (16, fn. 21)

30 Writers differ. Eastwood, in the 'Arab Who's Who' (CO 733/248/22) puts the sentence at 15 years.

31 Kedourie (1969: 48–49) thinks it was the Military Administration which decided to make the Mufti of Jerusalem Grand Mufti of the whole of Palestine. Kupfershmidt (1987: 19) thinks the title was a feature of British rule in Egypt with no basis in local custom.

32 For an account of the nature of the protests, see Kedourie (op. cit.: 54). Also Porath (1974: 189–91).

33 For an account of this meeting, see Kedourie (op. cit.: 51). Also Mattar (op. cit.: 26). For a slightly different version of the discussion which took place, described by Haj Amin, see Taggar (op. cit.: 23).

34 Apparently, this was thoughtfully prepared according to Jewish dietary rules. (Mattar op. cit.: 27)

35 'A particularly doubtful feature of the Order of December 1921 was the provision for the election of a President whose tenure for office should be indefinite'. (CO 733/222/7, Memorandum: Palestine SMC)

36 The AE had demanded his removal from his post (see CO 733/175/3, Minutes).
37 Kimmerling (2000: 71):

> Ottomanism was a convenient identity and ideology for the urban elites ... At the same time, for the peasantry and lower classes the most important identities were those of the clan, the region and perhaps the ancient primordial grouping around the Qays and Yaman factions. Islam provided some common denominators to bridge gaps between fellahin and effendis, poor and rich, ignorant and literate, however it did not offer a sense, at that time, of being a partner in an all-embracing Umma Islamiyya. In short, Islam was a part of the more embracing Ottomanism.

Similarly Muslih (op. cit.: 1) writes that 'Ottomanism remained the dominant ideology in the Arab territories which lay to the east of the Suez until the defeat of the Ottoman Empire in 1918.' According to Muslih, 'a belief that the preservation of the Ottoman Empire was the best means of defending Islam against the encroachment of the European powers' (ix). Regarding the Qays/Yaman political divide, see ibid.: 32–37: this division dates back to pre-Islamic Arabia, where the peninsula was split into the North (Qays), and South (Yaman) tribes. As Islam spread into the Fertile Crescent, so did this schism, the underlying motivation of which was political control of areas. When the Ottomans reasserted central power over warring factions in their provinces, these rivalries simply transferred from the field to the local councils (*Majlis Idara*). Muslih also states that in Jerusalem, Gaza and Jaffa, contrary to Nablus and the Judean hills, competition between notable families was not connected by the Qays/Yaman friction, but rather, it was stimulated by the prestige and power which could be yielded via certain public posts, such as that of Mayor, or Mufti.
38 Pan-Arabism never disappeared entirely from Palestinian politics and re-emerged with the formation of the Istiqlal party in the 1930s.
39 Members of the Zionist Executive quickly grasped the potential of the animosity between the two emerging political camps in Palestine, crudely identified according to the Husseini/Nashashibi divide. In the summer of 1921, the Zionist Executive made a formal advance to opponents of the AE and the MCAs. They funded the National Muslim Association (NMA) whose brief was to support Jewish immigration and oppose the AE, even encouraging its anti-Christian stand. They supported the NMA both morally and financially (see CO , Political Report for Feb. 1923). The NMA's strategy was to diametrically oppose their compatriots: 'The Moslem National Society instituted by Mr. Kalvarisky and now referred to in AE Bulletins as the "Moslem-Jewish Society", in sending telegrams asking for the speedy ratification of the Mandate, has caused some annoyance' (CO, HC Samuel to SSC Churchill, Political Report for July 1922). Ragheb Nashashibi formed the Arab National Party in November 1923. The party publicly opposed Zionism, but Fakhri Bey Nashashibi, Ragheb's nephew, whose notorious reputation preceded him (he is described in the 'Arab Who's Who' as 'useful to the police', 'a nasty bit of work', 'according to the Arab proverb, you couldn't trust him alone with a cat', 'no principles, no scruples, trusted by no one' (op. cit.)), approached the Zionist executive for finance of this venture.
40 Comments on this statement in the form of minutes imply that Melchett's overstated the situation.
41 For a detailed portrayal of Christian involvement in political activity, see Tshimoni (1978: 77–84).
42 This is a demand which was reiterated time and again, in the context of protests against 'taxation without representation' and 'direct colonial rule' (see CO 733/167/6, HC to SSC, 15 Jan. 1929, and HC to SSC, 18 June 1929).

43 For instance, Wauchope explains that one of the complaints against him in an increasingly loud and violent press campaign, is 'the fact that his holding of the English instead of leading a campaign directed against this government is a betrayal of the Arab cause'. (CO 733/278/13, HC to SSC, April 1935)

44 Its members consisted of the Haj Amin Husseini, the Grand Mufti, as President, and the heads of the major parties: Ragheb Bey Nashashibi of the National Defence Party; Dr. Hussein F. Khalidi of the Reform Party; Jamal Bey Husseini of the Palestine Arab Party; Abdel Latif Salah of the National Bloc; Yacoub Ghossein of the Youth Congress; Awni Abdel Hadi of Istiqlal, as Secretary; Ahmed Hilmi Pasha of Istiqlal, as Treasurer. The other members were Fuad Saba, a Protestant, and Secretary of the AHC; Yacoub Farraj, a Greek Orthodox member of the Opposition (the National Defense Party); Alfred Rock, a Greek Catholic supporter of Haj Amin.

45 In his memoirs, H.F.K. does not refer to himself as either the leader or the founder of the Reform Party, but merely as one of its Executive Secretaries, although British official documents identify him as the founder/leader. Why?

46 WWI may or may not have made the world safe for Democracy, but it did make 'the British Empire safe for hierarchy'. Cannadine leaves Palestine out of his study of the Settlement Dominions, Indian Empire, Crown Colonies and League of Nations Mandates.

47 Cf. Sartre (1963: 7): 'They picked out promising adolescents; they branded them, as with a red-hot iron, with the principles of Western cultures; they stuffed their mouths with high sounding phrases, grand glutinous words that stuck to the teeth.' This is in relation to a native élite class who are educated /trained in the mother country.

48 Marlowe (1961) also raises the same issue. Referring to the Sheriffian family of Western Arabia and the Sunni Magnates of Iraq, he writes:

> It was a collaboration which was, in appearance and to some extent in fact, so reluctant as to seem indistinguishable from resistance. For it was necessary for the collaborators, by hard bargaining, to justify the results of collaboration to political opponents and personal rivals and to try and demonstrate that these results had been obtained not by collaboration but by resistance. (31).

49 The Sheriffian princes from Arabia installed in Mesopotamia, Transjordan and Syria were not exactly 'local'.

50 Chancellor, who was in favour of Arab 'self-government', informing a deputation of the AE that whilst the Mandate provided for local autonomy in Palestine, and Municipal Council elections represented progress towards representative institutions, 'the interests of the people of Palestine' shall not take precedence over Britain's 'international obligations'. (CO 733/167/6: HC Chancellor to SSC Amery, 15 Jan. 1929)

51 In 1921 at the Cairo Conference, SSC Churchill refused to meet a delegation of the AE (see below). On 1 March 1922, Churchill told an Arab Delegation in London that he did not recognize them as representative of the Palestinian population: since no official machinery for representation existed, they were not a Delegation of which he would take heed. Taggar (op. cit.: 33) points out that this was contrary to Ottoman custom, in accordance with which the heads of various communities would be considered as representative of the people. When Jamal Husseini, the Mufti's nephew, visited London in December 1929, he was met with some coolness by the Colonial Office. His visit was tolerated as long as he restricted his opining to matters relating to the SMC and did not touch on political questions (see CO 733/178/1, Minute). HC Chancellor had reported that the AE did not want Jamal Bey to discuss politics in London, but recommended that he be granted an interview 'if a satisfactory reason is given'. Minutes on the front of a file dealing with his visit read:

> I do not like this at all ... In support of his request for an interview Jamaal sends us a letter of introduction from Mr. Philby, which is about the worst commendation to HMG that the wit of man could devise'. (ibid., Wilson)

Jamal Husseini's demands for 'justice', by which he meant 'not redress of practical grievances due to conflict of interests between Jews and Arabs, but the grant to Palestine of some form of representative government' was pronounced 'unthinkable', even with the High Commissioner holding an ultimate veto (see CO 733/178/1, note of an interview between Jamal Husseini and Secretary of State on 19 Dec. 1929, made by Williams). When an Arab delegation was preparing to visit London in 1930, Chancellor explained to them that the constitution of this delegation was crucial. The HC

> did not want them to go there and find that there was no one to receive them. Now, in such circumstances the SSC would ask him who the delegation were and whom did they represent. He wanted to be able to say that they were really the representative leaders of the Arab population of Palestine. (Chancellor Papers, box 14, File 3, Notes on meeting with the Mufti, 7 Jan. 1930: ff. 1–9)

Note that Chancellor was also advising that this delegation should be nominated and not elected, and we may wonder in that case what is meant by 'representative of the population of Palestine'. Similarly, the delegation was to proceed to London unsure of which topics they would be allowed to bring up in negotiations, a matter to be decided by the SSC, according to the HC (see Chancellor Papers, Box 14, File 3, 'Meeting with the Arab Delegation': ff. 54–64). In the wake of a general strike, as tension in Palestine reached unprecedented levels, the AHC was invited to London in 1936 to discuss a possible Legislative Council. They refused, despite HC Wauchope's best efforts to convince them otherwise, on the basis that the assurances they sought regarding land sales and immigration had not been granted. (CO 733/307/10, Minutes of interview between HC and the Arab leaders, 21 April 1936)

Chapter 5

The last word:

The unusual suspects

Paper dolls, labelled targets. These were dangerous days for Palestinian politicians, their status in perpetual flux. The government did what they promised and they arrested, deported, imprisoned, or chased the political leaders out of the country. H.F.K. was one of them. A 'moderate' (distinguished in this case from 'collaborator' – but how would we know, since 'moderate' and 'extremist' are the two gross and un-nuanced colonial categories) by the Mandatory. Regardless of his smooth political incline, of his placatory approach, H.F.K. was ultimately as obsolete and insignificant as the Mufti who fell from grace, as the collaborators who accepted the rules of the game, as the pan-Arabists who denounced Imperialism, as the Islamic preachers who swore Jihad, as the rebel who died on the land he could never save.

The following is an excerpt from the diaries of H.F.K. in which he recounts his arrest in Jerusalem and his deportation to the Seychelles. I include it with reference to an activity encouraged by Foucault (1991: 6): 'questioning the document'. Historical analyses need not (should not) be restricted to establishing continuities or proving the causality between events, and may extend to questioning the status of a particular text. So historians do not merely inquire into the meaning of a document, into whether it is authentic, whether it may have been tampered with and whether it is telling the truth. Historians are also responsible for turning certain documents into 'monuments'. It is those documents which are recognizable to society which are transformed into 'monuments' of that society's history. (ibid.: 7) Is the following document 'recognizable' to us? Can it ever be 'monumental' in that sense?

H.F.K's career demonstrates the uselessness, danger and inappropriateness of moderation under a colonial situation. He kept his deportation/exile diary in English. His tone is obedient and objective, if taut and contained. His attention to the minutest detail may be a deliberate diversion from the violent, surreal upheaval of his life and forceful separation from his home and family. He keeps the full extent of the slight at bay – or, one feels, he may well unravel. The document, with its placid language, its light and polite turn of phrase, beautifully embodies the powerlessness and inconsequentiality of the native élite. Discourse-wise, they are suspended between claims to nativism (by the peasant) and claims to modernity (by the colonialist). The symbolic resonance of the document rivals its historical relevance as literature from the front: the native is subject to the barbarism and whim of the colonialist, to his swift response, regardless of how well he speaks English, or how moderate or modern he is. As H.F.K. is seized and ceremonially removed from Palestine, even though he does his best to sanitize his rage, our naïve heart sinks with the realization that there simply is no cure for the native condition, it is fatal and inescapable. Whether you are a frenetic, feverish peasant or a soft spoken government doctor from town: humiliation is in store.

Hfk Diary – Volume I – Our trip to the Seychelles Islands

Thursday the 30/9/37

When I awoke at about 7 am on Thursday the 30/9/37, I never dreamt that next day I would be on board one of H.M. Ships bound for an unknown destination. Well, this is going to be the record of my trip to the Seychelles and a diary of our stay there. I am writing now while sitting on the north western veranda of Villa Curio in Port Victoria – Mahe Island.

I think I better record what happened on Thursday before I left Jerusalem. I had a very busy day before noon at the municipality preparing the agenda for my Council meeting due at 3pm. In the afternoon I went home at about 1pm and returned to the municipality at 3pm sharp. Farraj, Darwish, Dajani and [illegible] did not come, all the others were present. We had a long agenda to deal with. With the exception of a few hot words between me and Auster on the question of the Cadre, the meeting terminated successfully at 7.30pm. I thought that before going home I better clear all my trays and issue the necessary instruction to Heads of Department, arising out of the meeting. In fact I left nothing outstanding. At 8pm Rasim came to the municipality and we stayed there till 9pm. He told me all about his trip to Gaza, Beersheba and the North. From the municipality we went to uncle Moustafa's house where we stayed about an hour and then went home. Rasim stayed with me till 11pm.

I stayed late tonight chatting with Wahide about children's schools and so on, when I ultimately went to sleep about 12 midnight.

Friday 1/10/37

I was just opening my eyes and still dozing when one of the children, I think it was Leila, came into our room on tip-toe and whispered something to Wahide. My wife got out of bed and returned a few minutes later to awake me. She told me there was a police officer and two constables outside asking for me and she looked scared and worried. I did not believe it at first, but when I realized I was not dreaming, I got out of bed, pulled an overall over my pyjamas and looking out of the window saw about four constables in my garden. I entered the sitting room to find Mr. Riggs of the CID waiting there. He had a worried look. He began by saying:

'Well my dear doctor I am so sorry, it's my unpleasant duty to inform you that you are under arrest.'

'Under arrest!' I couldn't believe my ears. 'What for? May I know' I said.

'I'm afraid I don't know' he replied 'it's the instruction of the AG Mr Rice'.

'But I think I'm entitled to know the reason Mr. Riggs' I said 'will you allow me to ring up Mr. Rice.'

'Surely you can' he said.

I rang up Mr. Rice whom I fortunately found in his office. He couldn't tell me on the telephone. But he would come to my house if I told Mr. Riggs. I conveyed the message to Mr. Riggs. He left at once. I returned to Wahide who was waiting patiently to hear the news. I could not tell her at first that I was under arrest. I had to say something and soothe her. I said they wanted me at police headquarters to ask a few questions. She would not believe what I said, because she was expecting something one day and especially deportation.

In a few minutes Mr. Rice arrived. He was very kind, and said he had nothing to do with it, neither did he advise government to take such a step, that the orders came from the OAG and I should pack up a few articles of clothing, as I and others were going for a trip to Haifa. I thought of the Acre Concentration Camp at first; but he said he was under the impression that we are going to sea. I asked for half an hour to shave, dress and prepare. 'You will shave on the ship. If you will be ready in about 15 minutes, I will be grateful. I have arranged for you to go in a closed car, and not a police van, and I shall tell Riggs to send off the constables and take you in his private car. Fuad Saba will be going with you. *I wonder whether you may happen to know where Jamal Husseini is?* He is not at home.'[1] 'He may probably be at Jericho', I replied. ' I wish you a good journey', he said 'and God be with you'. I could just see a tear in each eye, as he gripped my hand firmly and said goodbye. I think Rice is a fine man and I am grateful for his coming in person to explain matters and say goodbye. I am sure he has nothing to do with our deportation. I told Riggs to wait for me while I dress. Wahide was waiting for me to hear what Rice had to say.

'Well old girl' I said 'will you pack up my things as quick as possible – I am going on a sea-journey'.

Wahide began weeping. I tried to say a few consoling words. I know I stammered something, as tears flew out of my eyes. I dressed hurriedly while Wahide was packing. The children with open eyes were around us wondering what was it all about. I turned to Adel and told him that now his turn had come. I am leaving them God knows for how long, and I wanted him to behave properly towards his brothers and sisters, and that I depended upon him to take my place at home and be a good boy. His eyes sparkled and he promised he would. I am sure I can depend upon him. I had to say goodbye and kissed my wife and children again and again. Wahide was weeping bitterly and when I sat in the car and waved my hand to them for the last time they were standing on the veranda, I felt a lump in my throat and tears rolled out of my eyes. Who knows whether I will come back one day to see them all fit and healthy. Riggs was very touched and he gulped and there were tears in his eyes also.

We drove up to Mount Scopus Police Training School, I and Mr. Riggs. We were met there by Inspector Black the H/OC. He was very kind too – knowing all my first aid services to the Police Force. Riggs left and I stayed in Mr. Black's office awaiting further orders from the H/IG.

At about 8am Fuad Saba was brought into the office of Inspector Black too. He told me they came to his house at about 6.30am; but he was still unaware as to where we were to be taken. He thought we were going to Acre. But I gave him the (hint?) and told him that we were going to Haifa to the sea … We waited for some time until his bags came from home. I again spoke to Mr. Rice on the telephone. He said we were going on board a ship but our destination was still unknown to him. At 9.15 sharp word was passed that the cars were ready and we were to proceed.

Our luggage was put in a police tender carrying a machine gun and crew of four British constables. We drove in an Austin with a constable in plain clothes on the wheel and another constable in [?] with a drawn revolver in his lap. I thought we would take the Nablus road but to my astonishment we took the Nablus road into Jerusalem and then the Jaffa road. Many Arabs saw us especially Lifta villagers who stood gaping at me. I asked the driver which direction we were going and he said it was Jaffa. I was a bit perturbed as I am sure Rice told me we were going to Haifa. Possibly they have changed their minds when we at last reached the outskirts of Jaffa near the square opposite [Awni?] Bey's house, a police officer stopped us and directed our car to Tel Aviv! A motorcycle driven by a British constable went before us with two police tenders behind. The motorcycle driver was stopping all cars on the road to open a way for us and I felt like a HC. It was great fun I told Saba. We drove out of Tel Aviv with Jews glaring at us. The monkeys – they did not realise however who were the two occupants of the [?] car.

We passed Petach Tikvah after having thought we were to embark at the Tel Aviv jetty. But not until we passed that blooming colony, heading for Haifa, did we realize that the authorities did not want us to pass through Nablus and Jenin. They may have been afraid of Abu Jildeh coming to the rescue.

On the outskirts of Haifa we were met by another British police officer with two tenders of constables armed to the teeth, who directed our car driver to follow.

We did that and by God they were driving at 70 and 80 kilometres through the streets of Haifa. I thought they were mad. We narrowly escaped two or three collisions with other cars.

When we passed the port area and headed on to the Nazareth road I looked at Fuad. Could they have changed their mind again and are taking us to Acre? But as soon as we reached Shell bridge we swung to the left and we drove into the oil area. From there we could see a few ships and a man of war standing outside the port. We wondered I and Fuad whether it would be a merchant or a battleship. At 12.15 we reached the Shell's Jetty and there in front of us was a motor launch full of British [?] we now naturally knew our destination.

Our luggage was transferred to the launch. Our car was surrounded with constables with drawn revolver. We went on board and headed for the battleship. It was a rather big one and when we came near we saw it was HMS Sussex a cruiser of over 10 000 tons carrying about 600 sailors and officers.

We went aboard and were met on the ship's stairs by a senior officer and about a dozen sailors standing in a line. When we passed them, they and the officer gave us a naval salute. Fuad tells me he saw Mr. Keith-Roach D-C and Pasha of Haifa standing bare headed behind the row of sailors. I didn't see him myself. He didn't seem to take any notice of us. But why was he there gaping at us? If I meet him again I shall tell him what I think of him. They took us into a small room which looked like a small dining room. We had lunch in a suffocating atmosphere as it was so hot we were sweating like hell, in spite of the constant motion of two electric fans.

At 1.30pm all of a sudden the door opened and in came Rashid Al Haj Ibrahim the Branch Manager of the Arab Bank at Haifa. He was astonished to see us there as he thought he was to be alone. Well three are better than one I said. He had lunch and told us that while at the bank about 10am he was requested to see the DSP, he realized he was being arrested and would be taken to Acre. He was detained at Police barrack for two hours where he hurriedly arranged his affairs with his son. At last he was put in a car brought to the Shell jetty and taken on board the Sussex. He also had a naval salute.

At 3.30pm I heard some movement on board and I saw Hilmi Pasha descending the stairs. We had been removed into an enclosure of canvas hurriedly prepared for our detention with a few easy chairs a writing pad and a pack of cards. There was a captain in charge of us with four sentinels. The place was suffocating and I felt very tired and oppression around the heart as if I was having a heat stroke and was on the point of calling the ship's doctor. We asked them to [?] a fan [?] in the enclosure which they did at once.

The treatment up to this hour was rather courteous but with a reserved attitude. We were not allowed to leave the enclosure without escort.

Rashid Eff.[2] was asked whether he would like to order anything from shore provided his letter was written in English. I arranged that for him and he asked for his baggage and a long list of articles.

Well so far so good.

After the arrival of Hilmi Pasha we again said four is better than three. We discussed matters and we realized that the authorities were arresting the Arab Higher Committee for deportation and we began wondering what happened to the other members? And where will they send us? We thought of Malta, Cyprus, [?] Islands and even Seychelles.

But why have they arrested Haj Ibrahim? He is not a member of the AHC. He laughingly said he was in lieu of Auni Bey![3] The Pasha then related his story. He was at his orange grove at Beit Hanoun near Gaza. Early in the morning his son came in to his room and informed him that the house was surrounded with police men. He dressed hurriedly and met a British and a Palestinian officer (a Jaouni), who informed him they had a warrant for his arrest. He protested, but what was the use of protest. He was put in a car and had a police tender as escort. Poor Pasha he had nothing with him except a small valise with one pyjama and a few odd articles. He was driven through the new Jaffa-Haifa road then to the Shell jetty and was brought on board. When the Pasha arrived I received a letter from Mr. Rice the A/IG [?] which read as follows:

'From Rice to Dr. Khalidi Haifa. Mrs. Khalidi asks me to pass the following message. That the children are well. You are not to worry. Take care of your health, and whenever it is possible for you to write, say where and how you are. Ends. Adieu. Your wife is very brave. Good luck. Rice'.

At 8pm we were called to dinner. The food was good and the fruits plentiful. After dinner we returned to the hellish canvas enclosure where we stayed till about 11pm. A naval officer came and escorted us to our sleeping quarters. We had to pass the seamen's quarters most of whom were in swings of the roof and [?] at us as if we were strange creatures! We at last came to a big ward with 8 beds which looked like the ship's hospital which in fact it was as we learned afterward. Saba slept on the lower bed and I slept in the upper one while the Pasha and Rashid slept in the two lower ones. There was plenty of air circulation from special ventilating holes ... I thought I must have a bath as I have perspired more than I have done before in my life. I went into the bathroom and gee wiz! There was no douche[4] but a bath tub and one or two basins. I could not manipulate the hot and cold water ... I decided to risk it. Preferred the cold water to the boiling. Well it was most refreshing and I felt a changed man after it. I slept well that night ...

The captain came at 6.30am and told us to be ready in 15 minutes as we were wanted on deck. He then said we could have a little more time. 7.30 would do. He asked whether we would like to have anything. We asked for tea and cigarettes. He went himself and brought Turkish and English cigarettes. We thanked him. I must say he was very polite and obliging. A fair haired officer with a small moustache. He remained standing near the door of the hospital the whole time.

At 7.30 sharp a senior naval officer who seemed to be the second in command came into our cabin and said: 'We have tried gentlemen to make you as comfortable as possible on this ship and we have done our best. You will now be transferred to another ship.' We were asked to see that our baggage is OK which we did.

This is Saturday the 2/10/37

A minute later an officer called 'Mr. Mayor, will you kindly come with me. One by one please.' I did so. He walked in front and I was escorted by two sailors with my overcoat on my left arm and my walking stick in my right hand. My face must have looked rather serious and grave. I had a feeling of a man who was being taken to face the firing squad. But I didn't mind it really as my conscience is absolutely at rest.

I walked along mounted stairs and was on deck the Sussex. I looked out and the shore was far away and we must have steamed out of Haifa Harbour when I was asleep. Lying side by side of the Sussex was what looked to me like a kind of steam launch (the tonnage of the Sussex is 10 000 tons). We went on board the small ship, from a hanging stairs, walked a few metres and descended into a cabin. There was the usual row of sailors, a tall officer (a rather big man, surely a plus six footer) and another officer.

When all of us arrived an officer came in and informed us that he was instructed to search our luggage, which he did. Naturally we had nothing but apparently it was a matter of routine and formality rather than actual searching. I had already handed my revolver and its license to Cpt. Riggs Friday morning. After the search the officer showed us a bell which we were to ring twice for the steward in case we needed anything like drinks or cigarettes. He was assisted in the search by another officer whom I was informed was the Asst. M.O. of the Sussex, and who was detailed to accompany us on our journey to look after our health as small ships like the one we were on do not carry doctors.

The cabin we were in was rather a nice one it contained one bunk, a small camp bed and a sitting room with two comfortable armchairs an improvised couch 2 chairs, a good table, cupboards and chest of drawers, a book case, a map of Spain and a few other articles. It looked cosy and nice. I had practically consumed all my cigarettes and had to fall back on Rashid Eff. for my supply. He luckily had brought some with him about 25 [?] of [?] cigarettes.

At 8am sharp the ship began to move ahead straight west to south. We began guessing our course. Rashid said it was Cyprus, the Pasha said Malta, I thought it was Egypt. When we were told that we could use the drawers to put our things in, we knew it was not a short journey. We tried to get some information from this officer but his reply was that he did not know himself. They receive orders to proceed to a given direction and not to a known destination. We knew now that we were on board HMS Destroyer Active, known as H. 14 carrying 120 and its tonnage 1330. Well compare 1330 tons with 10 000 tons and you will realize the difference between the Sussex cruiser and the Active Destroyer. We further knew that we were accommodated in the Captain's cabin (the six footer gentleman) and that the officer searching our baggage was the second in command called Mr. Barker age 31 married and the doctor called F.W. Baskerville a 1933 graduate married also.

At 11am we were allowed to go on the rear deck which is usually called the quarter deck and is reserved for the officers. 3 deck chairs were at our disposal and 2 other smaller chairs. The sea was quite calm and we felt relieved breathing the fresh and cool air of the Mediterranean sea. We were informed by Mr. Barker that he used to be on board another destroyer called HMS Hunter. It was a brand new one launched this year and detailed to carry anti-piracy work in the Mediterranean. It struck a floating mine off the shores of Spain and sank with 8 men killed and 30 wounded. He was one of the survivors. They were transferred to the Active which was built in 1929 and was lying in reserve at Portsmouth. Men were recruited and she was brought to Malta, when she received orders to proceed to Haifa and meet the Sussex.

At about 11.30 and all of a sudden, the Destroyer changed her course and turned north east. We were astonished and tried to find the reason; but no one would tell us. The ship continued changing course and at about 12.30 we were asked to go below to have lunch. We came to the cabin and found all port holes closed. We asked the sentinel to open them, but he replied they had to be closed till further notice.

At about 2.45pm I looked out of the closed port hole and found land ahead. We were approaching Jaffa port.

Again we asked have they changed their minds? And are they taking us back to Acre?

At about 2pm we saw two (2) motor launches heading from the port in the Destroyer. When the first came near we saw a police officer and one or two in civilian clothes. It was the port's boat. All of a sudden we saw Yacoub Gossein in it and we realized why the destroyer changed course after heading for Egypt.

Gossein had the usual naval salute and then he was a few minutes later sitting with the four of us.

We were now five.

And here is the story he gave us:

On Friday morning rumours were circulated of government action in arresting leaders. He thought of buzzing off, which he did. Police came and surrounded his house at Wadi [?] but did not find him. On Friday afternoon govt. issued a proclamation he said to the effect that{:} whereas of the state of unrest prevailing in the country for some time and the acts of terrorism which were crowned lately by the murder of the late Mr. Andrews considers the AHC responsible normally for this state of affairs and it has therefore been decided to arrest and deport the following gentlemen:

Jamal Husseini
Hilmi Pasha
Dr. Khalidi
Rashid Haj Ibrahim
Yacoub Gossein
Fuad Saba

The declaration further said that government has further decided to deprive the Mufti Haj Amin Husseini of all his official posts.

[?] a lot of other people were being arrested including Fahmi Husseini Mayor of Gaza and confined at Acre concentration camp.

The news worried us a lot especially [holding?] the AHC morally responsible for the terrorism taking place in the country.

Monday the 17/10/37 [in Mahe, Seychelles]
I was awakened at 6am by the hammering of rain on the roof. It must be falling down in sheets. That reminds me that I must look, in what available records we have, today and find out the rainfall in Mahe.

As I sat in bed at 6 I began thinking of home. It is now still 4am in Jerusalem and I wonder whether Wahide is still sleeping. I tried to do some wireless brain transmission and concentrating began calling her name. Did she hear I wonder? I shall ask her when I return home. I then whistled my usual tune to Leila. Pierre came in and asked what I wanted. Damn it, I didn't want Pierre, I wanted Leila to come in. Well I did not want to disappoint the boy and told him to get me a cup of tea and hot water for shaving and prepare the bath.

Friday the 22/10/37
I wonder whether Wahide is now thinking of me as she awoke. I am sure she will not forget me. She may now at this moment be talking to me. I wonder what she does all day long alone when the children all go to school. That was what passed through my brain as I sat in bed gazing at the ceiling and massaging my massive abdominal fat. I do this every morning. I think I am reducing.

Notes

1 Jamal Husseini, member of the AHC and nephew of Haj Amin Husseini. He escaped.
2 Eff.: Short for Effendi, an Ottoman title.
3 Auni Bey, founder of the anti-imperialist Istiqlal party and an ideological thorn in the side of the mandatory. In 1936, they said of him: 'Auni Bey and his influence was definitely in the direction of encouraging terrorism. I could not say that he was actually giving instructions to blow up this bridge or to waylay that patrol, but he was all along putting steam behind the terrorist campaign.' (See CO 733/297/3, minute interview between HC and Shertock, 2 Feb.1936, in Telegram SSC to HC on 17 June 1936.)
4 Douche (Fr): shower.

Bibliography

Abacarius, F. M. (1946) *Palestine Through the Fog of Propaganda*, London: Hutchinson and Co.

Abboushi, W. F. (1977) 'The road to rebellion: Arab Palestine in the 1930s', *Journal of Palestine Studies*, 6, 2: 23–46.

Abu El-Haj, Nadia (2001) *Facts on the Ground: archaeological practice and territorial self-fashioning in Israeli society*, London and Chicago: University of Chicago Press.

Adas, M. (1979) *Prophets of Rebellion: millenarian protest orders against the European colonial order*, Chapel Hill: The University of North Carolina Press.

Afzal-Khan, F. and Sheshadri-Crooks, K. (eds) (2000) *The Pre-Occupation of Post-colonial Studies*, Durham, NC: Duke University Press.

Akpan, N. U. (1956) *Epitaph to Indirect Rule: a discourse on local government in Africa*, London: Cassell and Co.

Al-Hout, B. N. (1979) 'The Palestinian Political Elite during the Mandate Period' *Journal of Palestine Studies* 9, 1: 85–111.

Antonius, G. (1938) *The Arab Awakening*, London: Hamish Hamilton.

Apthorpe, R. (ed.) (1960) *From Tribal Rule to Modern Government*, Lusaka: the Institute.

Aref Al Aref (1974) *Bedouin Love, Law and Legend*, New York: A.M.S. Press.

Arnon-Ohanna, Y. (1981) 'The bands in the Palestinian Arab Revolt 1936–39, structure and organization', *Asian and African Studies* 15: 229–47

Asad, T. (ed.) (1973) *Anthropology and the Colonial Encounter*, London: Ithaca Press.

——(1976) 'Class transformation under the mandate', *MERIP Reports*, No. 53.

——(1991) 'Afterword: from the history of colonial anthropology to the anthropology of Western hegemony', in G.W. Stocking (ed.) *Colonial Situations: essays on the contextualization of ethnographic knowledge*, Maddison, WI: University of Wisconsin Press.

Ashforth, A. (1990) *The Politics of Official Discourse in Twentieth-century South Africa*, Oxford: Clarendon Press.

Atran, S. (1989) 'The surrogate colonization of Palestine, 1917–39', *American Ethnologist* 16, 4: 719–44.

Attridge, D., Bennington, G. and Young, R. (eds) (1987) *Post-Structuralism and the Question of History*, Cambridge: Cambridge University Press.

Baer, G. (1978) 'The economic and social position of the village Mukhtar in Palestine', in G. Ben Dor, (ed.) *The Palestinians and the Middle East Conflict*, Israel: Turtledove Publishing.

Baldensperger, P. J. (1913) *The Immoveable East: studies of the people and customs of Palestine*, London: Pitman.

Balfour-Paul, G. (1999) 'Britain's informal empire in the Middle East', in J. Brown and R. Louis (eds) *Oxford History of the British Empire,* vol. 4, Oxford: Oxford University Press.

Barghuti, Omar (1922) 'Judicial courts among the Bedouin of Palestine', *The Journal of the Palestine Oriental Society* 2: 34–65.

Barker, F., Hulme, P. and Iversen, M. (eds) (1966) *Colonial Discourse/Postcolonial Theory*, Manchester and New York: Manchester University Press.

Basheer, T. (1969) *Edwin Montagu and the Balfour Declaration*, London: Arab League Office.

Ben Dor, G. (ed.) (1978) *The Palestinians and the Middle East Conflict*, Israel: Turtledove Publishing.

Ben Nefissa, S. (1999) 'The Haq el Arab: conflict resolution and distinctive features of legal pluralism in contemporary Egypt', in B. Dupret, M. Berger and L. Al-Zwaini (eds) *Legal Pluralism in the Arab World*, The Hague and Boston: Kluwer Law International.

Benjamin, A. (ed.) (1991) *The Lyotard Reader Jean-Francois Lyotard*, Oxford: Blackwell.

Benton, L. (1999) 'Colonial law and cultural difference: jurisdictional politics and the formation of the colonial state', *Comparative Studies in Society and History* 41, 3: 563–88.

Bentwich, N. (1932) *England in Palestine*, London: Kegan Paul, Trench, Trubner and Co. Ltd.

Berry, S. (1992) 'Hegemony on a shoestring: indirect rule and access to agricultural land', *Africa* 62, 3: 327–55.

Bhabha, H. K. (2004) *The Location of Culture*, London: Routledge.

Bivona, D. (1997) 'The erotic politics of indirect rule', *Prose Studies* 20, 1: 90–118.

Blomley, N. (1994) *Law, Space and the Geographies of Power*, New York and London: Guildford.

——Delaney, D. and Ford R. T. (eds) (2001) *The Legal Geographies Reader: law, power and space*, Malden, MA: Blackwell.

Blue, G. (2002) 'Introduction', in G. Blue, M. Bunton and R. Croizier (eds) *Colonialism and the Modern World: selected studies*, Armonk, NY: M. E. Sharpe.

——Bunton, M. and Croizier, R. (eds) (2002), *Colonialism and the Modern World: selected studies*, Armonk, NY: M. E. Sharpe.

Bohannan, P. (1967) 'Africa's Land', in G. Dalton (ed.) *Tribal and Peasant Economies: readings in economic anthropology*, Garden City, NY: Natural History Press.

Bowden, T. (1975) 'The politics of the Arab rebellion in Palestine 1936–39', *Middle Eastern Studies* 11, 2: 147–74.

Brown, J. and Louis, R. (eds) (1999) *Oxford History of the British Empire*, vol. 4, Oxford: Oxford University Press.

Brown, R. (1960) 'Indirect rule as a policy of adaptation', in R. J. Apthorpe (ed.) *From Tribal Rule to Modern Government*, Lusaka: the Institute.

Brunette, P. and Wills, D (eds) (1993), *Deconstruction in the Visual Arts*, Cambridge University Press.

Bryman, A. (ed.) (2001) *Ethnography*, London: Sage Publications.

Budeiri, M. (1997) 'The Palestinians: tensions between nationalist and religious identities', in J. Jankowski and I. Gershoni (eds) *Rethinking Nationalism in the Arab Middle East*, New York: Columbia University Press, 1997.

Bunton, M. (1997) 'The role of private property in the British Administration of Palestine 1917–36', D. Phil. thesis, University of Oxford.

——(1999) 'Inventing the status quo: Ottoman land law during the Palestine Mandate, 1917–36', *International History Review* 21, 1: 28–56.

——(2000) 'Demarcating the British colonial state: land settlement in the Palestine Jiftlik villages of Sajad and Qazaza', in R. Owen, (ed.) *New Perspectives on Property and Land in the Middle East*, Cambridge, MA: Harvard Centre for Middle East Studies.

Burman, S. and Harrell-Bond, B. (eds) (1979), *The Imposition of* Law, London: Academic Press.

Cameron, D. (1939) *My Tanganyika Service and Some Nigeria*, London: Allen and Unwin.

Cannadine, D. (2001) *Ornamentalism: how the British saw their empire*, London: Allen Lane.

Cell, J. W. (1999) 'Colonial Rule', in J. Brown and R. Louis (eds) *Oxford History of the British Empire*, vol. 4, Oxford: Oxford University Press.

Césaire, A. (1972) *Discourse on Colonialism*, New York: Monthly Review Press.

Chakrabarty, D. (1997) 'Postcoloniality and the artifice of history: who speaks for "Indian" pasts?', in R. Guha (ed.) *A Subaltern Studies Reader 1986–1995*, Minneapolis and London: University of Minnesota Press.

Chambers, I. (2002) *Migrancy, Culture, Identity*, London: Routledge.

Chanock, M. (1991) 'Paradigms, policies and property: a review of the customary law of land tenure', in K. Mann and R. Roberts (eds) *Law in Colonial Africa*, London: James Currey.

Chatterjee, Partha (1986) *Nationalist Thought and the Colonial World: a derivative discourse?* London: Zed for the United Nations University.

——(1989) 'Subaltern Consciousness', in Guha (ed.) *Subaltern Studies VI: writings on South Asian history and society*, Delhi and Oxford: Oxford University Press.

——(1992) 'Their own words? An essay for Edward Said', in M. Sprinker (ed.) *Edward Said, A Critical Reader*, Cambridge, MA: Blackwell.

——(1993) *The Nation and Its Fragments: colonial and post-colonial histories*, Princeton, NJ: Princeton University Press.

Chinhengo, A. (2000) 'The colonial clash of conceptions of land and law in Southern Africa and the genesis of the *Zimbabwe Land Question*'. Paper presented at the Third International Crossroads in Cultural Studies Conference, University of Birmingham, 21 June.

Cohen, M. J. (1973) 'Sir Arthur Wauchope, the army, and the rebellion in Palestine, 1936', *Middle Eastern Studies* 9, 1: 19–34.

——and Kolinsky, M. (eds) (1992), *Britain and the Middle East in the 1930s: security problems 1935–1939*, London and New York: MacMillan.

Cohen, S. A. (1976) *British Policy in Mesopotamia 1903–1914*, London: Ithaca Press.

Cohn, B. S. (1987) *An Anthropologist Among the Historians and Other Essays*, Oxford: Oxford University Press.

Colson, Elizabeth (1971) 'The Impact of the Colonial World on the Definition of Land Rights', in V. Turner, (ed.) *Colonialism in Africa 1870–1960 (volume 3), Profiles of Change: African society and colonial rule*, Cambridge: Cambridge University Press.

Comaroff, J. (2001) 'Symposium introduction: colonialism, culture and the law – a foreword', *Law and Social Inquiry* 26, 2: 305–14.

——(1989) 'Images of empire, contests of conscience: models of colonial domination in South Africa', *American Ethnologist* 16, 4: 601–85.

——and Comaroff, Jean (1992) *Ethnography and the Historical Imagination*, Boulder, CO: Westview Press.

Cooper, F. (1994) 'Conflict and connection: rethinking colonial African history', *The American Historical Review* 99, 5: 1516–45.

——and Stoler, A. L. (1989) 'Introduction, tensions of empire: colonial control and visions of rule', *American Ethnologist* 16, 4: 609–21.

Cosgrove, D. and Daniels, S. (eds) (1988) *The Iconography of Landscape: essays on the symbolic representation, design and use of past environments*, Cambridge: Cambridge University Press.

Crapanzano, V. (1985) *Tuhami: portrait of a Moroccan*, Chicago: University of Chicago Press.

Cromer, Earl of (Evelyn Baring) (1908) *Modern Egypt* (2 vols), London: MacMillan and Co.

Dalton, G. (1967) *Tribal and Peasant Economies: readings in economic anthropology*, Garden City, NY: Natural History Press.

Danaher, G., Schirato, T. and Webb, J. (2000) *Understanding Foucault*, London: Sage Publications.

Darwin, John (1999) 'A third British Empire? The dominion idea in imperial politics', in J. Brown and R. Louis (eds) *Oxford History of the British Empire*, vol. 4, Oxford: Oxford University Press.

Derrida, Jacques (1981) *Dissemination*, Chicago: Chicago University Press.

——(1982) *The Margins of Philosophy*, Brighton: Harvester Press.

Dirks, N. B. (ed.) (1992) *Colonialism and Culture*, Ann Arbor: University of Michigan Press.

Doumani, B. (1992) 'Rediscovering Ottoman Palestine: writing Palestinians into history', *Journal of Palestine Studies* 21, 1: 5–28.

Dupret, B., Berger, M. and Al-Zwaini, L. (eds) (1999) *Legal Pluralism in the Arab World*, The Hague and Boston: Kluwer Law International.

Eagleton, T., Jameson, F. and Said, E. (eds) (1990) *Nationalism, Colonialism and Literature*, Minneapolis: University of Minnesota Press, 1990.

Edney, M. H. (1997) *Mapping an Empire: the geographical construction of British India, 1765–1843*, Chicago and London: University of Chicago Press.

Emerson, R. (1937) *Malaysia: a study in direct and indirect rule*, New York: MacMillan and Co.

Fanon, F. (1952) *Peau Noire, Masques Blancs*, Paris: Editions Du Seuil.

——(1963) *The Wretched of the Earth*, New York: Grove Press.

Falah, Ghazi (1983) 'The role of the British administration in the sedenterization of the Bedouin tribes in Northern Palestine 1918–48', Durham University Centre for Middle Eastern Studies *Occasional Paper Series*.

Farah, Randa (2002) 'The significance of oral narratives and life-histories', *Al-Jana Magazine*, Beirut: Arab Resource Center for Popular Arts.

Finn, Mrs (1897) *The Fellaheen of Palestine, notes on their clans, religions, warfare and law*, Palestine Exploration Fund Quarterly Statement, 1897.

Firestone, Yacov (1981) 'Land equalisation and factor scarcities', *Journal of Economic History* 41, 4: 813–33.

——(1990)'The land equalising Musha', in G. Gilbar (ed.) *Ottoman Palestine, 1800–1914: Studies in economic and social history*, Leiden: E. J. Brill, 1990.

Fisch, Yorg (1991) 'Law as a means to an end', in W. J. Mommsen and J. A. De Moor (eds) *European Expansion and the Law: the encounter of European and indigenous law in 19th and 20th Century Africa and Asia*, New York: Berg.

Forman, G. (2002) 'Settlement of title in the Galilee: Dowson's colonial principles' *Israel Studies* 7, 3: 61–83.

——and Kedar, A. (2003) 'Colonialism, colonization and land law in Mandatory Palestine: the Zor al-Zarqa and Barrat Qisarya land disputes in historical perspective', *Theoretical Inquiries in Law* 4, 2: 491–540.

Foucault, Michel (1991) *The Archaeology of Knowledge*, London and New York: Routledge.

——(1995) *Discipline and Punish: the birth of the prison*, New York: Vintage.

——(2001) *The Order of Things: an archaeology of the human sciences*, London: Routledge.

Fox, R. G. (1992) 'East of Said', in M. Sprinker (ed.) *Edward Said, a critical reader*, Cambridge, MA: Blackwell.

Friesl, E. (1988) *The Balfour Declaration in Historical Perspective*, University of Cape Town: Kaplan Centre Papers.

Ganguly, K. (1990) 'Ethnography, representation and the representation of colonialist discourse', *Studies in Symbolic Interaction,* vol. 3, Greenwich, CT: Jain Press.

Garnett, D. (1983) *The Selected Letters of T.E. Lawrence*, London: Jonathan Cape.

Geertz, C. (1993) *The Interpretation of Cultures: selected essays*, London: Fontana Press.

——(2000) *Local Knowledge*, New York: Basic Books.

Gilbar, G. (ed.) (1990) *Ottoman Palestine, 1800–1914: studies in economic and social history*, Leiden: E. J. Brill.

Gluckman, M. (1963) *Order and Rebellion in Tribal Africa*, London: Cohen & West.

Goadby, F. and Dhoukan, M. (1935) *The Land Law of Palestine*, Tel-Aviv, Palestine: s.n.

Goodrich-Freer, A. (1924) *Arabs in Tent and Town*, London: Seeley-Service.

Goody, J. (1995) *The Expansive Moment: the rise of social anthropology in Britain and Africa 1918–1970*, Cambridge: Cambridge University Press.

Gottschalk, L. (1969) *Understanding History: a primer of historical method*, New York: Alfred Knopf.

——Kluckhohn, C. and Angell, R. (eds) (1945) *The Use of Personal Documents in History, Anthropology and Sociology – prepared for the committee on appraisal of research*, New York: Social Science Research Council.

Graves, P. (ed.) (1950) *Memoirs of King Abdullah of Transjordan*, London: Jonathan Cape.

Graves, R. (1927) *Lawrence and the* Arabs, London: Jonathan Cape.

——and Liddell Hart, B. H. (1963) *T.E. Lawrence to His Biographers, Robert Graves and Liddell Hart*, London: Cassel and Co.

Greaves, R. W. (1949) 'The Jerusalem Bishopric, 1841', *The English Historical Review* 64, 252: 328–52.

Guha, R. (1983) *Elementary Aspects of Peasant Insurgency in Colonial India*, Delhi and Oxford: Oxford University Press.

——(ed.) (1986) *Subaltern Studies II: writings on South Asian history and society*, Delhi: Oxford University Press.

——(1987) 'Introduction', in B. S. Cohn (ed.) *An Anthropologist Among the Historians and Other Essays*, Oxford: Oxford University Press.

——(1988) and Spivak, G. C. (eds) (1988), *Selected Subaltern Studies*, New York and Oxford: Oxford University Press.

——(ed.) (1989) *Subaltern Studies VI: writings on South Asian history and society*, Delhi and Oxford: Oxford University Press.

——(1989b) 'Dominance without hegemony and its historiography', in R. Guha (ed.) *Subaltern Studies VI: writings on South Asian history and society*, Delhi and Oxford: Oxford University Press.

——(1997) *A Subaltern Studies Reader, 1986–1995*, Minneapolis and London: University of Minnesota Press.

Gurr, R. T. (1970) *Why Men Rebel*, Princeton, NJ: Princeton University Press.

Gusfield, J. R. (ed.) (1970) *Protest, Reform and Revolt: a reader in social movements*, Chichester: Wiley.

Hall, H. D. (1948) *Mandates, Dependencies and Trusteeships*, London: Stevens for the Carnegie Endowment for International Peace.

Hammersley, M. (1922) *What's Wrong With Ethnography? Methodological Explorations*, London and New York: Routledge.

Hardy, M. J. L. (1963) *Blood Feuds and the Payment of Blood Money in the Middle East*, Leiden: E.J. Brill.

Harley, J. B. (1988) 'Maps, knowledge and power', in D. Cosgrove and S. Daniels (eds) *The Iconography of Landscape: essays on the symbolic representation, design and use of past environments*, Cambridge: Cambridge University Press.

Harris, R., Kedar, A., Lahav, P. and Likhovski, A. (eds) (2002) *The History of Law in Multicultural Society: Israel 1917–1967*, Dartmouth UK: Ashgate.

Hoare, Q. and Smith, G. N. (eds) (1991) *Selections from the Prison Notebooks of Antonio Gramsci*, London: Lawrence and Wishart.

Hobsbawm, E. and Ranger, T. (eds) (1983) *The Invention of Tradition*, Cambridge University Press.

Hodgkin, T. (1972) 'Some African and Third World theories of imperialism', in N. Owen and B. Sutcliffe (eds) *Studies in the Theory of Imperialism*, Harlowe: Longman.

——(1986) *Letters from Palestine 1932–1936*, London: Quartet.

Hodgson, M. and Ballinger, W. G. *Indirect Rule in Southern Africa (no.1)Basutoland*, Lovedale: Lovedale Press.

Holder, J. and Harrison, C. (eds) (2002) *Law and Geography*, Current Legal Issues, vol. 5, Oxford: Oxford University Press.

Holub, R. (1992) *Antonio Gramsci: beyond Marxism and postmodernism*, London and New York: Routledge.

Hyam, R. (1999) 'Bureaucracy and trusteeship in the colonial empire', in J. Brown and R. Louis (eds) *Oxford History of the British Empire,* vol. 4, Oxford: Oxford University Press.

Hyamson, A. M. (1918) *Great Britain and the Jews*, London: The Edinburgh Press.

——(1950) *Palestine Under the Mandate 1920–1948*, London: Methuen & Co.

Inden, R. (1992) *Imagining India*, Oxford: Blackwell.

Jabbour, G. (1970) *Settler Colonialism in Southern Africa and the Middle East*, Beirut: P.L.O. Research Centre.

Jankowski, J. and Gershoni, I. (eds) (1997) *Rethinking Nationalism in the Arab Middle East*, New York: Columbia University Press.

John, R. and Hadawi, S. (1983) *The Palestine Diary*, vol. 1, Beirut: The Palestine Research Centre.

Johnson, N. (1982) *Islam and the Politics of Meaning in Palestinian Nationalism*, London and Boston: Kegan Paul International.

Joll, James (1977) Gramsci, London: Fontana.

Jones, G. (2002) 'Camels, chameleons and coyotes: problematizing the "histories" of land law reform', in J. Holder and C. Harrison (eds) *Law and Geography*, Current Legal Issues, vol. 5, Oxford: Oxford University Press.

Kabha, M. (2003) 'The Palestinian press and the General Strike, April–October 1936: *Filastin* as a case study', *Middle Eastern Studies*, 39, 3: 169–89

Kamuf, P. (ed.) (1991) *A Derrida Reader: between the blinds*, London and New York: Harvester.

Kazemi, F. and Waterbury, J. (eds) (1991) *Peasants and Politics in the Modern Middle East*, Florida: International University Press.

Kedar, A. (2002) 'On the legal geography of ethnocratic settler states: notes towards a research agenda', in J. Holder and C. Harrison (eds) *Law and Geography*, Current Legal Issues, vol. 5, Oxford: Oxford University Press.

Keddie, N. R. (1968) *An Islamic Response to Imperialism*, Berkeley and Los Angeles: University of California Press.

Kedourie, E. (1960) Nationalism, London: Hutchinson.

——(1969) 'Sir Herbert Samuel and the government of Palestine', *Middle Eastern Studies* 5, 1: 44–68.

——(1978) *Britain and the Middle East, 1914–1921*, London: Harvester Press.

——(1984) *The Chatham House Version and Other Middle Eastern Studies*, Hanover and London: University Press of New England.

——and Haim, S. (eds) (1982) *Zionism and Arabism in Palestine and Israel*, London: Frank Cass and Co.

Kennedy, D. (1996), 'Imperial history and post-colonial theory', *The Journal of Imperial and Commonwealth History* 24, 3: 345–63.

Khalidi, R. (1980) *British Policy Towards Syria and Palestine, 1906–1914: a study of the antecedents of the Hussein–McMahon correspondence, the Sykes–Picot Agreement and the Balfour Declaration*, London: Ithaca Press for St. Antony's College.

——(1987) 'A question of land', *Journal of Palestine Studies* 17,1: 146–49.

——(1988) 'Palestinian peasant resistance to Zionism before World War I', in E. Said and C. Hitchens (eds) *Blaming the Victims: Spurious Scholarship and the Palestinian Question*, London and New York: Verso.

——(1997) 'The Formation of Palestinian Identity 1917–23', in J. Jankowski and I. Gershoni (eds) *Rethinking Nationalism in the Arab Middle East*, New York: Columbia University Press.

——and Stein, K. W. (1988) 'Letters', *Journal of Palestine Studies* 17, 4: 252–57.

Khalidi, T. (ed.) (1984) *Land Tenure and Social Transformation in the Middle East*, Beirut: American University of Beirut.

Kidder, R. L. (1979) 'Toward an integrated theory of imposed law', in S. Burman and B. Harrell-Bond (eds) *The Imposition of Law*, London: Academic Press.

Kiernan, V. G. (1969) *The Lords of Humankind: European attitudes towards the outside world in the imperial age*, London: Weidenfeld and Nicolson.

Kimmerling, B. (2000) 'The formation of Palestinian collective identities: the Ottoman and Mandatory periods', *Middle Eastern Studies* 36, 2: 48–81.

Klieman, A. S. (1968) 'Britain's war aims in the Middle East', *Journal of Contemporary History* 3, 3: 237–51.

——(1970) *Foundations of British Policy in the Arab World: the Cairo Conference of 1921*, Baltimore and London: Johns Hopkins Press.

Klug, H. (1995) 'Defining the property rights of others: political power, indigenous tenure and the construction of customary land law', *Journal of Legal Pluralism and Unofficial Law* 35: 119–48.

Knightley, P. and Simpson, C. (1969) *The Secret Lives of Lawrence of Arabia*, London: Nelson.

Kolinsky, M. (1992) 'The Collapse and Restoration of Public Security', in M. J. Cohen and M. Kolinsky (eds), *Britain and the Middle East in the 1930s: security problems 1935–1939*, London and New York: MacMillan.

Kuper, A. (1993) *The Invention of Primitive Society: transformation of an illusion*, London: Routledge and Kegan Paul.

Kupferschmidt, U.M. (1987) *The Supreme Muslim Council: Islam under the British Mandate for Palestine*, Leiden: E. J. Brill.

——(1978) 'Attempts to Reform the Supreme Muslim Council', in G. Ben Dor (ed.) *The Palestinians and the Middle East Conflict*, Israel: Turtledove Publishing.

Lachman, S. (1982) 'Arab rebellion and terrorism In Palestine 1929–39: the case of Sheikh Izz Al Din al-Qassam and his movement', in E. Kedourie and S. Haim (eds) *Zionism and Arabism in Palestine and Israel*, London: Frank Cass and Co.

Landry, D. and McLean, G. (eds) (1996) *The Spivak Reader*, New York: Routledge.

Larsen, N. (2000) 'DetermiNation: pC, Poststructuralism, and the problem of ideology', in F. Afzal-Khan and K. Sheshadri-Crooks (eds) *The Pre-Occupation of Postcolonial Studies*, Durham, NC: Duke University Press

Lawrence, T. E. (1939) *Oriental Assembly*, edited by A.W. Lawrence, London: Williams and Norgate.

——(1939) *Secret Despatches from Arabia*, London: Golden Cockerel Press.

——(1927) *Revolt in the Desert*, London: Jonathan Cape.

——(1966) *Seven Pillars of Wisdom*, New York: Doubleday.

Lees, G. R. (1905) *Village Life in Palestine*, London: Longmans.

Liddell Hart, B. H. (1934) *T.E. Lawrence*, London: Jonathan Cape.

Likhovski, A. (1995) 'In our image: colonial discourse and the Anglicization of the law of Mandatory Palestine', *Israel Law Review* 29: 291–359.

——(1998) 'The invention of Hebrew law in Mandatory Palestine', *American Journal of Comparative Law* 46, 1: 339–73.

——(2002) 'Colonialism, nationalism and legal education: the case of Mandatory Palestine', in R. Harris, A. Kedar, P. Lahav and A. Likhovski (eds) *The History of Law in Multicultural Society: Israel 1917–1967*, Dartmouth UK: Ashgate.

——(2003) 'Establishing and blurring borders: law, Arab nationalism and Arab colonial discourse in Mandatory Palestine', *Tel Aviv University Law Review* 27: 627 (Hebrew).

Litowitz, D. (2000) 'Gramsci, hegemony and the law', *Brigham Young University Law Review* 2: 515–51.

Lloyd, G. A. (1933) *Egypt Since Cromer*, London: Macmillan.

Louis, R., Winks, R. and Low, A. (eds) (1999) *Oxford History of the British Empire*, vol. 5, Oxford: Oxford University Press.

Low, D. A. (1973) *Lion Rampant: essays in the study of British imperialism*, London: Frank Cass.

Lugard, F. J. D. (1928) 'The Dependencies of the British Empire and the responsibilities they involve', address delivered at Birkbeck College, London.

——(1959) *The Diaries of Lord Lugard*, (4 volumes), edited by Margery Perham, London: Faber and Faber.

——(1965) *The Dual Mandate in British Tropical Africa*, London: Frank Cass.

Lyotard, J.-F. (1997) *The Post Modern Condition: a report on knowledge*, Manchester: Manchester University Press.

Mack, J. E. (1998) *A Prince of Our Disorder*, Cambridge, MA: Harvard University Press.

McCarthy, C. and Crichlow, W. (eds) (1994) *Race, Identity and Representation in Education*, London: Routledge.

McHoul, A. and Grace, W. (eds) (1997) *A Foucault Primer*, New York: New York University Press.

McKenzie, J. (1995) *Orientalism: history, theory and the arts*, Manchester: Manchester University Press.

McTague, J. J. (1980) 'Zionist–British negotiations over the draft Mandate for Palestine, 1920, *Jewish Social Studies* 42, 3/4 281–92.

——(1983) *British Policy in Palestine, 1927–1922*, Lanham, MD: University Press of America.

Madden, F. and Fieldhouse, D. K. (eds) (1982) *Oxford and the Idea of the Commonwealth: essays presented to Sir Edgar Williams*, London: Croom Helm.

Maghraoui, A. (2006) *Liberalism Without Democracy*, Durham, NC and London: Duke University Press.

Malinowski, B. (1960) *Argonauts of the Western Pacific: an account of native enterprise and adventure in the Archipelagoes of Melanesian New Guinea*, London: Routledge and Kegan Paul.

Mamdani, M. (1996) *Citizen and Subject – contemporary Africa and the legacy of late colonialism*, Princeton, NJ: Princeton University Press.

Mann, K. and Roberts, R. (eds) (1991) *Law in Colonial Africa*, London: James Currey, 1991.

Malpas, S. (2003) *Jean-François Lyotard*, London and New York: Routledge.

Marlowe, J. (pseud) (1946) *Rebellion in Palestine*, London: The Cresset Press.

——(1961) *Arab Nationalism and British Imperialism: a study in power politics*, London: Cresset Press.

Marx, E. (1967) *Bedouin of the Negev*, Manchester University Press.

Mattar, P. (1983) 'The role of the Mufti of Jerusalem in the political struggle over the Western Wall 1928–29', *Middle Eastern Studies* 19, 1: 104–18.

——(1988) *The Mufti of Jerusalem: al Hajj Amin al-Husayni and the Palestinian National Movement*, New York: Columbia University Press.

Mbembe, A. (2001) *On the Postcolony (studies on the on the history of society and culture)*, Berkeley: University of California Press.

Meek, C. K. (1949) *Land Law and Custom in the Colonies*, London and New York: Oxford University Press.

Memmi, A. (1966) *Portrait du Colonisé*, Paris: Jean-Jacques Pauvert.

Migdal, Joel (ed.) (1980) *Palestinian Society and Politics*, Princeton, NJ.: Princeton University Press.

Mignolo, W. (2000) '(post)Occidentalism, (post)coloniality, and (post)subaltern rationality', in F. Afzal-Khan and K. Sheshadri-Crooks (eds) *The Pre-Occupation of Postcolonial Studies*, Durham, NC: Duke University Press.

Miller, Y. (1980) 'Administrative policy in rural Palestine: the impact of British norms on Arab community life, 1920–48', in J. Migdal (ed.) *Palestinian Society and Politics*, Princeton, NJ: Princeton University Press.

——(1985) *Government and Society in Rural Palestine, 1920–1948*, Austin: University of Texas Press.

Mitchell, T. (1991) *Colonising Egypt*, Berkeley: University of California Press.

Mommsen, W. J. (1991) 'Introduction', in W. J. Mommsen and J. A. de Moor (eds) *European Expansion and the Law: the encounter of European and indigenous law in 19th and 20th Century Africa and Asia*, New York: Berg.

——and J. A. de Moor (eds) (1991) *European Expansion and Law: the encounter of European and indigenous law in 19th and 20th Century Africa and Asia*, New York: Berg.

Monroe, E. (1964) *Britain's Moment in the Middle East, 1914–1956*, London: Methuen and Co. Ltd.

Morrell, W. P. (1966) *British Colonial Policy in the Age of Peel and Russell*, London: Frank Cass.

Morris, H. F. and Read, J. S. (eds) (1972) *Indirect Rule and the Search for Justice: essays in East African legal history*, Oxford: Clarendon Press.

Mosely Lesch, A. (1979) *Arab Politics in Palestine 1917–1939: the frustration of a national movement*, London: Cornell University Press.

Muslih, M.Y. (1988) *The Origins of Palestinian Nationalism*, New York: Columbia University Press (Institute for Palestine Studies series).

Nadan, A. (2001) 'The rural economy in Mandate Palestine 1921–47: peasants under colonial rule', PhD thesis, London School of Economics.

Nandy, Ashis (1988; 1st edn. 1983) *The Intimate Enemy: loss and recovery of self under colonialism*, New Delhi: Oxford University Press.

——(1995) 'History's forgotten double in history and theory', *History and Theory: world historians and their critics*, theme issue 34: 44–66.

Nashif, T. (1977) 'Palestinian Arab and Jewish leadership in the Mandate period', *Journal of Palestine Studies* 6, 4:113–21.

Nelson, C. and Grossberg, L. (eds) (1988) *Marxism and the Interpretation of Culture*, Urbana and Chicago: University of Illinois Press.

Neocleous, M. (2003) 'Off the map: on violence and cartography', *European Journal of Social Theory* 6, 4: 409–26.

Niall, L. (2004) *A Derrida Dictionary*, Malden, MA: Blackwell.

Nicolet, C. (1991) *Space, Geography and Politics in the Early Roman Empire* (Jerome Lectures 19), Ann Arbor: University of Michigan Press 1991.

Nilson, H. (1998) *Michel Foucault and the Games of Truth*, Basingstoke: Macmillan.

Nimr, S. (1990) 'The Arab Revolt of 1936–39 in Palestine: a study based on oral sources', PhD thesis, Exeter University.

O'Hanlon, R. (1988) 'Recovering the subject: subaltern studies and histories of resistance in colonial South Asia', *Modern Asian Studies* 22, 1: 189–224.

——and Washbrook, D. (1992), 'After Orientalism: culture, criticism and politics in the Third World', *Comparative Studies in Society and History* 34, 1: 141–67.

Oxford University Press (1937) *Oxford University Summer School on Colonial Administration – Summary of Lectures*.

Owen, N. (1999) 'Critics of Empire in Britain', in J. Brown and R. Louis (eds) *Oxford History of the British Empire*, vol. 4, Oxford: Oxford University Press.

Owen R. (1972) 'Introduction', in R. Owen and B. Sutcliffe (eds) *Studies in the Theory of Imperialism*, Harlowe: Longman.

——(1994) 'Defining Traditional: some implications of the use of Ottoman land law in Mandatory Palestine', *Harvard Middle Eastern and Islamic Review* 1, 2.

——and Bob Sutcliffe (eds) (1972) *Studies in the Theory of Imperialism*, Harlowe: Longman.

——(ed.) (2000) *New Perspectives on Property and Land in the Middle East*, Cambridge MA: Harvard Centre for Middle East Studies.

Palestine Exploration Fund Quarterly Statement (1905) 'A history of the Fellahin during the first half of the 19th century, from native sources', *Occasional Papers on the Modern Inhabitants of Palestine*.

Pandey, G. (1989) 'The colonial construction of "communalism"': British writings on Banaras in the nineteenth century', in R. Guha (ed.) *Subaltern Studies VI: writings on South Asian history and society*, Delhi and Oxford: Oxford University Press.

Parry, B. (1992) 'Overlapping territories and intertwined histories: Edward Said's post-colonial cosmopolitanism', in M. Sprinker (ed.) *Edward Said, A Critical Reader*, Cambridge, MA: Blackwell.

——(1996) '*Resistance theory/theorising resistance or two cheers for nativism*', in Barker, F., Hulme, P. and Iversen, M. (eds) *Colonial Discourse/Postcolonial Theory*, Manchester and New York: Manchester University Press.

Patai, R. (1949) '"Musha" tenure and co-operation in Palestine', *American Anthropologist* 51: 436–45.

Pearlman, M. (1947) *Mufti of Jerusalem: the Story of Haj Amin el Husseini*, London: Victor Gollancz.

Perham, M. (1967) *Colonial Sequence 1930 to 1949: a chronological commentary upon British colonial policy especially in Africa*, London: Methuen.

Porath, Y. (1971) 'Al Haj Amin Husayni, Mufti of Jerusalem – his rise to power and the consolidation of his position', *Asian and African Studies* 7: 121–56.

——(1974) *The Emergence of the Palestinian–Arab National Movement 1918–1929*, London: Frank Cass.

——(1977) *The Palestinian Arab National Movement from Riots to Rebellion (vol. 2) 1929–1939*, London: Frank Cass.

Power, J. (1992) 'Individualism is the antithesis of indirect rule', *Journal of Southern African Studies* 18, 2: 317–47.

Prakash, G. (ed.) (1990) 'Writing post-Orientalist histories of the Third World: perspectives from Indian historiography', *Comparative Studies in Society and History* 32, 2: 383–408.

——(1992) 'Can the "Subaltern" ride? A reply to O'Hanlon and Washbrook', *Comparative Studies in Society and History* 34,1: 168–84.

——(1994) 'Subaltern studies as postcolonial criticism', *The American Historical Review*, 99: 5: 1475–90.

——(ed.) (1995) *After Colonialism: imperial histories and postcolonial displacements*, Princeton, NJ: Princeton University Press.

Pratt, M. L. (2000) *Imperial Eyes – travel writing and transculturation*, New York and London: Routledge.

——(1985) 'Scratches on the face of the country; or, what Mr. Barrow saw in the land of the Bushmen', *Critical Inquiry* 12, 1: 119–43.

Reilly, K. (2002) 'Forward: colonialism and the modern world, Selected Studies', in G. Blue, M. Bunton and R. Croizier, (eds) *Colonialism and the Modern World: selected studies*, Armonk, NY: M. E. Sharpe.

Reyntgens, P. (1991) 'The Development of the Dual Legal System in Former Central Africa', in W. J. Mommsen and J. A. De Moor (eds) *European Expansion and the*

Law: the encounter of European and indigenous law in 19th and 20th Century Africa and Asia, New York: Berg.

Robinson, F. (1999) 'The British Empire and the Muslim world', in J. Brown and R. Louis (eds) *Oxford History of the British Empire*, vol. 4, Oxford: Oxford University Press.

Robinson, K. (1965) *The Dilemmas of Trusteeship: aspects of colonial policy between the wars*, London: Oxford University Press.

Robinson, R. and Gallagher, J. with Denny, A. (1981) *Africa and the Victorians: the official mind of imperialism*, London: Macmillan.

Robinson, R. (1992) 'Non-European foundations of European imperialism: sketch for a theory of collaboration', in N. Owen and B. Sutcliffe (eds) *Studies in the Theory of Imperialism*, Harlowe: Longman.

——(1982) 'Oxford in imperial historiography', in F. Madden and D.K. Fieldhouse (eds) *Oxford and the Idea of the Commonwealth: essays presented to Sir Edgar Williams*, London: Croom Helm.

Robinson Divine, D. (1983) 'Islamic culture and political practice in Mandated Palestine, 1918–48', *The Review of Politics* 45, 1: 71–93.

Royle, N. (2003) *Jacques Derrida*, London and New York: Routledge.

Said, E. (1978; 2nd edn 1995) *Orientalism*, Harmondsworth: Penguin.

——(1988) 'Foreword', in R. Guha and G. Spivak (eds) *Selected Subaltern Studies*, New York and Oxford: Oxford University Press, 1988.

——(1994) *Culture and Imperialism*, London: Vintage.

——and Hitchens, C. (eds). *Blaming the Victims: spurious scholarship and the Palestinian question*, London and New York: Verso.

Salamone, F. A. (1987) 'The social construction of colonial reality: Yauri Emirate', *Journal of Legal Pluralism and Unofficial Law* 25: 47–70.

Salant, E. (1934) *Constitutional Laws of the British Empire*, London: Sweet and Maxwell.

Samuel, H. (1945) *Memoirs*, London: Cresset Press.

Sanbar, E. (2001) 'Out of place, out of time', *Mediterranean Historical Review* 16, 1: 87–94.

Sanders, Ronald (1984) *The High Walls of Jerusalem: a history of the Balfour Declaration and the birth of the British Mandate for Palestine*, New York: Holt, Rinehart and Winston.

Sartre, J.-P. (1963) 'Preface' to F. Fanon *The Wretched of the Earth*, New York: Grove Press.

Sayigh, R. (2002) 'Editorial – the history of Palestinian oral history: individual vitality and institutional paralysis', *Al-Jana Magazine*, Beirut: Arab Resource Center for Popular Arts.

Scheid, K. (1998) 'Editorial – oral history is an activist project', *Al-Jana Magazine*, Beirut: Arab Resource Center for Popular Arts.

——(2002) 'The illiterate woman, she talked to us', *Al-Jana Magazine*, Beirut: Arab Resource Center for Popular Arts.

Selznick, P. (1970) 'Institutional vulnerability in mass society', in J. R. Gusfield (ed.) *Protest, Reform and Revolt: a reader in social movements*, Chichester: Wiley.

Seton-Williams, M. V. (1948) *Britain and the Arab States: a survey of Anglo-Arab relations 1920–1948*, London: Luzac.

Shamir, R. (2000) *The Colonies of Law: colonialism, Zionism and law in early Mandate Palestine*, Cambridge: Cambridge University Press.

Sheffer, G. (1971) 'British policies and policy making towards Palestine 1929–39', D. Phil. Thesis, University of Oxford.

——(1973) 'Intentions and results of British policy in Palestine: Passfield's White Paper', *Middle Eastern Studies* 9, 1: 43–60.

——(1978) 'British colonial policy-making towards Palestine (1929–39)', *Middle Eastern Studies* 14, 3: 307–22.

Sheshadri-Crooks, K. (2000) 'At the margins of postcolonial studies: part I', in F. Afzal-Khan and K. Sheshadri-Crooks (eds) *The Pre-Occupation of Postcolonial Studies*, Durham, NC: Duke University Press.

Shohat, E. (2000) 'Notes on the postcolonial', in F. Afzal-Khan and K. Sheshadri-Crooks (eds) *The Pre-Occupation of Postcolonial Studies*, Durham, NC: Duke University Press.

——(2006) *Taboo Memories, Diasporic Voices*, Durham and London: Duke University Press.

Simensen, J. 'Jurisdiction as politics: the Gold Coast during the colonial period', in W. J. Mommsen and J. A. De Moor (eds) *European Expansion and the Law: the encounter of European and indigenous law in 19th and 20th Century Africa and Asia*, New York: Berg.

Simson, H. J. (1937) *British Rule and Rebellion*, Edinburgh: Blackwood.

Sluglett, P. (1999) 'Formal and informal empire in the Middle East', in R. Louis, R. Winks and A. Low (eds) *Oxford History of the British Empire*, vol. 5, Oxford: Oxford University Press.

——and Farouk-Sluglett, M. (1984) 'The application of the 1858 Land Code in Greater Syria: some preliminary observations', in T. Khalidi (ed.) *Land Tenure and Social Transformation in the Middle East*, Beirut: American University of Beirut.

Snyder, F. G. (1981) 'Colonialism and legal form: the creation of "Customary" law in Senegal', *Journal of Legal Pluralism* 19: 49–90.

Spivak, G. C. (1988) 'Can the subaltern speak?', in C. Nelson and L. Grossberg (eds) *Marxism and the Interpretation of Culture*, Urbana and Chicago: University of Illinois Press.

——(1988) 'Subaltern studies: deconstructing historiography', in R. Guha and G. C. Spivak (eds) *Selected Subaltern Studies*, New York and Oxford: Oxford University Press.

——(1996) 'Subaltern talk: interview with the editors', in D. Landry and G. MacLean (eds) *The Spivak Reader*, New York: Routledge.

—(1999) *A Critique of Postcolonial Reason: toward a history of the vanishing present*, Cambridge, MA and London: Harvard University Press, 1999.

Sprinker, Michael (ed.) (1992) *Edward Said, A Critical Reader*, Cambridge, MA.: Blackwell, 1992.

Starr, J. and Collier, J (eds) (1989) *History and Power in the Study of Law: new directions in legal anthropology*, Ithaca, NY: Cornell University Press.

Stein, L. (1961) *The Balfour Declaration*, London: Vallentine Mitchell.

Stein, K. W. (1985) *The Land Question in Palestine, 1917–1939*, Chapel Hill and London: University of North Carolina Press.

——(1990) 'The Intifada and the 1936–39 Uprising: a comparison', *Journal of Palestine Studies* 19, 4: 64–85.

——(1991) 'Rural change and peasant destitution: contributing causes to the Arab Revolt in Palestine, 1936–39', in F. Kazemi and J. Waterbury (eds) *Peasants and Politics in the Modern Middle East*, Florida: International University Press.

Stocking, G. W. (ed.) (1991) *Colonial Situations: essays on the contextualization of ethnographic knowledge*, Madison, WI: University of Wisconsin Press, 1991.

Stokes, E. (1959) *The English Utilitarians and India*, Oxford: Clarendon Press.

——(1960) *The Political Ideas of English Imperialism. An inaugural lecture given in the University College of Rhodesia and Nyasaland*, London: Oxford University Press.

Stoyanovsky, Y. (1928) *The Mandate for Palestine. A contribution to the theory and practice of international mandates*, London: Longmans.

Stewart, F. H. (1987) 'Tribal law in the Arab world: a review of the literature', *International Journal of Middle East Studies* 19, 4: 473–90.

——(1994) *Honor*, Chicago: University of Chicago Press.

Suleiman, M. (1966) *T.E. Lawrence: an Arab view*, London: Oxford University Press.

Sutcliffe, B. 'Conclusion', in N. Owen and B. Sutcliffe (eds) *Studies in the Theory of Imperialism*, Harlowe: Longman.

Swedenburg, T. (1995) *Memories of Revolt: the 1936–1939 rebellion and the Palestinian national past*, Minneapolis and London: University of Minnesota Press.

Sykes, Christopher (1953) *Two Studies in Virtue*, London: Collins.

——(1965) *Crossroads to Israel*, London: Collins.

Taggar, Y. (1986) *The Mufti of Jerusalem and Palestine Arab Politics, 1930–1937*, New York and London: Garland Publishing.

Tidrick, K. (1989) *Heart Beguiling Araby*, London: I.B. Tauris.

——(1990) *Empire and the English Character*, London: I.B. Tauris.

Tomlins, C. (2003) 'In a wilderness of tigers: violence, the discourse of English colonizing, and the refusals of American history', *Theoretical Inquiries in Law* 4, 2: 451–90.

Tshimoni, D. (1978) 'The Arab Christians and the Palestinian Arab national movement during the formative stage', in G. Ben Dor (ed.) *The Palestinians and the Middle East Conflict*, Israel: Turtledove Publishing.

Turner, V. (ed.) (1971) *Colonialism in Africa 1870–1960 (Volume 3), Profiles of Change: African society and colonial rule*, Cambridge: Cambridge University Press.

Tyler, S. A. (2001) 'Post-modern ethnography: from document of the occult to occult document', in A. Bryman (ed.) *Ethnography*, London: Sage Publications.

Tyler, W. P. N. (2001) *State Lands and Rural Development in Mandatory Palestine, 1920–1948*, Brighton: Sussex Academic Press.

Vashitz, J. (1983) 'Dhawat and Ismaiyyun: two groups of Arab community leaders in Haifa during the British Mandate', *Asian and African Studies* 17: 95–120.

Vereté, M. (1970) 'The Balfour Declaration and its makers', *Middle Eastern Studies* 6: 48–76.

Verrier, A. (ed.) (1995) *Agents of Empire: Anglo-Zionist intelligence operations 1915–1919. Brigadier Walter Gribbon, Aaronsohn and the NILI Ring*, London: Brassey's.

Victor Gollancz and the New Fabian Research Bureau (1933) *The Protection of Colonial Peoples. A study in British colonial policy*, London: Victor Gollancz.

Wasserstein, B. (1991) *The British in Palestine: the mandatory government and the Arab-Jewish conflict 1917–1929*, Oxford: Blackwell.

——(1977) 'Clipping the claws of the colonisers: Arab officials in the Government of Palestine, 1917–48', *Middle Eastern Studies* 13, 2: 171–94.

Weber, E. (ed.) (1995) *Points … Interviews 1974–1994, Jacques Derrida*, California: Stanford University Press.

Weintraub, S. and Weintraub, R. (eds) (1968) *Evolution of a Revolt: early post-war writings of T.E. Lawrence*, University Park and London: Pennsylvania State University Press.

Westrate, B. (1992) *The Arab Bureau: British policy in the Middle East 1916–1920*, University Park: Pennsylvania State University Press, 1992.

White, C. M. N. 'Indirect rule', in R. J Apthorpe (ed.) *From Tribal Rule to Modern Government*, Lusaka: the Institute.

Wolf, Lucien (1919) *Notes on the Diplomatic History of the Jewish Question*, London: Spottiswood.

Woolf, L. (1920) *Mandates and Empire* (6 pamphlets), London: League of Nations.

Woodward, E. and Butler, R. (1952) (eds) *Documents on British Foreign Policy*, series i, vol. iv, London: HMSO 1952.

Young, R.(1996) *White Mythologies*, London: Routledge.

Official Archives: Public Record Office, The National Archives, London

CO 733 Colonial Office, Palestine, Original Correspondence.

CAB 23
Cabinet Conclusions
CAB 24
Cabinet Papers
CAB 27
Cabinet Palestine Committee 1930
FO 371
Foreign Office, Palestine, General Correspondence
WO 32............War Office

Official Publications

The Constitutions of All Countries, vol. i, British Empire, HMSO 1938.

Hansard 5th Series: Parliamentary Debates. House of Lords, House of Commons, 1928–39.

Palestine and Transjordan, Geographical Handbook Series, Naval Intelligence Division, 1943.

Palestine Mandate, League of Nations

Cmnd. 1785, 1922

Palestine Order in Council 1922

Palestine Defence Order in Council 1931, 1936

Statement of British Policy in Palestine (Churchill White Paper)

Cmnd. 1700, 1922

Statement of British Policy in Palestine (White Paper on Wailing Wall)

Cmnd. 3229, 1928

Report of the Commission on the Palestine Disturbances of August 1929 (the Shaw Commission Report)

Cmnd. 3530, 1930

Statement of British Policy in Palestine (White Paper on Shaw Commission Report)

Cmnd. 3582, 1930

Palestine Report on Immigration, Land Settlement and Development (by Sir John Hope-Simpson)

Cmnd. 3686, 1930

Statement of British Policy in Palestine (Passfield White Paper)

Cmnd. 3692, 1930
Palestine Royal Commission Report (the Peel Report)
Cmnd. 5479, 1937
Reports by the Mandatory to the Council of the League of Nations on the
Administration of Palestine and Trans-Jordan for the Years:

1929, Colonial No. 47.
1930, Colonial No. 59.
1933, Colonial No. 94.
1934, Colonial No. 104.
1935, Colonial No. 112.
1936, Colonial No. 129.
1937, Colonial No. 146.
1938, Colonial No. 166.

Summary of the Report of the Palestine Royal Commission, Series of League
of Nations Publications, VI. A. Mandates.

Private Papers, Archives And Manuscripts

Aref Aref,
Diaries (Arabic).
MEC
Neville Barbour
Papers
Middle East Centre, St. Antony's College, Oxford University (MEC)
Norman Bentwich
Papers
MEC
Edgar Bonham Carter
Memoranda on Palestine and Mesopotamia.
MEC
Chancellor Papers
Rhodes House Library, Oxford University
Dr. Eliot Forster
Diaries
MEC
Kermack Stuart Grace
Memoirs of work in Palestine judicial service 1920–30
MEC
Dr. Hussein Fakhri Khalidi
Memoirs (Arabic) and Diaries (English)
Private collection, with Leila Husseini in Amman, Jordan
T.   E. Lawrence *War Diaries*. British Library Additional 45914.

Ivan Lloyd Phillips in R.E.H. Crosbie Papers, file I.
MEC
Elizabeth Monroe.
Miscellaneous papers relating to the Balfour Declaration
MEC
Le Ray Hugh Granville (LRHG)

'Annual reports of Director of Surveys 1920–39. Material on land law, land tax, and distribution of land in mandate period.'

MEC
Palestine Police Old Comrades Association Collection (PPOCAC) (donated by Ted Horne in late 2003, un-catalogued):
-    Col. Raymond Cafferata Papers
-    De Lacy Personal Papers
-    Harold Price (former head of CID., Palestine Police 1932–37) Personal Papers
-    Mandate Period Notices from the Arab Revolt
-    Palestine Police Magazine
-    Ted Horne Photographic Album 'Arab Rebellion'
-    Ted Horne 'Palestine Diary'
-    Col. Harry Rice

    -

Intelligence Report, Arab Revolt 1938.

H.M. Wilson, 'School Year in Palestine 1938–39'.
MEC

Reference Books

Center for Documentation and Knowledge. *The Arab Documents 23: the Historical Documents on Arab History in the Archives of the World Conference* (United Arab Emirates, March 2002).

Index